Slow Wood

Slow Wood

Greener Building from Local Forests

Brian Donahue

Yale

UNIVERSITY PRESS

New Haven and London

Published with assistance from Highstead Foundation,
and from the Louis Stern Memorial Fund.

Yale University Press books may be purchased in quantity for educational, business,
or promotional use. For information, please e-mail sales.press@yale.edu (U.S. office)
or sales@yaleup.co.uk (U.K. office).

Set in Bulmer type by Integrated Publishing Solutions.
Printed in the United States of America.

ISBN 978-0-300-27347-2 (hardcover : alk. paper)
Library of Congress Control Number: 2024934156
A catalogue record for this book is available from the British Library.

This paper meets the requirements of ANSI/NISO Z39.48-1992 (Permanence of Paper).

10 9 8 7 6 5 4 3 2 1

For Liam and Maggie

Contents

Slow Wood

Introduction

"AT A CERTAIN SEASON OF OUR LIFE we are accustomed to consider every spot as the possible site of a house," observed Henry Thoreau. For Faith and me, that season lasted thirty years.

Thoreau never got his fingers burned by actual possession. Owning no property was something he wore as a badge of honor, claiming that before buying a farm it would be better to "go round and round it as long as I live, and be buried in it first, that it may please me the more at last." For a long time, we lived by that philosophy, too—longer than Thoreau, in fact. By dying young, he kept his hands clean. We didn't.

Thoreau's home farm, his real estate, was all of Concord, which he called the most estimable place in the world to have been born, and in the nick of time. He died in the nick of time, too: had he lived just a few more years he would have seen an amusement park spring up at Walden Pond, which would have killed him. But his luck held.

Had Faith and I enjoyed such luck, we could have made the same bold claim about having gone freely round and round Weston without ever being saddled by owning a piece of it, either. But we outlived Thoreau, leapt into shared ownership of a farm (with friends, in a more rural town, two hours away), and built a house that pleases us very much—in spite of our burned fingers. And so, we stepped into a season of life never traveled by Thoreau.

Sauntering around Concord untrammeled by the bonds of property, stealing across neighbors' back pastures to reach their woodlots by devious routes calculated to keep him out of sight of the kitchen window and barn door, Thoreau observed that he had "frequently seen a poet withdraw, having enjoyed the most valuable part of a farm, while the crusty farmer supposed that he had got a few wild apples only." Echoing Emerson, Thoreau claimed that the highest use of nature is to enjoy its beauty, an opportunity too often wasted on the owner. The farmer, he wrote, keeps his eyes on the ground, trudging behind his oxen, his back bent beneath the heavy yoke of the market economy, desperately hoping his herd of cows will pay for his bootlaces. The idea that farmers (and the rest of us) mortgage our souls and labor in the dirt to gain superfluous material possessions, bargaining away the freedom to lift up our heads and enjoy the best of nature, or any other higher purpose, is at the heart of *Walden*.

I remember that freedom, and, as is only natural, I want it back. When I was in high school, my friends and I roamed the rewilding farm-land on the fringes of the expanding postwar suburbs of Pittsburgh, seek-ing wild birds and wild fruit. We were young and untroubled by fences, being both free of fear and fleet of foot. Any notable bird or edible plant was fair game for trespass. We chased after crows harassing owls, and we harvested elder flowers and cattail bloom spikes that were not legally ours—figuring that the owner probably didn't want them anyway. I re-member the exhilaration of being seventeen years old, cresting a hill on a fall afternoon and gazing into an unforeseen valley of fields and woods, with no earthly responsibility except to pay attention: to be, as Thoreau put it, forever on the alert.

But the brash young fellow crowing about the poet tasting the cream and leaving the lowly farmer only the skimmed milk comes off as irritat-ingly smug to anyone who has done any farming, as I now have. It may be that the farmer enjoys the cream as well and knows more of its worth than Thoreau allows. Sponging the cream without shoveling the manure invites the populist scorn summed up on pickup truck bumper stickers during the spotted owl controversy in the Pacific Northwest: "Are you an environmentalist, or do you work for a living?"

I am an environmentalist, and I do work for a living. I believe that with the right kind of work, we can escape that bind. It may be that the cream tastes better when you have worked for the milk, freedom be damned. The trick is to avoid shoveling shit in payment for (supposedly healthier) skim milk or allowing anyone else, poet or plutocrat, to hog the cream.

There was another Henry Thoreau who knew this perfectly well—who enjoyed not just walking in nature but working in it, too. That Tho-reau surfaced just a few pages away, cheerfully framing his house in Walden Woods with a borrowed ax. The land belonged to Emerson and the rent was the house itself, which the Sage of Concord retained after young

Henry returned to village life, moving back to look after Emerson's place while the elder philosopher was touring Europe, in fact. The Walden house (or most of it) eventually wandered off to the other side of Concord—oddly enough, settling on land that was later owned by Emerson's grandson and great-grandson, who once showed me what he claimed were its famous timbers, stacked under an old barn. At least, that's what I thought he was claiming—he was a bit cagey about it. As for the ax, Thoreau returned it sharper than he received it, the only interest he paid on his construction loan. Who lent him the ax is a mystery, although the circumstantial evidence points to Bronson Alcott: the ax was dull. That is the trout in the milk, in this case.

Why Thoreau even needed to borrow an ax is puzzling. He says it was an ordinary narrow felling ax, not a broad ax, and he was a competent woodsman who surely owned one himself. At any rate, he plainly enjoyed felling and hewing the white pine timbers for his house, working on a "pleasant hillside" on "pleasant spring days" and "chatting pleasantly over the chips which I had made" when a rambler heard the sound of his ax. Who was the poet then, and who the crusty old farmer? Which part of those pine trees was the cream and which the skimmed milk? The lofty tops laid low, the chips, the rough-hewn roof beam and sills?

Such a working relationship between people and nature benefited both parties, according to Thoreau. He claimed that "before I had done I was more the friend than the foe of the pine tree, though I had cut down some of them, having become better acquainted with it." Now *that* is a salutary message for any environmentalist who lives in a wooden house! But what could the pines have possibly gained from having their good friend cut down some to get better acquainted with them, you might ask? A fair question—but as it happens, there are more white pines in Concord today than there were before our Yankee ancestors (Henry's, and Faith's, and mine) arrived in New England and started chopping.

It is possible to cut pine trees and still have pine forests. Most other native trees of our region have not fared so badly either, though few have made out quite so well as white pine—for if white pine has gained ground, something else must have lost it. Around Concord that would be pitch pine, among other trees, likely because of a comparatively recent decline in landscape fire. The story is a twisted one that varies from century to century, from species to species, and from place to place.

I should know. By chance, Thoreau's people were neighbors of ours. His grandmother Mary Jones grew up across the street from us in Weston, and I have logged woodlots that were once cut by Mary's father, Elisha, her grandfather, Josiah, and her great-grandfather, Deacon Josiah Jones, who bought that land in 1665 and who was among the founders of our town. Besides logging them, I have studied them in some detail. Like the more famous woods surrounding Walden over in Concord, some of those wood-lots in what is now the Weston Town Forest have been cut at least *six times* (that I know of) since English settlement, and they are still going strong. Others were sojourners in civilization for a time, serving as cow pastures or hay meadows, and have since returned to forest.

I suspect that the wormy chestnut paneling in my Weston study was salvage-logged in that woods after the blight came through in 1923—I could show you the stumps. They are now mixed with more recent white birch and red oak stumps that I made myself, sixty-two years after the blight, which have rotted away faster than the chestnut. You would see that today those woods are growing big, beautiful pines and oaks in spite of all the trees that Thoreau's forebears and their successors, including me, have removed. Indeed, the trees growing there today are bigger and better *because* I removed some of the others, if you ask me. Not better in any eco-logical sense, but better in the quality of their timber without paying any discernable ecological price, I mean to say. It doesn't always work out so well for the trees when people cut forests, but in this case, it has. We can have our woods and cut them, too.

This book is about cutting down trees to become better acquainted with them, by building with the resulting timber. Applying that philoso-phy at our new farm, Faith and I built a timber frame house primarily with trees cut from our woodlot. Over the past four decades I have cut a few more trees than those Thoreau felled for his house; my tally is probably not yet in the thousands but is at least high in the hundreds. I must be an even better friend of the trees than he was. There isn't any less tree volume standing in the woods because of the ones I cut—there is probably more. Most of mine were cut for firewood, a few for timber, and the two are re-lated: we cut firewood mainly to improve the growth of timber.

But this story is about more than our own enduring friendship with the beautiful forest that surrounds us: it is about others who work in the woods or work with that wood to make beautiful things—our forester, logger, sawyer, architect, timber framer, millworker, carpenter, cabinet maker, and (not to neglect what lies beneath the roots of trees) the stoneworkers who cut our kitchen counters and the mason who built our stove. It is also the story of the ways we Americans have managed our forests, built our houses, and heated them since before Thoreau's time. It is about this country's broken but still reparable relationship between our woodlands and our wood, about how we might care for our woods better, while still making good use of them.

Slow Wood is a plea that we return that working relationship—that close friendship with nature, however fraught—to the heart of conservation. This is not a rejection of preserving wild, unmanaged places as well—far from it. And it is the opposite of an endorsement of the industrial extraction of wood that American forests have suffered for the past two centuries and continue to endure. Although I have great respect for the people who do that work, all too often I can't say as much for the results. Under the corporate ownership that supplies most of our wood, the skills and sympathies of loggers are as grossly exploited as the woods they work in and would be delighted to care for better. This book calls for beautiful and sustainable ways of building with wood that are intimately connected to beautiful and sustainable ways of caring for woodlands.

There is more we could be building with wood, and in the process of harvesting that wood we could be fostering biodiversity, protecting watersheds, sequestering carbon, and rebuilding rural communities. It is not all that complicated, just good, slow silviculture—often preached, but seldom practiced. For generations, my mentors (starting with my neighbor Mary Jones Dunbar Minot's grandson, Henry) and colleagues have toiled to bring about such a transformation in the way we work with our forests, but the remorseless logic of the market economy scorns such social and environmental affections and shrugs us off. We need your help, environmentalists!

For readers tempted to build their own place in the woods, this book is humbly offered as guidance. For those, mostly younger, who yearn to work directly with woodlands or wood products themselves, this book is offered as encouragement: many of my students dream of becoming farmers (which I also encourage), but I have helped persuade a few to become foresters as well. For the rest of you, this story of building a modest home from our lovely woods is presented as a metaphor for the larger work of green building and forest conservation that we all need to undertake, as consumers, yes, but much more as *citizens,* if we are ever to live beautifully on this beleaguered planet.

Henry Thoreau ultimately lived a village life, as Faith and I now have, too. He is mostly remembered as a cranky individualist who withdrew from society to live alone in the woods—a well-deserved reputation, considering the inspiring though irritating book he wrote about that experience. For that he is widely admired, frequently imitated, and routinely excoriated. But it is worth remembering that his two years and two months in the woods were cast as a youthful experiment and that he lived most of his life with his family in Concord center. Thoreau was a quirky character, all right, but he was no hermit: he followed his "crooked bent" in plain sight, not in isolation. His frequent trips to town while living at the pond, to conduct business or visit with family and friends, were not an abdication of his principles or a failure of his go-it-alone resolve—they were an ongoing part of his village life, which he rejoined in full swing once his sojourn in the woods was over, joking that it was the other way around. As a sojourner in civilization again he helped run the family pencil (later plumbago) business, surveyed farms and woodlots for neighbors, explored and catalogued the surrounding countryside on foot and by boat, and, of course, wrote about it. All the while, he was a deeply committed citizen of town and national affairs, especially the abolitionist campaign to end slavery. That was a village life, productively engaged with his community.

I think about this as we retire from our own village life in Weston, where we have been engaged in town affairs ourselves for over forty years, and move to the country at last—but also to another village. There is a perennial urge in American culture for urbanites to flee to rural places, whether as a footloose youthful adventure or a more mature withdrawal to a vacation or retirement home, for those with sufficient means. This movement ebbs and flows but is currently once again in full flood, thanks to internet sites like "Cabin Porn" and now the Covid pandemic and climate change. The way it plays out will have consequences for rural forests and villages and for the future of the planet.

Faith and I now have modest but sufficient means ourselves, which we didn't think much about while our beloved parents were still living. Whenever I visited home my mother would lead me through the folders that contained my folks' financial records and wills, and I would dutifully take notes about where everything was filed, without paying any attention to the size of the sums. This began decades ago, when she was no older than I am now. When the time finally came for my brothers and I to take the contents of that file drawer seriously, it dawned on me that it held the means to help Faith and me to buy a farm and build a house, just as we had always dreamed. We came to understand the power of generational wealth, which we had studiously ignored up to that point.

As someone who has spent a lifetime working to conserve land, it seems to me that with such privilege comes responsibility. If affluent people build country places *only* for their own enjoyment, that is indeed pornography—or something worse than porn, closer to assault. I don't object to stressed-out, over-connected, self-incarcerated urban inmates of social media prison cells gazing longingly at images of rustic homes in nature, hand-crafted from organic materials, and fantasizing about an uncomplicated, unplugged rural lifestyle, if that is what "cabin porn" means. I have had such ecorotic fantasies all my life, and Faith and I have acted on them more than once, in our own way—and learned, of course, that they are anything but simple. But if such people also act on their fantasies, purchasing country property and building on it only as a private respite from modern turmoil, that can easily become just another prettified form of nature consumption, worsening the dilemma it aims to solve. That is how consumer capitalism does its dirty work.

This book contains graphic photographs of nesting, too, so I want to be careful to declare our fidelity to a different set of principles, and here they are: those with the means to move to the country should be encouraged, if not required, to site their houses so that the surrounding farmland and woodlands remain intact and to donate generously to their conservation. They should contribute to (and politically support) mechanisms by which working farmers and loggers can also gain secure access to land and policies by which affordable housing is constructed for everyone. Their rural sojourn should not be just a transient escape from modern industrial civilization: it should aim to help transform the reality that enables it. If they believe this is not their business, I believe they are wrong. In a time of planetary crisis, we can ill afford to indulge individualistic retreats to rural isolation and quaintly evoked craft traditions, no matter how appealing. The revival of those traditions needs to be connected to some larger purpose. We need to lead a village life, caring for the local landscape and community, and we must stay engaged with the wider world, wherever we may settle. As did the more mature Henry Thoreau, in his own crooked way.

As for *building* your house, which is the main subject of this book: think of it as borrowing wood from the surrounding forest. The woods provide us with abundant but mostly unrequited goods and services, and among them, we have come to realize, is continually sequestering carbon. The older the woods grow the more carbon they store, out to some old-growth limit of which we have almost no surviving examples in our region to study so can only vaguely guess. Harvesting wood for building inter-rupts that process, at least temporarily. This is true whether the wood comes from a local woodlot or from the other side of the planet.

But people need houses, houses need wood, and the available alter-natives—steel, concrete, plastic—are generally far worse for the environ-ment. Therefore, trees—many, many trees—must be harvested somewhere, and with the removal of those trees comes the responsibility to safeguard and eventually return that borrowed carbon, with interest, and to see that the bank remains on a sound footing and continues to enlarge its capital. The longer we borrow the carbon, the better. Wood should be cut in ways that interfere as little as possible with the capacity of the forest to continue to grow, absorb more carbon dioxide, and otherwise stay healthy and beautiful. And the house itself should be built to hold its carbon as long as it can. It should be built for the ages. It should be made of slow wood, in other words: wood that stands for a long, long time in both the forest and the house.

There's an old story about a young fellow who comes into a lumber-yard and says he wants to buy some "four-by-twos."

The lumberman looks puzzled. "Four-by-twos?" he says. "What, you mean two-by-fours?"

The lad scratches his head. "Hang on a second. I'll find out."

He goes out into the parking lot. The lumberman watches him con-sulting there with a couple of older guys, sitting in a beat-up station wagon. He comes back in.

"That's right—two-by-fours," he says. "We want some two-by-fours."

"OK, two-by-fours," says the lumberman. "So, how *long* do you want them?"

The young man scratches his head again and goes back out to the parking lot. Eight-footers is the standard length for a two-by-four stud, but you never know—you can get tens, twelves, sixteens, whatever you need. Another animated discussion ensues, the other two men gesticulating for emphasis. Then he comes back in.

"We want them for a long time. We're building a house."

That was one of my mother's favorite jokes. Not as funny as the one about the penguins in the back of the convertible wearing sunglasses, perhaps, but still pretty good. You can see the "how long" pun coming a mile away, but that isn't the real joke—it's the "four-by-twos" that make it funny. The idea that these guys who don't even know what a two-by-four is called think they would be capable of building a house. Carpenters like the joke, too, or maybe they just laughed because I was the guy signing the checks.

There are plenty of ordinary two-by-fours in our house, hidden in the walls. But the structure of the house, the frame, is made of sterner stuff, drawn from our own woods: eight-by-ten hemlock plates and tie beams, eight-by-eight posts, four-by-eight joists, three-by-five cherry braces. How long do we want them? A long time. We want them to stand here longer than we do, longer than the trees that once grew alongside them, even as that forest keeps growing and changing. A few hundred years before the house inevitably burns down would be nice. We want those timbers to outlast the ancient trees some of them might have become—at which point they start bearing that good carbon interest. We just don't want them to outlive the forest.

We Buy the Farm

I GREW UP IN A REWILDING WORLD, though I didn't know it. The countryside north of Pittsburgh was returning to forest all around me. The abandoned farmland I roamed freely as a boy and then explored more deliberately in high school with my birdwatching, berry-picking friends was being overrun by deer berry, sassafras, and crabapple thickets. On the steep valley slopes there were older oak woods, with bigger trees. Only a small portion of the best land was still being farmed, and that was shrinking double time: the countryside was suburbanizing as fast as it was rewilding.

We liked the old woods best. Not many around where we lived were being logged, that I can recall—unless they were being cleared for new houses. But the developers generally headed first for the flatter, more open farmland. We encountered logging more frequently when we walked the countryside around Todd Sanctuary, in Butler County up north of us, about an hour farther out in the sticks—and when we saw it, we cursed it.

Today I would probably curse it because I thought it was bad logging; back then, I just hated it outright because I thought all logging was bad. Logging destroyed our stately old woods, leaving them a shredded shambles of their former beauty. I vaguely knew there had been more severe cutting in those woods sometime in the past, though I didn't know exactly when or how this might have shaped the regrown forests we revered. But I was sure any and all logging should be left in that past. I believed, instinctively, that recovering forests were best left alone, to regain their ecological wholeness. That is, I believed in what is now called "proforestation"—which I would define as a philosophy espousing the superiority of wild, unmanaged forests, while ignoring any serious consideration of where and how to harvest wood products.[1]

Once I moved to eastern Massachusetts to attend Brandeis Univer-

The original farmhouse and barn—now Tom and Joan's place. (Tom Chalmers)

sity and then dropped out to farm the Boston suburbs, I discovered a world where rewilding was more advanced—a condition that would no doubt have pleased Henry Thoreau. Or half-pleased him, because suburbia was more advanced, too, resulting in a landscape composed of a few woods and many houses, with farmland almost entirely squeezed out. By the 1970s, the great century-long wave of New England reforestation had crested, but the tide of development continued to advance. Now I walked in town conservation forests filled with tall pasture pines at least half a century old, oak woodlots that hadn't been cut for even longer, and dense red maple swamps that had once been hay meadows. This was also a transfigured agricultural landscape (which it took me some time to recognize), but it had been abandoned decades earlier than western Pennsylvania. I grew to love the place and call it home. And in time I got to know those woods a little better.[2]

There wasn't much logging going on in eastern Massachusetts, either, but my attitude about that soon changed. Instead of wanting to see less logging, or no logging, I came to think there should be *more* logging: in fact, I soon became a suburban logger myself. I learned how to cut down trees, and I enjoyed it. This was always a puzzle to my mother, who had me pegged as a tree hugger. Which was still true. It wasn't that I came to dislike wild forest; I just no longer thought of it as ecologically superior, as the only really good forest. Wild, unmanaged forest is special, and we do need *some*—indeed, far more than we currently have. I am not opposed to "setting aside" abundant wildlands, or more precisely to having more of them as an important part of the ecological mix. But I have come to believe that establishing wildlands is ultimately futile unless those wild reserves are surrounded by much larger, continuous, well-protected, well-logged forests.

Wild forests exist at the mercy of the rampant growth of industrial resource extraction, and all its consequences. We will end up with just as much wilderness in this world as human needs and desires can spare, and no more. Nobody is going to seriously grant us "half earth" and then honor that line, not under the global economic dispensation we have now. Therefore, the most pressing order of business is to reconfigure those needs and desires and reduce the impact of how we go about meeting them—which will inevitably still require cutting a lot of lumber and other wood products, because people do need decent houses, and wood is often the best material. We still need wood—lots of wood. Given that, the next order of business is to manage the forests that are producing that lumber so that they deliver a full range of ecological benefits, too. Wild forest and sustainably managed, productive forest must work together; it isn't that difficult to imagine, just less profitable for owners to practice. The challenge remains what it has always been: radically reforming the political and economic rules under which forests are owned and managed.[3]

That much of the argument is easy to make, whether you agree with it or not. I was thinking about it that way by 1980 when I was twenty-five years old, and we formed Land's Sake in Weston. It was my take on a long-running debate in the conservation community, between "spared earth" and "shared earth." The clincher, for me, is more subtle, and came more slowly. It is no more than an article of faith, and it is this: only by actively caring for the world we use can we build a culture and constituency resolute and powerful enough to protect forests in the long run. If we concentrate only on setting natural places aside, without building enduring bonds to the places we use and inhabit, we will remain too weak to enforce the terms of protection. This is a faith that you acquire by walking through woods that you first thinned forty years ago, and again twenty years ago, and seeing the results: big, beautiful trees. This stuff really works.

I realize that few people can become foresters, loggers, landowners, woodworkers, or timber framers in their own right, and enjoy such a direct relationship with forests and wood. But I do believe that we can build an economy, and a culture, in which most people are exposed to elements of that beneficial connection throughout their lives, in part by walking in community forests and living in well-built, beautiful homes made of wood.

So I, too, am pro-forest, but not if it means being anti-logging. In the end, the flourishing of wildness depends on the quality of our care for the forests we use, which will be most of them for the foreseeable future. That is the central, "slow wood" tenet of this book.

We tested that slow wood philosophy in the conservation forests of Weston, the leafy suburb of Boston where Faith was born and I landed in 1975, at the age of twenty. It has indeed been slow going, but we have persisted for over forty years. Land's Sake, a non-profit community farm and forest organization, still works with the town conservation commission to tap maple trees, thin firewood, and sometimes even harvest timber, across several hundred acres of the two-thousand-acre town forest. Much of the work has been done by young people. After helping conceive the program and run it for many years I passed those duties on but continued to serve on the Land's Sake board. The first twenty years of that adventure are recounted in my previous book, *Reclaiming the Commons*. Faith and I are still connected to Land's Sake and Weston in numerous ways.

I have to admit Land's Sake has never harvested as much wood from the Weston town forest as I would have liked, especially compared with that wealthy community's profligate wood consumption: the houses just keep getting bigger, and who knows where the materials for them originate. But at least we have kept the conversation going by running chainsaws where the people who inhabit those houses can hear them. Mostly Land's Sake has cut firewood, which just about pays for itself and provides winter work for the farm crew, requiring minimal investment in equipment: a logging winch for the tractor, a mechanical wood-splitter (over my cheerfully ignored objections), and some bar and chain oil. The silvicultural purpose of thinning firewood is to improve the growth of the remaining timber. We have occasionally harvested oak and pine timber in Weston, but in general that has proven more difficult. Cutting timber in the suburbs is economically daunting because it requires a larger outlay for machinery, extreme care in execution, and trucking logs to distant sawmills, leaving slender profit margins at best. An alternative was getting a band sawmill of our own and going into the lumber business; we tried that twice but never got it off the ground. Logging is a tough business—to succeed at a small scale, you would need to build strong direct markets for local wood products. That is also what this book is about.

Harvesting timber is even more daunting politically. It removes bigger trees than cutting firewood, leaves bigger messes, and gets more suburbanites up in arms. More than once, when we did cut big trees, we had to defend ourselves before the conservation commission from outraged Weston woodswalkers. We expected it, we prepared for it, and we always prevailed; over the years, we built a strong reservoir of community support and knew how to draw upon it when needed. This was following what were, honestly, some pretty lightweight timber harvests, working with borrowed or improvised equipment. Gearing up to go beyond firewood thinning to conduct regular timber cutting on a scale that would make economic sense is a goal that has so far eluded Land's Sake, but we keep at it. Perhaps the next half century will prove more conducive to local timber harvesting than the last—the more modest, sustainable world we began preparing for in the 1970s has not arrived as quickly as some of us hoped. It better come soon, though, because as the well-managed Weston town forest grows beautifully older and the trees get bigger, we are running out of firewood to thin.

In time I was asked to serve on the conservation commission, and so I left the Land's Sake board. Faith joined in my place and helped build the organization's education program. (In fact, when Land's Sake named a new greenhouse for us a few years ago, her name came first!) As chair of the conservation commission, I worked with Land's Sake to keep the forest program going, and to this day I help mark trees and prepare cutting plans, which are then approved by the state district forester. During my commission tenure we introduced bow hunting on town lands, to control the population of marauding deer. That caused an even bigger stir than logging, as it often does in suburban towns—in many ways, whether or not to hunt deer is the same debate as whether or not to cut timber, but even more emotionally charged. Once again, we were patient and polite, and when challenged at town meeting, we prevailed by a wide margin.

While working to manage suburban forests, I got to know those woods in another way. I returned to Brandeis to finish my schooling in history, and, in time, joined the faculty there. I studied forest ecology with colleagues at the Harvard Forest in central Massachusetts and became an associate of that venerable institution as well. Working with old tax records, deeds, and probated estates, I began to reconstruct the history of landownership and land use across thousands of acres of Weston, as well as neighboring Lincoln and Concord. I was interested in how farmers managed their fields, pastures, and woodlots over many generations and in the changing social and ecological forces that drove those shifting patterns of use. I learned to recognize many of the signs of those complex changes in the woods.

These studies drove home to me the idea that the land is *always* changing. The forest may have returned, but it is different from the one that was here before European settlement, which itself was never stable. Complete ecological "restoration" is not in the cards, because in our region nature is not inclined to return to an established "climax" state, as I had been taught when I was younger. Working to restore a healthy, flexible relationship with the changing forest we have *now* is more to the point. I also gained respect for the Yankee farmers I was studying, whose treatment of the land was not as irredeemable as I had once assumed. If gaining sympathy for your subjects is one of the hazards of working with primary source material, I succumbed. I later discovered that several of the families I had been researching were in fact my own ancestors, on my mother's mother's side.[4] As it turns out, I am indelibly a colonial settler. These are my people.

Working with colleagues at Harvard Forest, my students and I put in place a network of ecological inventory plots across the conservation forests of Weston, Lincoln, and Concord. These plots, some of which are paired with deer exclosures, are designed to allow us (or somebody) to follow how the forest changes in the future as it responds to ongoing disturbances such as climate change, windstorms, fire, and the impact of pestiferous species such as hemlock woolly adelgid and deer. The network is also laid out to compare areas we have logged with others that have been set aside as wild reserves. This is yet another way to know the forest, through ongoing collection of scientific data.[5]

So, without really planning to, over nearly half a century I developed a deep, complex, intensely rewarding relationship with the forests and other natural systems of one little corner of the planet. There are many places in those Weston and Concord woods where I have gone walking, birding, and skiing hundreds of times, but I also know all the owners of these places back to the 1630s. Sometimes I know when they cleared the land (if they did, which was in 90 percent of the cases), how they farmed it, and when they allowed it to return to forest. I also have some idea how the Native people who preceded the European colonists might have lived with that same land, though I am far less confident speaking about that. Just looking around a piece of woods, I can usually tell what has happened during the past century and sometimes as far back as the Civil War, although I tend to be cautious about "reading the land" even that recently, unless I also have the documents, tree rings, and soil pits to back me up, as I have guessed wrong so many times. I often know when the town acquired the property, and in some cases I helped protect it myself. And in Weston I know when we logged it since then, which was often twice.

In some places I know details about things that happened before I was born—the chestnut blight that reached our part of New England in the 1920s, the Hurricane of 1938—from people who witnessed those events a century ago and told me about it. They are gone now, as are most of those who helped Land's Sake get started and who served on our town boards and land trusts in those days. But some of the younger ones remain and have become lifelong friends, so when I walk in those woods I think of them, too—and sometimes bump into them. I also think of young people who worked with us or were my students, who have gone on to do similar work in other places. For me, a walk in the Weston or Concord woods is now about many generations of people, some of whom I know and some I never met, as much as it is about generations of trees.

Whose woods these are I think I know, and the names still live in my head. Faith was born in Weston center. At one point, we lived within half a mile of the house where she grew up, another house where her mother grew up, and a third house where her grandmother grew up. Our children are fifth-generation Westonites, which is pretty unusual these days. Given our deep ties to that community and its land, and its convenience to our places of employment—Faith taught in local schools, I taught at a nearby university—it would have made sense for us to stay put until the end of our days. But we didn't, and our motivations for leaving are similar to those of many other urbanites and suburbanites who move to the country. There was a push, and there was a pull.

The push was financial: no way could we afford to buy a house in Weston, let alone a farm—which hardly exist there anymore, in any case. We came close to acquiring one of the smallest houses in town (where we lived happily through the 1980s) at family rates. But thanks to a plot twist worthy of Thomas Hardy—a lost relative, an untimely death—the deal fell through at the eleventh hour. Owning that house might have kept us in Weston; it is hard to know. Or we could have just gone on renting—over the years we lived in all or part of seven houses in Weston, two of them twice. All belonged to family or friends, and the last one, where we lived for twenty years (in different parts of the same rambling structure) and raised our children while the events in this book were taking place, stands on one of the few remaining private farms. We could have stayed connected to our Weston roots, invested our modest funds in something other than property, and gone on with our unusual but satisfying suburban farmer and woodlander lifestyle.

But then there was the pull. We had always wanted a farm "of our own." (I put that in quotation marks for reasons that will become obvious.) Faith and I didn't really like living in the suburbs, even though it was our town—you can only pull the homespun wool over your own eyes for so long. It wasn't that we became disillusioned with or outgrew the Land's Sake community farm and forest adventure, exactly: it was that both of us had been planning to move to the country since we were kids, before we even met. Farming in Weston was always supposed to be just a temporary gig, a kind of training exercise. And indeed, we had acquired the necessary skills for country living: we knew how to back a trailer, operate a tractor, load a spreader, sharpen a chainsaw, fence a pasture, build a woodshed, plant a garden, birth a lamb, tap a maple, cultivate pumpkins, get along with our neighbors, and make hay while the sun shines. We had been doing those rural things for decades, without ever leaving suburbia. As a girl, Faith had dreamed of moving to her grandparents' summer place in Temple, New Hampshire, but that was sold before she came of age. As for me, since 1975 I had been assuring friends that I was planning to leave Weston in five years. Thirty years later, that was still the plan. Then one evening I got a call from a friend who knew we were looking for a farm, telling me to come see this place, right away, and to bring my snowshoes.

That was in March 2007, and the friend was John O'Keefe. John is a forest ecologist who was then the director of the Fisher Museum at the

Harvard Forest and also a member of the board of the Mount Grace Land Conservation Trust, which protects farm and forest land in central Massachusetts. The circumstances surrounding this particular farm were unusual, he explained, and urgent. It was the largest of three adjoining properties, tucked away in a small valley near the Connecticut River, in the process of being protected by a state Agricultural Preservation Restriction. Under the APR program, which dates back to the 1970s, the Commonwealth purchases a conservation restriction (called an "easement" in most other states) on a farm so that it remains in private hands but can no longer be developed: the owner receives the difference between the land's agricultural value and its full market value. This was not one of those phony schemes by which the wealthy get tax breaks for "protecting" land that was never going to be developed anyway, sometimes deploying an inflated appraised value. This was a "working farm" easement. Anyone who purchases an APR property must continue to farm it, and the state checks annually to make sure legitimate agricultural activity is actually taking place.[6]

Getting a farm selected to receive an APR is highly competitive because there are many deserving properties and not enough funds to protect them all. Securing the APR requires a lot of lead time and up-front costs, so land trusts such as Mount Grace often step in to pre-acquire the restriction and later transfer it to the state when the funding comes through, which often depends in turn on federal sources and takes a couple of years. The land trust often raises these bridging funds by borrowing from local donors, and those loans have to be secured. The town conservation commission usually kicks in some money as well, to demonstrate local community support for the project.

Orchestrating all this is arduous enough, but this particular deal had gone totally haywire. Just as the state appraisal was being completed but before the APR agreement had been signed, the owners' personal situation changed and they decided to sell the property immediately, as they needed to cash out. To everyone's consternation, they put the farm on the market. A normal buyer would have been under no obligation to accept the unconsummated APR, so the project, and possibly the land, would have been lost.

Then an unusual thing happened. I have served on the boards of several land trusts and I have never heard of anything quite like it, and neither has anyone else I know (although I have heard different versions of this story, with interesting discrepancies I won't go into here). The president of the Mount Grace board, a man named Dick French, abruptly resigned without telling anyone why. Dick, who has some moxie, went down and bought the farm himself. He signed a purchase and sale agreement with the owners and arranged his own financing to back it. But he had no intention of ever actually owning the farm. He went back to Mount Grace and told the board he had frozen the property: now all that was needed was a buyer who would take it from him at closing, accept the APR, and cover his costs. And this person was needed in about a month. The scramble was on to find a conservation buyer who was also a legitimate farmer, and Mount Grace board members fanned out across the countryside in search of one. That's why John O'Keefe was calling me. So that weekend I threw my snowshoes in the truck, picked up John, and went to meet Dick and see the place.

I didn't really know what to expect—few things in life turn out to be as good as advertised. But then again, John is not known to exaggerate, and he would not be dragging me out here for nothing. We turned off onto a side road, then another side road, and then down a gravel road, which was a good sign. If you live on a dirt road, the volume and velocity of traffic past your front porch drops precipitously, and you can actually sit there and enjoy the evening. Neighbors are likely to walk on your road and say hello, without fearing for their lives or having to shout. That the road has never been paved is itself an indication that it isn't a very good way of getting anywhere else very fast. All country roads should be dirt roads.

The snow from a recent spring nor'easter was still lying a couple of feet deep in the woods, much more than we had left back in Weston—another good sign. I was feeling younger by the minute; I was going back in time, reliving a dream I first had when I was twenty. The winters really were colder back then, of course—by moving a hundred miles inland, I could even return to the *climate* of my youth. We came down the hill and out of a pine woods, and all at once we were in an open, gently terraced valley, with big old trees standing along the road (shagbark hickories and sugar maples, an arresting juxtaposition of south and north) and fields running off in all directions, flanked by hedgerows and little belts of woods, with more forest above. Then there was an old white farmhouse and a big red barn sporting a slate roof with a dead level spine, standing at a bend in the road. It was a place from another time, not from my own youth but rather from my grandfather's youth over a century ago. I am far from the only person to feel that way—it is pretty much a universal reaction. We later learned that many local people have their own pet names for our farm, such as "Hidden Valley" or "Paradise Valley." All places are important, but this one was magical.

We drove past the barn and parked by a broad wind-swept field of about twenty acres, in a spot plowed out by the highway department to turn its trucks. A little river just beyond the field marked the town line, but the bridge was closed because of flood damage a few years earlier, turning what was already a road less traveled into a dead end, serving only two farms. The bridge has since been repaired, but there is still hardly any traffic. Paradise, found.

We strapped on our snowshoes and started walking into the late-morning sun. Dick apologized that on such short notice he hadn't been able to arrange permission to view the house, but we could at least see the farm. I said I wasn't too concerned about the house; we could check that out later—what I really cared about was the land. This is a book about a new house that now stands on that property next to the old one, but at the time I really didn't care much about houses, though now I do. Dick didn't say anything then, but he told me later that was why he sold us the place: others who had expressed interest just wanted to see the house. We were the first who turned immediately to the fields and woods—we had the right priorities.

As we tramped across the big field I was captivated by a line of grand old trees along the little river, running high and noisy with snow melt, a few hundred yards to the west. I asked if those were really sugar maples, which seemed odd standing that close to the water. Dick said he thought they were and agreed it was unusual; he guessed the bank was pretty high on this side. And indeed, I then noticed that a line of sycamores just beyond the maples was on the far side of the stream, down in the narrow floodplain. We trudged on over the brilliant snow crust, talking about the history of New England's forests, the ways that different trees had been used and how they responded to generations of cutting, the discussion coming around to white pine, as it always does with Dick, who does colonial millwork. There was plenty of white pine in view, too, along the brook on the opposite, east side of the field and on up the slope that enclosed the little valley, mixed with hemlock and hardwoods that looked to be domi-

nated by oaks, stretching all the way to the top of the hill: this farm came
with a noble woodlot.

We kept walking south, through the softening snow. Past the big field
the open land rose twenty feet or so and narrowed atop a river terrace that
went on for another quarter mile, a long winding tail a few hundred feet
wide between the river on the right and the brook, beaver ponds, and
meadows on the left, flanked with handsome woods on either side. It
seemed like it just kept going and going. At last we reached the southern
end, a little five-acre field tucked into a bowl of high wooded hills where
the river and brook met, with lots of maple, pine, and hemlock, the back
of beyond. We turned around and tramped back out, the bright spring sun
now behind us, lighting up the forested hillside and shining on another
small farm and more woods lying away to the north, up the valley. It was
an astonishingly beautiful and diverse piece of land.

I drove home exhilarated. Faith and I were a few years either side of
fifty—still young and strong enough to tackle something like this. It was a
170-acre farm: fifty acres of fields and one hundred acres of woods, with
beaver pond, swamp, and riparian forest thrown in. It had a little bit of
everything as it ran from river bank to ridge top, enclosed in its valley by
several other farms and woodlands, two of them also to be protected in the
same complex conservation deal. That cherished old dream of moving to
the country, which we had reluctantly set aside time after time when we
chose to stay in (or return to) Weston to pursue the upstart dream of suburban community farming, had suddenly been offered to us all over again.

The only slight drawback was that we couldn't afford it—but that
had never stopped us before. In the past we had solved that problem simply by not owning anything: renting all those charming houses and working on community land that didn't belong to us—at least not in fee, but
only by common usufruct and the trusted position we had earned in the
community. In Weston, I had the keys to two thousand acres of forest and
farmland, without owning a single acre (I still carry them in my truck, actually). That strategy wasn't going to work this time: to pull this off, we
were going to have to borrow more than a dull ax. And we were going to
need help.

We never really considered farming on our own. Land in New England is expensive, and we doubted we could swing it by ourselves—at
least, not on the scale of a farm that would really fire our imagination and

test our resolve. For several years we had searched with two younger couples, until they found a place that was perfect for them but too suburban for us—it is now Simple Gifts Farm in North Amherst. We knew that if we didn't hurry up, one day soon we might have to settle for a more modest retirement farmette with a nice garden, an assortment of fruit trees, and maybe a pair of goats, but we weren't quite ready for those green pastures just yet. Therefore, we were going to need active and competent farm partners.

Beyond the cost of acquiring the land, there would be the expense and labor of running the place. We assumed we would keep some version of our day jobs, both because we would need the income but also because teaching and writing are rewarding for us. That meant the work of farming would have to be shared. Harmonious sharing of both labor and management can be complicated, of course, but it has compelling advantages. Farming in America often evokes a mythos of independent self-reliance, but our own experience, not to mention any unblinkered study of the nation's agrarian history, reveals that the resulting rural isolation has been a crushing cultural disaster. On the contrary, one should never farm alone.

Two things made buying this farm remotely possible for us: family and friends. On the family side, my father had died a few years earlier and my mother was showing the first signs of dementia, which worried her. She was anxious that her assets pass along to her children as quickly as possible, rather than staying tied up with her, where as she saw it they would be increasingly wasted. Besides substantial annual gifts, she was willing to make loans against the value of her estate, which was not enormous but enough to make a difference: it consisted of dad's TIAA annuity (which had some residual value beyond her life), some other investments, and her house in Pittsburgh, which she owned free and clear.

My two brothers and I availed ourselves of this family bank at times during those difficult years, and then we settled accounts after our mother died and our own houses were built. Faith and I could not have bought the farm and built our house on the strength of her earnings as a teacher and my professor's salary alone, but we were able to draw on the modest wealth accumulated by a professor in the previous generation. My father, who rose to eminence as a space scientist, once told us that in real terms his salary peaked in the mid-1960s, in the middle of his ascending career; this benchmark certainly tells us something about where this country has been going since the 1970s. In spite of that, his three children still had access to meaningful generational wealth, while many others, who have worked much harder all their lives than certainly I have, do not; this fact also tells us something about where we have been going.

Even so, in spite of modest but meaningful family wealth and a substantial discount on the land because of the APR, the price of the farm was too steep for us alone. We were going to have to split it with somebody else—to split the ownership, that is, not the property. We were going to own (as it says in old deeds) an "undivided moiety" of this place. Luckily, we had compatible friends to whom we could turn for that matching half. Tom Chalmers and Joan Meyer were about our age but had children a few years older, already on their way out of the Weston schools. Tom and I served together on the conservation commission, and for a few years he went in with Faith and me on a small flock of meat lambs, just for fun. I agreed to let Tom join in that enterprise to teach him a little about farming, but I quickly discovered that his innate competence is in fact an order of magnitude greater than mine—that is, anything mechanical that might take me an hour takes Tom six minutes. Okay, maybe ten minutes. Of those basic farming skills I mentioned earlier, the only two at which I excel Tom are running a chainsaw and growing pumpkins—and I only went back and added pumpkins to the list just now, so I could claim more than one.

Tom is an architect but has also made a living as a carpenter. His business around Weston was doing well at the time, this being the year *before* the Great Recession, thank goodness. Things were about to get tough for a few years, but Tom didn't know that yet. Joan had a demanding job as an environmental economist. She worked on fascinating cases that she often couldn't even discuss with us until they went to trial or were settled (and sometimes not even then), often involving someone who had knowingly violated environmental regulations for profit—her job was to figure out which shell company the miscreants hid the money under. Grifters would not want to mess with Joan. Tom's brother had a farm in Vermont with draft horses and a sugar bush, and I knew that Tom and Joan harbored a fantasy of someday moving to the country, too. So that evening I called him up and asked if they would like to buy a farm with us.

We all went out the next weekend and met with Dick French again, and this time we were able to view the house. It was in rough shape, but fixing up shaky old houses while living in them was something Tom and

Joan had done many times before; it was kind of how they rolled. They didn't exactly flip houses—just gently turned them over as they moved through the stages of life. Fortunately for us, when the owners of our prospective farm cut the APR deal with the state they had excluded not just the existing house but also a second lot in case any of their children might someday want to live nearby. The appraisal therefore assumed there would be another two-acre lot somewhere on the property, excluded from the protected farmland—and the uncompleted APR survey could still define where exactly that parcel would go.

It was a perfect setup: Tom and Joan could buy the existing house and fix it up, Faith and I could buy a lot and build another house there in about five years, and we all could form a partnership to own the rest of the land together, sharing the farm decisions and expenses right down the middle. Which is exactly what we did. We agreed that such an arrangement could only survive without tensions and resentments inevitably wrecking it if the stakes were equal, so no one was beholden to anyone else. So far, so good.

As for the land, the others were as enchanted as I was. The next evening, after we had a chance to talk it over, I called Dick and told him we wanted it. A few nerve-wracking days went by while Dick weighed other offers. Then he called me back and announced: "The land is yours." The whole thing took about two weeks. After dreaming about it for over thirty years, we had a farm of our own.

The closing took place in July, the day after my fifty-second birthday. I won't detail everything it took to get this deal to closing—I'll just say, for those who are conservationists, this would make an excellent case study for an MBA course on the subject. There was setting up the limited liability company to own the farm (and to lease the barn from Tom and Joan, since it stands on their lot), finishing the APR land survey that also set the boundaries of the house lots, getting the local conservation commission to approve the building envelope on our lot as it fell within the wetland buffer even though that lot did not yet legally exist (not to mention determining that the brook at that point was an intermittent rather than perennial stream, keeping us out of the more stringent provisions of the state's Riverfront Act), getting a perc test to make sure it was indeed a buildable lot, confirming the Chapter 61a "current use" property-tax abatement for farm and forest land would remain in place, completing an approved Natural

Resource Conservation Service (NRCS) farm conservation plan (one of the requirements of the APR process, as federal matching funds flow through NRCS), even agreeing with Mount Grace on a fallback partial-development option for the property, which would make their lenders whole in the event the state and federal money didn't come through and part of the land had to be sold—tellingly, that plan would have sacrificed the woodland to save the farmland. If you could understand that entire sentence, you should teach the course. I probably already know you.

Oddly there was no haggling over price, because that had already been fixed before we came into the picture—we just agreed to pay it, plus everybody's costs. At closing the property passed from the previous owners through Dick French to four separate buyers: Tom and Joan bought the existing house and barn, Faith and I bought an adjoining house lot, our new LLC bought 167 acres of beautiful farm and wood land, and Mount Grace bought the agricultural preservation restriction. I remember looking around the conference room and realizing that we were paying for both our own lawyer and Mount Grace's lawyer, who fortunately (and not coincidentally) had adjoining offices. A year or two after that the state funding did come through, but it came a few months later than anticipated, so we discovered we were liable for yet one more cost, tucked into the fine print (for extra credit on the take-home exam): paying interest to the lenders who had financed Mount Grace's pre-acquisition of the APR. Ah, yes— *we* were guaranteeing those loans. To those local philanthropic lenders' credit, they had been donating the interest up to that point.

One detail that does seem worth dwelling on is our choice concerning where to put the second house lot, which could have been anywhere on the property that had sufficient road frontage. We toyed with the idea of building our new home in a more isolated and private spot, as there were sites up the hill with noble views and another road that touched the back side of the woodlot. One corner in particular could have been carved out as a seat for a magnificent edifice overlooking our farm valley from a prominent eminence. That was certainly the most valuable potential house lot on the property, in normal real estate terms. It had that coveted "location" to the third degree.

But we remembered that we had come to work the land in common, not survey it. By lineage and inclination we were not lords but lowly peasants. Aspiring yeomen, not retiring gentry. The highest and best views could be occasionally hiked to, and so earned. Living close to the barn would put us together at the center of things and be less disruptive of the whole. Two houses set far apart would have created separate spheres of influence; instead, as it came to be, we share the same somewhat cluttered outlook, the same noises and smells. So, in consultation with our partners (who would lose something of their own pristine seat and have to put up with us), we chose to build right next door.

I mention this because exurban development in rural areas is not going to stop anytime soon, and in fact it is once again on the rise. This is not necessarily a bad thing: if the countryside is to become prosperous and well-tended, it must be resettled. But it should not be chopped all to pieces in the process. In most cases the best way is to cluster new buildings as close as possible to existing ones, to avoid defacing the working landscape with showy palaces and idle lawns plopped all over creation like cow pies. The catch is that people love their privacy and sense of personal control. I once heard a seasoned land use planner remark that the only thing suburban Americans hate worse than sprawl is density.

I can now faithfully report that when faced with this dilemma ourselves, we chose density. In fact, while we were working through the complicated process of buying the property, we were told point-blank by more than one local citizen that the community had worked long and hard to protect our little valley with its idyllic mix of fields, woodlands, and historic buildings, and they were counting on us not to mess it up. Since I had written a book called *Reclaiming the Commons,* which several of them had actually read, we were open to scrutiny. "Your coming has long been foretold," remarked one of those canny old hippies to me at a garden party, with a penetrating and skeptical eye. The first test is where you build. The next test is what you build.

It was an odd feeling for us, owning private property—having spent so much of our lives working on, and championing, the commons. Our contention that private ownership should play a subordinate (and shrinking) role within a larger context of growing common interest in land still held, but our home base along that spectrum had shifted. The common interest in property can be expressed in several ways. First of all, to "own" land is merely a temporary privilege. I am acutely aware of this not only as a person who looks to the future and considers his own mortality, but also as a historian who retains a vivid sense of the lives that have shaped our place in the past: people who labored as I do (only harder) and cared for the place as I do (only more) and then passed away, having left their mark for us to ponder. I firmly believe in the ancient agrarian creed that our duty as landowners is to pass the land along to the next in line in at least as good shape as we received it, if not a little better. I have good evidence that some of our predecessors felt the same. In a sense, then, any private tenure inevitably becomes common over time.

But beyond such glib observations that rest effortlessly on the unstoppable passage of time and certainty of death, I remain a strong advocate for deliberately moving a larger part of the landscape back into more formal common ownership right here and now, particularly at the local level. I say "back" because that's where it all came from not so long ago: on our place the experiment in private landownership is barely older than those big sugar maples along the river bank. When the *parents* of those trees were alive the Abenaki still held this land, and the alienating modern concept of owning private property in fee simple was as yet undiscovered, even back in England, let alone in America—even today, we are only a couple of generations of trees into it. We were naturally pleased when, a few years after we bought our farm, the town established a large community forest on property just north of ours, again under the leadership of Dick French and with assistance from the Franklin Land Trust and the Massachusetts Department of Conservation and Recreation. Land conservation continues in our little valley, and we have become part of that effort. Other local landowners have taken note of what we did and sought our advice in conserving their own land, which is as it should be.

Between the poles of unrestricted private ownership on one side and land held by the public in fee on the other lies the middle ground of private land that is covered by various sorts of conservation restrictions, or easements. A public agency or non-profit conservation organization usually holds the restriction, which at minimum prevents the landowner from building on the property but otherwise affords them normal rights to occupy and improve it. Such easements are often donated or sold at a discount by owners who want to see their land protected, and there are currently many more landowners who want to make such deals than there are funds to accommodate them.

Easements are well suited for protecting working farms and woodlands—at least those owned in small pieces, by people who really care for them. I am among the authors of the "Wildlands and Woodlands" vision for New England, which proposes that 80 percent of the region should remain forest and farmland, protected partly by outright common ownership and partly by such restrictions. It was interesting and instructive, while working to write and promote such a sweeping vision, to be part of seeing a small piece of it implemented on land we came to own. Farm and forest conservation on such a grand scale would still leave ample room for residential and commercial development in rural areas—far more room, in fact, than is ever likely to be needed. But it would concentrate that development, leaving forests and farms as much as possible unfragmented and intact. For us, it was an exciting new experience to take part not only in land conservation but in just such clustered rural development, in harmony with sustainable use of the surrounding natural landscape, by building our own house.

TWO

Fencing Out the Forest

IT WOULD BE A FEW YEARS BEFORE we were ready to start building. Meanwhile, Tom and I got to work on our new farm, which was also an old farm. First, as we intended to raise livestock, we needed a fence.

For years our place had been hayed by a local farmer who has a cow-calf operation and cut many fields in the neighborhood. We were happy to make the transition from his tenure to ours long and gradual. It was going to take us a few years to get the place fenced, acquire the nucleus of a herd, and get our own equipment, so in the meantime the old farmer kept cutting the hay, first for himself and later partly for us, in exchange for cash and some help wrapping bales. As is customary we didn't charge anything for the use of our land, the logic being that the farmer is doing the land-owner a service, keeping the field mowed and open, that is at least equal in value to the standing hay. As he was getting on in years while we were just coming into our prime, it all worked out pretty well.

I offer this as another tip for anyone moving to the country. You will surprise no one if you assume complete control of your place the moment you arrive: new broom sweeps clean. But remember, old broom knows the corners. If you take your time and honor existing arrangements, treating your new property like something others may have some history with and ongoing interest in, you may reap unexpected rewards. You will learn things about the neighborhood you might not otherwise have known, and you will secure ready access to neighborly assistance. For a purely hypo-thetical example, suppose years later you can't find the top half of your power take-off shaft after you have already filled your spreader with ma-nure and you suddenly realize that might be because some idiot left it *in-side* the spreader for safekeeping. After probing uselessly with a manure fork for a few minutes, you will know where to go borrow a substitute PTO shaft to take your spreader for a spin around the field and see if the old one eventually comes flying out the back, which it did.

Laying cable before hanging a gate: Tom, Brian, Liam, and Maggie (behind the fence). I am trying to cut the conduit with my trusty Felco pruners; Tom holds the tool that will do the job in a second. The fence line follows the edge of the woods. (Faith Rand)

To build a fence, you have to negotiate with the trees. This has always been the fundamental challenge of farming in our part of the world: holding back the forest. History suggests that like life itself this is a losing battle but fun while it lasts. In New England, the cultivated and the wild can't easily be kept apart: it takes work. The woods enclose the farm, they embrace the farm, they lean into the fields: they want it back, and they exude quiet confidence. That line between farm and forest is always changing. It is never a permanent boundary but only a brief truce, forever contested.

At one time not so long ago, we Yankee farmers were winning—we were too far ahead, in fact. Behind the present field edges, back in the woods, you will find rusted barbed-wire fences that run smack through the middle of trees; behind them again are stone walls relaxing back to glacial rubble; and everywhere you will cross blurring boundaries among mature stands of white pines, red maples, and curving oaks that mark once clean edges dividing pastures, meadows, and woodlots. By the time of the Civil War, the farmers seemed pretty much in command and likely to all but eliminate the wild forest forever, much to the chagrin of Henry Thoreau.

But now the trees have regained the upper hand. In spite of the monumental labor invested in those good fences by our great-great-grandfathers and their great and good neighbors, farmers have been steadily losing ground for generations. The forests of New England (along with many of its signature creatures such as bear, beaver, and deer), which had all but disappeared, have now returned in triumph. This is in many ways a good thing, but we farmers have mixed feelings about it, and we have not given up yet. On our farm my chief agrarian responsibility (besides growing pumpkins) is holding that line, and I take it seriously. I never get out of my truck without sticking my trusty Felco pruners in my hip pocket, in case I need to cut something. You never know what vegetation may be sneaking up behind you.

We fence to keep the stock in but also to keep the trees out. I admire the forest, but I know it to be a formidable and implacable foe of farmland. The forest would take everything back, if it could. Had Thoreau not died at forty-four, he would have seen an amusement park pop up at Walden Pond, as I mentioned earlier. I might have added that had he survived tuberculosis and lived to eighty-eight, he would have seen that establishment disappear back into the woods. I could show you the cinders of the old oval racetrack, but you would never even notice the rest. I'm not even sure where the dance hall was.[1]

The lower part of our field hadn't had its borders cut back in years. There had been no livestock to speak of on the place since about 1960, when the dairy farm three owners back went under. Overhanging branches and windfalls make it hard to hay right up to the edge of a field, and so every year the woods creep in stealthily behind the mower. Before building a new fence, our first objective was to push the trees back to where the fence line had run half a century earlier, hard against the older woods. That meant ten to twenty feet of young growth to clear in some places, branches from the larger trees behind them to lop off as high as we could reach with a chainsaw from the bed of the truck (which is not entirely safe, but everybody does it), a few leaners behind them again that were going to be nothing but trouble, so might as well cut them now: hemlock and pine, white and red oak, black cherry, chokecherry, chokeberry, sugar and red maple, black and white birch, a little ash, the odd beech, elm, and hickory thrown in, one or two serviceberries and plenty of muscular ironwood twisting in slantwise underneath.

Tom and I did this hard-driving work the second fall we owned the place, with the leaves off the trees but the ground still open, running two saws. We employed younger people (my former students) to help drag the brush out of the field back into the woods and to load the firewood. Tom had installed a woodstove at the old farmhouse, and I could haul wood home to satiate the three stoves we were feeding at our ramshackle old place in Weston (two for us, one for Polly, our beloved landlady and life-long friend), so we bucked and trucked firewood as we went. I hate leaving wood on the ground, and I dislike driving home with an empty truck. To this day, most of the firewood we burn to heat the two houses at the farm, and a good bit of what we burn back in Weston, is generated simply by maintaining those fence lines. Yes, the trees want the fields again, but we can heat our homes forever by resolutely beating them back. There is great satisfaction in that.

With our boundaries re-established, it was time to build a fence. Here we got an assist from President Obama and from you. As you may recall, the spring after the crash of 2008 a (woefully inadequate) federal stimulus package was passed, and a small part of those funds flowed through NRCS. With our farm conservation plan already in place, Tom and I were shovel-ready. Because our fields abut both the river and the brook, we qualified for a grant from the Environmental Quality Incentives Program to protect water quality on both sides. Cultivating crops, spreading manure, and pas-turing livestock can flush sediment and nutrients into waterways, unless mitigated by best management practices. Though we were pushing the trees back in some places, in others our fields ran right to the river bank. There we agreed to pull the line of our new fence back and let brush and trees grow up in between, establishing a riparian buffer. This protects the river from agricultural runoff and also shades it, which is desirable because as a cold-water stream, it harbors native brook trout.[2]

In exchange we got cost-sharing to build a six-wire, high-tensile elec-tric fence. It is a heck of a fence, if I do say so. We built two miles of it—exactly what it would have taken to fence an entire 160-acre quarter-section in Kansas, yet here we only enclosed about forty acres for the same yardage, but hey: this is New England. A mile of fence just doesn't go as far. NRCS paid a bit more than two dollars a foot, which is just about what it would have cost to hire a contractor to build the fence for us, so fair enough. But then the contractor would have had all the fun, and, besides, the materials were only half the cost. So Tom and I saw a legitimate opportunity to build the fence ourselves and pocket the difference to cover our own labor, which was considerable. It was the most profitable thing we have ever done on our farm, by far. Your tax dollars at work—though I doubt you were even paying us minimum wage. In return, you are welcome to come fish in the cold, shady stream—the state stocks it, besides the native brookies, so you might have some luck, if you time it just right. To keep faith with the public, although it is not a requirement, I maintain a trail along the river bank for you.

Tom took on the most exacting part of the job, which was building the corners and gate ends—the parts of a fence that need to be braced to take the strain of the high-tension springs in the line. My second piece of advice for aspiring young farmers (after never farm alone) is this: always farm with somebody who knows how to fix things. Especially if like me you are just a reformed intellectual, with recidivist tendencies. When an ancient piece of farm equipment breaks mid-task, as they often do, I typically waste the next few minutes cursing the universe and bewailing my fate, before settling down and figuring out how I'm going to get the job done some other way. Tom just gets happy, because a beneficent providence has granted him yet another opportunity to practice his welding.

We set the posts about one hundred feet apart, leaving room for a truck road outside the fence in the upper part of the field where we were creating our riparian buffer. In the lower part where we had pushed the woods back, we decided to use trees for posts (attaching pressure-treated two-bys to protect them from the wires) wherever we could, hating to surrender any of what we had worked so hard to recover. That was a mistake: you should always leave room behind your fence to run a tractor with a brush hog to keep the line clear. The livestock can mostly handle the front side of the fence; the back side is your responsibility. It's worth giving up a few feet of pasture in exchange for ease of maintenance, and you won't grow that much grass right next to the woods anyway.

We had 140 posts to put in the ground, the part of fencing that every farmer abhors: digging post holes. We didn't do it—instead we rented a post-pounder that ran off the rear hydraulics on our tractor. This thing was great: it had "High & Heavy Hitter" stenciled on it by some previous admirer. The high and heavy hitter held the posts plumb and drove them two feet into the earth, wham, just like that—they weren't even sharpened. Our bottomland soil is sand and gravel without much in the way of stones— not ideal for growing grass, perhaps, but great for pounding posts. They usually went in straight, but if they did hit a rock and go awry we just wrapped a chain and yanked them back out, moved over a foot, and sank them again. We drove all the posts in a single weekend.

With the posts in the ground and the corners built the rest of the job was straightforward, just a matter of incremental steps, the sort of thing you can put a few hours into whenever you want. We tacked six insulators to each post, ran wires through them from gate to gate, cut heavy springs into each wire, and ratcheted them tight. Then we put in fiberglass rod battens every thirty feet or so—two between each set of wooden posts—to keep the wires at the correct height and stiffen the fence. Finally, we flushed the posts to a uniform height, a foot above the top wire. Building a fence is a good way to let the neighborhood know that you mean business and are at least minimally competent, so it better look sharp. Naturally, the gate end that goes out of whack from the strain of the wires will be right next to the road. No amount of banging that effing post back down with the tractor bucket will ever fix it. But if all the other corners and gates are square and true, the crooked one will earn you more sympathy than scorn. The people you want to impress are the ones who know what they are looking at.

Building that fence took us about a year, chipping away at it. Tom and I got the last gates hung one soft and lovely evening in July, and we went out to celebrate with a late supper at a local tavern. We had the energizer wired in the barn but not yet hooked up, because we had a little conduit work left to do to run the juice out to the fence. When we returned, in the afterglow of sunset, we looked out in our brand-new pasture and danged if there weren't five head of cattle out there, grazing peacefully in the gloaming: two cows, two calves, and a heifer. Wow: fence it, and they will come! We ran around and closed all the gates, which we had left open because—well, because we didn't have any livestock. But now we did. In the morning we made some calls and learned whose cows these almost certainly were; we were also told that we should ask the owner to come fetch them with his trailer, not just turn them out the back gate to find their own way home through the woods. And in fact the cattle were now circling the pasture fence in a little procession, as if trying to remember how they got in, and making some noise about it, too. I *know* it was back here somewhere, they seemed to be saying. Where did it go?

A few hours later the owner arrived with his trailer, but when we went to show him his rambling cows and help him round them up, they were gone. Vanished, as mysteriously as they had appeared, and all the gates still shut tight. Apparently, these half-ton creatures had magically walked right through a six-wire high-tensile fence, or jumped over it, or something. To them, gates were mere formalities. Proving once again the importance of electricity to an electric fence, which is not a lesson you will be content to learn only once in your farming career. The following spring we bought five bred Devon heifers, and our own herd was begun. We immediately began to lose money, unless you count our labor as profit—the secret to success in farming. Building that fence is not only the most profitable thing we have ever done, it is almost the *only* profitable thing we have ever done, other than cut timber. But we did not get into farming to make money. We got into farming to cover our costs, to build something for the future, and to keep from losing our minds.

The fence is where the farm and forest meet: it defines which side is which, on our watch. It remains an active work zone. We mow behind the fence where we can, and once or twice a year I strap on the big Husky brush cutter and slip it along underneath the bottom wire to keep woody stuff from getting established; now that's a workout. That triangular brush cutting blade just pings harmlessly off the wire, by the way, rather than causing mayhem: letting a whirling piece of sharpened steel get anywhere near a wire fence seems like something you should perhaps avoid, but go ahead and swing—it's perfectly safe. Presuming all your wires are horizontal, of course—I wouldn't recommend it with wire mesh. Down in the lower pasture where the fence meets the woods I have been working for years with the chainsaw, endlessly cutting overhanging branches and small trees, keeping enough room behind the fence to comfortably swing the brush cutter. Every winter I re-clear a few hundred yards, and I can see now that holding even this narrow strip will be a lifelong battle, going around and around, because the woods grow back as fast as I can cut them. But again, we need the firewood.

It's funny—to cut one corner, we ran the fence a few hundred yards diagonally through the woods, and along that stretch nothing at all grows up under the wires, because there is no light. Not much ever falls on it, either. Maintaining a fence in the woods requires almost no work, so that might be your best option, instead of moving it out into the field: move it a few yards back under the trees, away from the light. In fact, other farmers have since told us we should have done just that. Live and learn. Generations of foresters will scold you for allowing stock in the woods, but as a farmer you have to play both sides of the ball. All the action is at the edge, where everything grows greedily toward the light: up, down, and sideways. Reaching out into the field for light makes it more likely that the trees will fall, and when they do fall, they fall on your fence. Luckily, one of the many virtues of high-tensile electric fencing is that once you cut off the fallen weight, the fence springs right back into place as if nothing ever happened. Well, you might have to replace a fiberglass batten now and then, but that's about it. Running a chainsaw and preserving fields has become my most abiding and congenial agricultural labor—it seems to be the work I was born to. The jury is no longer out on that.

This book is mostly about managing the forest and building our house, and I will get to that; but I wanted to start with the fence to make a couple of points about the nature of the woods and the nature of work. First, for us the woods exist in the context of the farm. The farm is why we are here, and the woods are part of the farm—two-thirds of it, in fact. Woodlots have always been an integral part of New England farms, even when they were reduced to less than one quarter of the landscape and pastures, fields, and meadows occupied all the rest. When I am working along the fence line I am constantly reminded that the two sides exist in a tension that is never resolved. Everything that is now open was once forest and may yet become forest again. But then again, most of what is now woods was once cleared, and in most cases it remained cultivated for a century or more before reverting to trees. It could become farmland again someday, too. We should think about this relationship from both sides at once and not lose too much sleep over a few feet, or even a few million acres, of slippage in either direction from generation to generation. Within reasonable bounds, either would be a desirable outcome, when compared to the alternative: subdivisions, or widely scattered McMansions.

Forest once again covers a majority of even densely settled southern

New England, and conserving that continuous forest provides important ecological benefits: water quality, wildlife habitat, carbon sequestration. Viewed from outside the fence, farmland is just one more interruption in the naturally wooded landscape, and the integrity of the forest is what counts. But the forest also exists within a continuous matrix of farms, or former farms. The forest comprises old woodlots and regrown pastures lying within particular ownerships, even if it sums to a majority of the landscape. This does not mean that the woods should be treated as just another crop—the forest does have emergent qualities that transcend its individual parcels and its production of timber. But on the other hand, we don't want to be so mesmerized by its transcendent eco-ness that we are afraid to mess with it. The woods are not fragile—they are powerful, resilient, and opportunistic. That is one thing you can stay well informed about by building a fence within their reach.

The second point has to do with the nature of that work. We know our farm mainly by working it. We do put our implements down now and then and walk the place (and our neighbors' places) for simple pleasure— along the river, down the brook to the beaver pond, or up to the woods on the hill. We maintain trails so others can walk, too. But we know the shape of the farm mostly through work: the way it looks in changing seasons, at odd hours, in rough weather, from unexpected angles. We have seen it mostly with tools in our hands or from the seat of a tractor. The wildlife that frequents it we most often encounter while working. I carry binoculars in the truck and wear them on the job when I can (a small pair works best). I know where the wild sapsucker nests, which is one dying tree along the fence I decided not to cut. I know where the barbed wire once ran not only from seeing it but also from time spent resharpening my chain after rediscovering it the hard way.

Beyond giving us ample opportunity to see and resee the shape of the farm, the work we do *creates* that shape, year after year. Our work determines what grows where and when: trees, grass, crops—the relentless surge of vegetation up out of the ground toward the sun, the animals that chew it back—the warp and weft of our world. What we see is shaped partly by what we plant, but much more by what we *cut,* and how frequently: felling trees, mowing hay, directing our animals where to graze. Farming in New England is mainly about harvesting the perennial growth of grass and trees, and mediating the bounds between them. The place where the work of crafting that growth is most intense, and where the character of the place is most sharply defined, is along that edge where field and forest meet.

This creative outdoor work is deeply rewarding in at least three ways. First there is the enjoyment of the produce that comes from it, without which the work would have no purpose: meat from the livestock that graze the grass and clover, firewood that warms us, timber that frames our house. The meat and timber we mostly sell, but we do consume some of it ourselves, so our work rewards us in that most direct and satisfying way. Second is the landscape that is created by that harvesting, with its interplay of woods and fields in different shades and textures of green. If one "owns" land, that privilege comes with a duty to care for it responsibly—to minimize the impact of the farm on the quality of water in the river, for example. As soon as you acquire a cow, you are also entrusted with the well-being of brook trout. The health and beauty of the landscape finds an unerring mirror in the flavor of the food and figure of the wood we consume. If you don't think that a grilled steak tastes better when you are looking out over the pastures that provided the meat, not to mention the hedgerows that provided the oak and maple coals for the grilling (and maybe a little hickory bark for smoke flavor), I am here to suggest that your palate might benefit from further education.

And if you can feel the lingering ache of maintaining those pastures and hedgerows in your muscles, your steak will taste better still. Because third, and not to be overlooked, is the physical pleasure and satisfaction of doing the work that creates both the produce and the landscape—of employing the body to carry out the intention of the mind to impose a desired human order on the boisterous growth of nature. This last point is so simple I am almost embarrassed to mention it, but I guess I better. Outdoor manual labor *feels good.* While washing the dishes, I listen to authors on National Public Radio talking earnestly about their new book on mindfulness and living in the moment or about the latest study confirming the importance of physical exercise to the health of not just the body but also the mind. No kidding; really? Who would have thought it? Or yet another book about how we no longer spend enough time outdoors, in nature, and how we should take more walks.

"You fools," I cry, "just go outside and *work!* Plant a garden, or something. You'll get all three at once." Not only that, I will only have to write one book instead of three, which leaves me more time to go out and work, too. Think of the savings! I would rather work on our farm than write about it, by a ratio of roughly two to one, as long as I am able. Conceivably that last third, this writing bit, helps curate mindfulness—and why does everything need to be curated these days? Why does everything suddenly need to be resilient or vibrant? "Don't shout at the radio," Faith scolds me; "you're upsetting the children." But I know she agrees with me, and by now the children are just amused, rolling their eyes. They've heard it all before.

Good wood, good food, and a well-tended landscape are the most obvious symmetrical products of good work, but the work itself is pleasant and satisfying, and that is actually the main reason anybody does this anymore: we like the work!

Economists among you will have noticed that I have more or less restated the labor theory for determining the value of a good, with a second value appended, which is the creation (or at least maintenance) of health and beauty in nature. There is, of course, an eternal conflict concerning how value earned by work compares with value determined by exchange—and about the inordinate share of that value those who dominate the exchange rake off. I have a producerist mentality: I firmly believe that our economy should be structured so that those who work on farms, or in the woods, or at making food and wood products, and who manage their affairs prudently, are assured a decent living. I know a few such producers who have found their niche and succeeded financially, which is a wonderful thing and my hat is off to them. But they are pretty rare. They are competing within a system of large-scale, industrialized extraction, processing, and marketing of food and wood that has the advantage of externalizing the costs of environmental damage, exploited labor, poor health, and ruined communities. Our side is trying to produce good, healthy food and wood, beautiful landscapes, and thriving equitable communities all at once, and *by virtue of the same work,* without also producing dead zones and red tides and people with diabetes but no health insurance as side products. The other side is churning out commodities as cheaply as possible without worrying about algae blooms, disabilities, and underpaid immigrant workers living in the shadows and then proclaiming, "See, you elitists just aren't *efficient!* No ordinary people could ever afford the artsy-fartsy stuff you make." Yeah, right: ordinary people who have been systematically impoverished!

Shouting at the radio again, I know—but we do need to transform

that economic reality. In the meantime, given the world as it exists, I know
many people who do farm and forest work as a sideline without expecting
to make much or any profit, or who do it as employees of non-profit organizations that find other sources of revenue to help pay their salaries, or
who barely break even and still keep at it I don't know how. I applaud all
of them, and I consider it all "real" farming. I've met retired dairy farmers,
older than I am, who now run a logging business. If you know anything
about the economics of the forest industry you scratch your head, because
that's a short hop from the frying pan straight into the fire—but then you
look at the careful work they do in the woods and you realize exactly why
they are out there, other than to keep themselves busy puttering around
with a forwarder and a feller-buncher in their golden years. They do it
because they love the work.

It is safe to say that, with rare exceptions, none of us who try to farm
and log responsibly are planning to get rich. Some may have more modest
(but still often unrealized) dreams of earning a middle-class living, and
others may be subsidizing their outdoor work habit some other way, but
trust me, few are motivated by the prospect of big profits. We do it, over-
whelmingly, because we love the work. We love the physical challenge of
using the body—augmented by modest mechanical power—skillfully to
manage the growth of the land and create beautiful things. If we could do
the work by sitting at our laptops and sending robots to do it for us by
clicking on a screen (the way I am writing now) without being physically
engaged except at the eyeballs and the fingertips, that satisfaction would
virtually disappear. What satisfies is going out and seeing if the body is
capable of carrying out the work at hand—of wrestling with the difficulties
of reshaping the natural world while confronting gravity, inertia, friction,
and the wayward behavior of water in all its mercurial phases. Not to mention the independent notions of other living creatures who may not fully
share your ambitions. That is good for the body and the soul, and that is
the main reason that people do this kind of work.

I don't want to seem naïve about the joys of outdoor manual labor,
although after doing my share for nearly fifty years I suppose I have earned
the right to romanticize it if I want. As a historian, I am keenly aware that
most of the people who have labored in the bosom of the earth, down
through the ages, have been brutally exploited by a long train of extortion-
ists: emperors, feudal warlords, plantation owners, party commissars, or

(most devious of all in that parade of cruel masters) the market economy. If a person is sweating out unremitting toil for a grossly inadequate (or nonexistent) wage, as remains largely the case today in our globalized food, farm, and forest economy, that work becomes drudgery or outright slavery, even if it is intrinsically satisfying for a body to do. Before the industrial era, even the comparative few who farmed with something resembling a freehold competency (or some other reasonably secure and unmolested form of tenure) faced demands of physical labor that were unrelenting, rewarded only by the pinched level of material comfort the earth could provide, at least by modern standards. I am not advocating a return to medieval working conditions—I like my chainsaw and tractor, and I recognize the importance of an industrial economy to general human well-being, given coming on ten billion of us to provide for.

I am sure those who worked the land with preindustrial tools reveled in their energy and strength when they were young and then their skill and judgment when they were older. But it also ground them down by the time they reached my age, which is about when colonial New England fathers typically handed the reins over to their youngest son, now fully grown (the elder children having already departed to neighboring farms or towns). The work of colonial farm mothers (while also rewarding in many ways) was never done, and it was cumulatively even more grueling. Many kinds of manual labor, if too strenuous, awkward, or repetitive, will wear the body to lameness. I have had my share of back problems over the years and sometimes I do feel a bit worn down, but not too badly yet, and the aches and pains I endure the morning after a good workout with a chainsaw and splitting maul aren't that different from what I feel after a long day lecturing and sitting in faculty meetings, or grading papers, or hiking or cross-country skiing for that matter. Never mind staring at a screen like this. It seems possible that (at least so far) I would be in *worse* shape than I am without all the outdoor work I have done.

Sometimes in the middle of the term, when the schoolwork gets me bogged down and I can't get out to the farm for a few weeks, I start to feel like crap. I am fortunate: the diversified farming and logging I've done has usually been a satisfying mixture of machine and hand work, and I have seldom done the same task for more than a few hours before moving on to something else, which keeps drudgery at bay. I have tried to arrange my days, my weeks, and my years so that they are a shifting balance between farm and desk work. There are those who find it fulfilling to work outside day after day, year after year—a calling that I deeply admire—but I am not one of them.

For physical work to be fully enjoyable, it must take place under circumstances that do not render the worker trapped and excluded from enjoying other earthly pleasures. Most of those who have performed farm labor for the past ten thousand years, since the invention of agriculture, have not enjoyed such happy circumstances. But they should have, and now they can—if we ever get this yoke off our necks. Today that yoke is global capitalism, which consigns most manual labor to the poor and exploited, and whose acolytes then deride as romantics those who profess to enjoy such work by reminding us how miserable it is to be poor and exploited. As if misery and poverty were the natural and inescapable condition of those who labor with their bodies, rather than something unjustly imposed upon them.

The world seems to be reaching a point where robots and artificial intelligence will be capable of providing almost all the goods and services that we could ever need or want (and many more that we don't), while at the same time the world is full of people who need to purchase those goods and services and who also need to feel satisfied with their existence. If machines can do all the work, I guess productivity goes to infinity and becomes a useless measure of value, so we better come up with something else. This evidently poses a gnarly problem to the market economy: what are all these people supposed to do so that they can earn money and continue to consume the stuff they are no longer needed to make?

But to me this seems less of a dilemma and more like an opportunity: the world would be better off if more, not fewer, people were well rewarded for doing satisfying work such as farming, logging, and making comely products from the resulting food and wood in ways that enhance health and beauty, rather than sacrificing health and beauty on the altar of efficiency. I mean this most sincerely: as a society we ought to be employing *more* people to care for the land and do it well—which means, *less* efficiently. We can afford it. The land is not being well cared for the way we are doing things now, and we are all suffering mightily as a result. We are paying for that suffering, but through a scurrilous accounting trick the market credits the work someone has to do subsequently to mitigate that suffering as yet *more* economic growth, rather than debiting that treatment as the needless and stupid expense it really is.

If a person grows food or cuts wood in ways that avoid causing damage in the first place, that is a marvelous gain that never gets credited: an opportunity benefit, we ought to call it. Instead, it gets punished by the market for being inefficient. The virtues of a deliberately slower approach are coming to be widely understood and lauded, if not yet fairly compensated, in the world of food. We also need to celebrate and reward such direct, wholesome work in the world of wood. In other words, we need slow wood.

The Woods

BUYING THE FARM PRESENTED FAITH and me with a once in a lifetime opportunity to build a house. But as I have said, we weren't ready to leap into that adventure right away. We needed time to marshal our resources, and we weren't going to extricate ourselves from Weston overnight: the kids were still in school, we had our teaching jobs, and we were deeply entangled in town affairs. We had to take it slow—which was a good thing.

We knew roughly where the house would go, as the site was tightly constrained by the setbacks from the brook along one side and Tom and Joan's lot on the other. So we built a tent platform for weekend visits and camped out. When it was cold we slept over at the farmhouse, which Tom was methodically renovating. One thing we remember best from those early years was the brilliance of the autumn stars, especially looking to the dark north from our little bowl of a valley. They convinced us we really were out in the country at last, and they reminded us that our little world is part of a big cosmos, something all too easy to forget in the suburbs, where the glow of city lights wipes out the night sky. We started thinking about what kind of house to build on that spot, and how to build it.

For us those two questions were closely linked, in ways they may not be for most homebuilders. I am not here to promote any particular architectural style—that is a matter of taste, according to your own experiences. Now that I pay more attention to houses, I find most styles attractive in their own way, if well designed and ably built. Naturally, I dislike overblown mish-mash McMansions as much as anyone. Most of the rest look fine to me, and I remember all the houses we have lived in fondly, in spite of their defects—most often lack of insulation, which we remedied where we could. My own life has been, in many ways, a tug of war between the progressive pull of Modernism and a backward yearning for older traditions,

Planting maples by the river. Sugar maples are in bloom around the barn, with the farm woodlot on the hill dominated by oak and pine. (Faith Rand)

and I'm not about to come down on one side or the other as representing the best direction for the future. I think we're going to need to hold on to a small part of each and jettison a much larger part of both. I have stronger opinions about the second part of the question: *how* the house is built. To summarize: I think building "little boxes" is just fine, as long as they're *not* made of ticky-tacky.

I doubt this is the top concern of most people building their dream house. With a preferred look in mind, having a certain size and a desired set of features, you engage the services of an architect, builder, or some combination thereof. Probably you start with a fantasy that is more than you can afford, whittle your way down to reality, and end up spending more than you planned for less than you wanted. How the house is actually built and what materials go into it is generally left to the professionals—aside from features that are particularly visible, such as granite countertops or oak floors. Where the building materials come from or how the house is put together to keep it from falling down is seldom determined by the homeowner; the contractors purchase whatever is up to code from their usual suppliers, and most of the wood disappears into the walls.

Not so with us. We knew we wanted a timber frame house, and we wanted it to come from our woods. We wanted a house that was more or less a form of Andy Goldsworthy art: to express the landscape not just in its design and setting, but in the very stuff from which it was made, inside and out. We wanted to see the wood doing its work. When you walk into our house, you know right away why it won't fall down. My brother Kevin, a structural engineer who was in San Francisco in 1989, declared that our house would come through an earthquake unscathed. It has that combination of strength and, well, resilience.

We can't remember exactly when we decided we wanted a timber frame—it just seems like we always did. Of course, most American houses are framed with lumber, but usually with many light members, mere four-by-twos, stick-framed: a perfectly sound way to build, but to us, perfectly boring. By "timber frame" here I mean heavy timbers, preferably having traditional mortise-and-tenon joints, securely pegged together.

Neither of us had ever lived in such a house, that we knew of. Faith grew up in a nineteenth-century Greek Revival in Weston center; it may have been either timber-framed or stick-built, but there was no way you could tell from inside its many small rooms. I grew up in Pennsylvania first

in a postwar brick ranch house and then in a two-story house of no particular style that I can name, but *inside* those houses my parents' tastes in art
and furnishings ran strongly to mid-twentieth-century Modernism. My
mother, in particular, detested neocolonial houses, with their hanging por-
tico lamps and ostentatious pillars. About the time I left for Boston, the
family moved to a more congenial modern house in Ann Arbor, which I
visited once or twice annually for thirty years and much admired.

The house that made the deepest impression on me was on Fair-
haven Bay in Concord, about a mile southwest of Walden Pond. I lived
there for two years in my mid-twenties, doing almost nothing except working in the woods and thinking about the future. I don't think that structure
was timber-framed, but it had a powerful Arts and Crafts feel to it and
showed a lot of wood inside, mostly pine. It had initially been a summer
house; we winterized as best we could and installed a couple of woodstoves. It had time-burnished pine flooring, paneling, and board and batten doors, rustic pine furniture, and dark oak beams (salvaged, I believe,
from some machine shop) running across the living room ceiling. Sadly,
the Bay House is remembered today only by a few metal wicker chairs, left
sitting by the old terrace wall where it once stood. Since I am still doing
research in those woods, once or twice a year I sit for a few minutes in one
of those chairs to look out over the bay and think about the past.

None of the many houses Faith and I lived in together were overtly
timber-framed. But we have put in thousands of hours stacking hay and
birthing lambs in several old New England barns, with their massive timber frames. Back when Land's Sake had a band mill, I once sawed pine
timbers to build a new hayloft in one of those barns. That addition was
built "post and beam" rather than strictly timber-framed—that is, it used
metal fasteners (20d spikes) instead of mortised joints and wooden pegs—
but still, it gave us a feeling for the structural principles involved, and those
new pine timbers sure looked cool, and robust. So we did rub up against
timber frames over the years; we just never inhabited one.

Like many others, we had our eyes opened to timber framing as a
viable modern construction method in 1989, when *This Old House* broad-
cast a project about building a home in Concord. The homeowners in that
episode had been hoping to turn their old barn into a new house, but pioneering timber framer Tedd Benson found that the structure was too far
gone, so instead they built a barn-like house in its place, from scratch. The

crew paid a visit to a woodlot in Maine where the pine trees were cut, chiseled the joinery by hand on site, and held a community house-raising. Faith and I weren't all that interested in building anything resembling a barn—we worked in barns, so we wanted to come home to something a little cozier. Still, here was a popular home construction program showing how the structure of a house could come straight from the woods and remain visible in a satisfying, deeply rooted, tree-affirming sort of way. I remember thinking, well heck, we could do that. All we needed was a place to do it.[1]

Oddly enough, when *This Old House* tackled a timber frame again twenty years later, I became part of the show. The 2008–9 season featured homeowners in Weston who planned to donate their existing home for affordable housing (by moving it to a smaller lot down the road) and to build a new timber-framed house in its place. Once again, Tedd Benson served as the framer in this reprise of the classic Concord episode. By then I was on the Weston conservation commission, and the owners had to come before us because part of their landscaping was in the wetland buffer zone. That was routine; we approved their application with an order of conditions to protect the resource. In the process, they told us about their exciting timber frame project, which they had designed to reflect the look of several old Weston barns they particularly admired (barns, it so happened, in which Faith and I had worked or partied, or both). As staunch environmentalists, they were especially pleased that Bensonwood was going to recycle some Douglas fir timbers and some ancient live oak crucks, originally from South Carolina, that had recently been unearthed by the Big Dig in Boston, where they had once been part of a wharf. No living trees would be harmed in the making of *this* new house!

Using reclaimed wood like that is all very well, except that characterizing it as especially environmentally conscious reinforces the illusion that we can somehow keep building houses without cutting trees. By chance, these folks had stumbled upon a commission infiltrated by rogue conservationists who were actually in *favor* of cutting trees—so we immediately offered them some of ours. We saw an opportunity to showcase the principles of sustainable forestry and building with local wood, even in the suburbs. The owners, producers, and builders agreed to source some of the upper timbers for their house from the Weston town forest and to add that story line to the show. We marked a thinning of a middle-aged white pine stand out in Jericho Forest. Land's Sake felled the trees and skidded them to a field by the road, where a solid citizen from central Massachusetts named Michael Moore and his daughter set up their band mill and sawed the timbers. We filmed the whole thing on a cold March morning, slogging through rain, sleet, and snow—nothing fazed that old camera crew.

After those local timbers were sawn, ironically, they were trucked up to Bensonwood's shop in New Hampshire where all the joinery was cut, before returning to Weston and finding their place in the new house. So, the timbers were "local" via about a hundred-mile round trip. But they allowed us to get our message across: you can't really protect forests by separating them from human needs, obtaining your lumber by some magical sleight-of-hand like digging it out of the mud. Designating wilderness is fine, but more broadly you protect forests by taking good care of them while honestly cutting trees to build houses. The design of that particular house, both outside and in, struck us as a bit over the top with its exaggerated rusticity—but again, that is a matter of taste. The project reaffirmed for Faith and me that building a timber frame house from our own woods was indeed plausible. We had seen it on television—in fact, we had helped *put* it on TV. And by that time, we had acquired a farm at the other end of the state upon which to give it a try ourselves.[2]

We wanted to build our house with wood from our property—that much, we knew. But we didn't yet know exactly what that would mean. We knew we wanted a timber frame house, and we had plenty of timber suitable for framing—pine, oak, hemlock. We knew we wanted a mix of woods that went nicely together. We had been imagining the interplay of elements like the frame, the flooring, and the cabinets, as we scrolled through the galleries of timber framing company web sites and paged through books and magazines. But we had no clear understanding of how trees could be taken from the forest and rendered back in usable form. Who in Massachusetts still does such work? Because Land's Sake once sawed rough lumber to make barns and sheds, I understood that first step well enough; but I had only a vague notion about what happened to wood, after it was sawn, to make the more finished lumber products that typically go into a house. What particular parts of a house come from what parts of which trees, and how?

We knew we wanted the house to reflect the forest. But we didn't want to design around a few species we liked and then just cherry-pick them from our woods. That might express the forest in some sense, but it seemed fraudulent. Just a fancy gesture—not the thrifty, Yankee way. I suppose if we had the time, skill, and equipment to do all the work ourselves it might have answered, but we didn't. It made more sense to see whether a silvicultural treatment and timber sale could improve our woodlot, provide revenue to cover the harvest costs, and at the same time generate materials to build a house. That way the house would reflect the forest in a more solid way—it would express a particular moment in the life of the forest and the work that was being done to shape its future. There would still be a nice assortment of species to choose from. In fact, one could imagine a wide range of houses and timbers that would express that same forest work in different ways. That became our philosophy—though in truth it is clearer to me now, in retrospect. At the time we just had a notion that we should first consult with the woods, before our choices for house design and timbers were irretrievably pegged home. Start with the woods, and work toward the house.

To consult with the forest, we needed a consulting forester. I turned to my friend Susan Campbell, who was running the Massachusetts Forest Stewardship program at the time, to get her recommendations. We walked the woods, and Susan was suitably impressed by the big oaks on our hill. She immediately asked if there was any way we could run pigs up there to eat the acorns. Pigs? This surprised me, although the thought had crossed our minds, too: the oak woods stood upslope from a pine stand that had recently been logged off by the previous owners, and it seemed possible to establish a permanent hog pasture on the open land there and run the pigs up the hill for a few weeks in the fall during heavy oak mast years, using temporary fencing. There are a few heritage hog farmers around the country raising forest-foraging pigs like that, and in fact we had just visited one up in Vermont. It wasn't a bad idea—it just wasn't something I expected to hear from a forester. Convincing farmers to *stop* their livestock from chewing up the woods has sort of been Forestry 101 since Gifford Pinchot, so I'm like, what have they been teaching you down there at the Yale Forest School these days, Susan?[3]

But maybe times have changed. Unlike a century ago New England now has plenty of forest and not much livestock left to degrade it, unless you count deer. The real danger to woodlands these days is houses being plopped smack in the middle of them by new owners who say they love them so. Progressive foresters like Susan are trying to promote innovative non-timber forest products to help landowners glean more value from their woods, so that they might be more likely to protect them. This could be ginseng, fiddleheads, mushrooms, or any number of off-beat things beyond mere cordwood and timber. So in places it might be pork finished on acorns, a little pannage for some smoking Yankee version of *jamón ibérico*. You wouldn't want pigs rooting up *every* oak woods in the land, but a few experiments in agroforestry and eco-gastronomy here and there might not be such a bad idea, either. If I were a celebrity chef or retired venture capitalist you might be paging through a fancy picture book about just such a project. In fact, we do raise heritage pigs these days, but their shady corner is much closer to home. After due consideration Tom and I decided putting a pig pasture way up on the hill was too logistically challenging, and so we stuck with more conventional silviculture there. But the point was made: there are many "multiple-value" ways of managing different parts of your woods.

For a consulting forester, Susan pointed us to Lincoln Fish, among others. I knew Lincoln by reputation and had met him at one or two land conservation gatherings, so I gave him a call. On a crisp morning in January 2009, Lincoln, Tom, and I strapped on snowshoes and took a walk up the hill. It was twelve degrees below zero, and we were elated because it had been almost that cold back in Weston, too—cold enough to seriously knock back the hemlock woolly adelgid that has been ravaging forests on the East Coast for decades and was just then moving into our state. It was pleasant to think that as we tramped doggedly upslope through the mountain laurel thickets, keeping the blood moving, all across the wooded hills and vales of Massachusetts tiny adelgids were quietly freezing to death, and thousands of hemlocks were breathing a sigh of relief, at least for now. Here on the southern edge of the north woods a frigid night and a frosty morn is a thing to be cherished, these days. Following our walk around, Lincoln produced a stewardship plan with prescriptions that translated our goals for the forest into silvicultural treatments.

A forest stewardship plan delineates the various "stands" on the property, discrete areas with trees of a similar age and mix of species, defined by topography and history. Given the size, density, and quality of those trees, the forester offers prescriptions for each stand that are tailored to the owner's goals—usually some combination of harvesting timber and

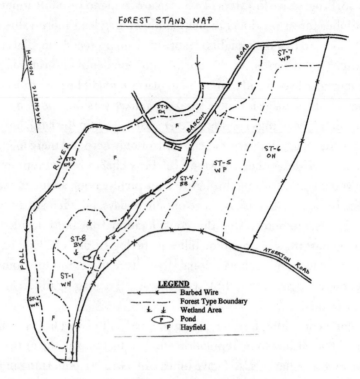

FOREST STAND MAP

Forest stand map of our farm, drawn by Lincoln Fish as part of the forest stewardship plan he prepared for us.

firewood, enhancing habitat for wildlife, and recreational use. There is no one right way to manage a forest. The degree of management can vary from intensive to infinitesimal, depending on the owner's wishes. In our case, those wishes varied from stand to stand: our woodland is diverse, and our wishes for it are equally diverse.

We live in what is sometimes called the "transition hardwoods" forest zone, though it seems to me that *all* forest regions are transition zones, given the dynamics of post-glacial plant migration of the past few millennia, let alone the dramatic agrarian disturbances of the past few centuries—not to mention the rapid climate change that now transcends even those error bars. In western Massachusetts there are elements of the "central hardwoods" forest that stretches from southern New England to Arkansas (dominated by oak, hickory, and the ghost of chestnut), mixing with elements of the "northern hardwoods" forest that runs from northern New England to Minnesota (dominated by sugar maple, beech, and yellow birch). The leading softwoods that inhabit this belt of silvic tension are white pine and eastern hemlock. What a glorious mixture of trees and of woods—it excites me just thinking about it, never mind looking at it, or even better, touching it. At our farm, with its climb from river bank to ridgetop, we have a little bit of all that to enjoy and to work with.

For an overview of our woods we actually have to start on the far side of the river. It turns out our farm came with an extra six acres we didn't even know about until well into the process of buying it. This parcel wasn't part of the APR, so it wasn't covered by the farm survey. It just popped up at closing—like wait, what's this here? It isn't even in the same town. It has no road frontage and is completely inaccessible, except on foot: you have to wade across the river (which is truly a glorified brook; where I grew up, we would call it a creek), which we do about once a year to visit our secret property. We own from the river right up to the top of the steep valley slope on that west side, a lovely woods composed of majestic oaks and maples. It is nice to look at, and fortuitously it protects us from anyone who might contemplate building a palace at the edge of the neighboring property to lord it over our valley (exactly what we chose not to do ourselves, on the east side), because we own the trees that would block the view. We would never think of cutting a tree over there, and we can't reach them anyway—at least, not from our own land.

Why do we own this little piece of woods? The story we have heard is too good to be true, so I will pass it on. Our farm was owned for about forty years by an eccentric recluse—about that, there is no dispute. Apparently, at one time the post office in our town refused to deliver mail to the two farms down here—presumably the boxes were out at the end of our dirt road, almost a mile away up the hill. However, the neighboring town did make deliveries to the single farm in the valley on that side. So, in 1969, the old man bought a few steep, worthless landlocked acres across the river and erected a mailbox on the far side of the bridge—only a quarter-mile stroll on flat ground to get his *National Geographic* (of which he kept a large collection) at his new address. Presumably there was some other reason he really bought that land, but we will never know. I am looking at it from my window right now, and I am not complaining. Just beyond that piece of land sits an old house that I can barely see in winter, and not at all in summer; our trees blocking the view from that house site may prevent a new one from ever being built there.

To us, this little piece of land should stay forever wild. In fact, we are donating an easement to a local land trust to give it permanent protection, like the rest of the farm. Every place should have some wilderness. What Thoreau called *wildness*—life pasturing freely—is a quality that exists everywhere, in a sense: it is the hummingbird visiting the morning glory on your porch, or the bacteria crawling on your skin. But we do need legally defined wild*lands* that are untrammeled by human manipulation, and we need them at every scale. Of course, wilderness advocates are primarily concerned with protecting large wild reserves that can be ruled by natural processes at large, but we also need smaller wild places in every community, and perhaps on every property. These are often (as in this case) places that are either too hard to get to or too easy to mess up for timber harvesting to be a good option, though they should be more than that. They are places of humility—a tithe to nature.[4]

Back on our side of the river, the farm is blessed with a strip of riparian forest that is more than a mile long, though seldom much more than a hundred feet wide, with the river along one side and our pastures along the other. At the southern end where the valley narrows, this forest is dominated by hemlocks, at least looking from below (ST-2 on the forest stand map shown here). Even during dry spells it retains that wonderful damp, earthy smell of a dark woods after a rain, where fungus rules. Boles of large, straight white pines, along with red oaks and other hardwoods, shoot up through the hemlock canopy. This stand is easily accessible, and the pine and oak timber is valuable. But we have no interest in cutting it. So close to the river, it has immense ecological and aesthetic value just the way it is. Our stewardship plan calls for doing next to nothing (I have cut a few dying trees that were going to fall on the fence). From the south end of our farm for more than another mile downstream the river rushes through a narrow, densely wooded ravine, thick with hemlock, black birch, white pine, and maple, until it opens up again near its confluence with the Connecticut. We are working with our neighbors to protect more of this hidden stretch of wild country.

The northern half of our narrow riparian forest, where the river winds between bottomland farms, has a different character (ST-3). It is dominated by sugar maple: ancient mother trees up to four feet in diameter along the edge of our fields, and thrifty daughter trees one to two feet thick from there to the river. Other hardwoods mix in—oak, hickory, basswood, ash, beech—but the maples are so pervasive that Lincoln thinks the stand might once have been managed as a sugar orchard, by removing other species. I'm not sure about that given the density of small and intermediate stems, and I don't see any taphole scars; but in any case, we're going to keep it that way. Again, hard maple timber is quite valuable but we wouldn't want to cut heavily so close to the river, and we want the big trees for their sap, at least in theory. I would say we have enough trees for several hundred taps. Collecting and boiling sap is no game for old folks (as we know from forty years' experience), so whether we ever assemble the right crew to make syrup again is anybody's guess. In any case, our forest stewardship plan calls for this stand to remain a sugar bush, managed with light thinning—cutting from the bottom, as it's called. We have even planted a few more maples ourselves, along bare stretches of the river bank.

Across the fields at the eastern side of the valley is a lazy brook that occupies an older channel of the river, fed by seepage from the base of a steep gravel slope. Along the brook are several small beaver ponds and a few acres of wet meadow. At the south end of the meadow lies a rich bottomland forest of about fifteen acres, easily accessible from the fields (STs-1, 8). This stand is suitable for long-term timber management. It was once topped by white pines, but most of the largest had been logged a few years before we bought the property, along with some low-value firewood. This left a vigorous, well-stocked stand—a promising mixture of middle-aged pine and oak of excellent quality, together with younger sugar maple, shagbark hickory, and black cherry at the north end, by the meadow. The previous owners had engaged a forester for a management plan (of which we have a copy), and a nice job had been done: minimal damage, and most of the best trees left to keep growing. There wasn't much we needed to think about doing there for at least fifteen or twenty years.

The east side of the brook presents a trickier proposition. Just beyond the brook a steep slope rises—the kind you can only climb by holding onto small trees, if you are over fifty. Or descend the same way, if you are even over forty. This is the sheer edge of a bench of sand and gravel that was graded into the valley from the north thousands of years ago by meltwaters sweeping into glacial Lake Hitchcock, which occupied the Connecticut River valley as the ice receded. The broad terrace hems our little valley along its eastern flank, widening toward the south, standing as much as one hundred feet above the brook at the south end of the property. All along it are springs where the ground flow of water from above breaks out, intermittently feeding the brook. The narrow bottom and steep gravel slope are thick with black and yellow birch, sugar and red maple, oak and hemlock maybe half a century old (ST-4).

　　This ten-acre stand reminded me of my early days in the Weston town forest, although the species composition was more northerly: middle-aged and heavily overstocked, from a silvicultural point of view. At least a third of the trees could have been cut and never missed, allowing the higher-quality stems to expand their crowns and keep growing. Many were going to die anyway, as the stand matured, not to mention the impact of maraud-ing beaver. But given the brook, the slope, and the many intervening springs and sloughs, the stand wasn't accessible for harvesting such low-value trees. Instead, our stewardship plan called for pre-commercial "timber stand improvement," which means cutting or girdling the lower-quality trees without removing them. But in truth we've never gotten around to that work, and in time a new idea has taken its place. These woods are the nearest to our house, so we made a simple footbridge over the brook and began to extend trails up and downstream, and climbing a draw in the steep slope to reach the bench above. Along the trails we have started making small plantings of native wildflowers and wild edibles, like mayapples and ramps, creating a woodland garden of a few acres. Once we began planting flowers, of course, we discovered others that were already there—another example of how working on a place inspires it to reveal itself. Research has shown that many shrubs and wildflowers that were presumably much more common in the pre-European forest have been slow to re-establish on abandoned farmland—in other words, most of the reforested landscape. The trees came back on their own, but the viburnum and spring beauties need our help—even more so now, as climate change throws them another curveball. This wildwood gardening project falls somewhere between set-ting aside wild places on the one hand and cutting and harvesting timber on the other; no doubt it will engage us more and more as we grow older and enjoy the woods closer to home.[5]

　　On top of that broad gravel bench, the picture changes entirely. Up there were old pastures that had been abandoned many decades earlier and invaded by white pines, which have been growing very well. The northern end of this extensive pine stand, above our upper hayfield and meeting the dirt road where I first drove into the valley, had never been cut (ST-7). It, too, was overstocked, as foresters say—denser than is ideal for the growth of all the trees, which is just how nature does it: first overstocking and then allowing the passage of time to do the thinning. By the time we arrived, the tall trees looked to be almost a century old (in fact, they started growing around 1920); it was a motley mix of pasture pines, some perfectly straight and many spindly and crooked, growing too thickly.

The southern twenty acres of the bench, by contrast, had been cut heavily just a year or two before we bought the place, leaving behind only a few score, widely spaced, very tall pines about sixteen inches in diameter (ST-5). Their lofty, compact crowns were now perched incongruously high above a tangled explosion of blueberries, blackberries, sweet fern, and birch and pine seedlings that carpeted the suddenly sun-drenched earth beneath. This is where we thought about housing the pigs, but didn't. We did get a few years of good berry picking from it—a woods-warming gift for having bought the place. We later determined, by counting rings, that this part of the pasture had been relieved of its cows and handed over to the pines somewhat later than the north end, around 1940—a few years after the barn had been fitted with a concrete block foundation and forty tie-stalls in the new cellar. Oddly enough, as New England cow herds have steadily grown in size since the Civil War (with the number of those herds shrinking, of course), the pastures required to support them have just as steadily decreased. Cows have been increasingly fed in and around the barn, with hay, sileage, and purchased feed brought to them. Letting cows walk to pasture went out of style long ago, though some of us are now trying to bring it back. The result was a remarkable explosion, spanning roughly the lifetime of Robert Frost, of white pine.

In this pasture pine stand we had been left with the aftermath of a "seed tree" cut, designed to permit the most valuable trees to continue growing for another ten or fifteen years before final harvest and, at the same time, to jump start the next stand to follow. Because young pines (which are constantly being replenished by the mature trees) need lots of light to take off, such a cut was appropriate for this sandy, well-drained site, though it was a bit shocking to behold—a close cousin to a clear-cut. My main silvicultural quarrel with it, looking at the relatively slender girth of the remaining trees, was that it had come too early. A lighter first cut—removing the lower-quality trees but allowing many more of the better ones to keep growing for a few more decades before initiating such a heavy regeneration harvest—would have been better, it seemed to me: they had taken too much of the potential value too soon and shortened the life of the stand. Perhaps the previous owners needed money, which often drives people to cut trees, even those who swear they would never dream of such a thing, until they do. At least their forester left the best timber and made a clean start for the future, rather than allowing a "high grade" cut that would have taken *all* the valuable trees and bequeathed us only the poor ones.[6]

Ecologically speaking, that harvest created early successional habitat where we could hear towhees and whip-poor-wills and pick berries for a few years—not such a bad thing, as long as it is confined to a small percentage of the landscape at any given time. Even the Audubon societies of Massachusetts and Vermont are now promoting heavy cutting of this kind for the sake of the increasingly rare open habitat, through their "Foresters for the Birds" programs. Open habitat has become rare because we have just about run out of pastures to abandon in New England, so we have to resort to cutting places that were abandoned earlier and grew back, of which we have plenty—a century-long cycle actually predicted by Robert Frost in "Something for Hope." The chief danger of a seed tree cut in white pines is windthrow, as the species is shallow-rooted and the residual trees lose the buffering protection of their tightly packed companions and stand there isolated and exposed. Indeed, we could see that, since the harvest, several had been blown down already. Our stewardship plan called for harvesting the remaining pines within a decade or so, before the saplings springing up underneath became so large they might be excessively damaged by the logging operation. Now that a regeneration cycle had been so decisively initiated, we were more or less obliged to see it through.[7]

Above the pine terrace our land rises steeply again to the top of the ridge (ST-6). This final slope is composed not of sand and gravel outwash but of hard-packed glacial till, the thin skin and protruding bones of New England that gives us our flinty reputation. There is even a hint of a stone wall at our eastern boundary, the only one on the property. Till soils were deposited by the ice grinding south for tens of thousands of years, until the interglacial thaw that began about eighteen thousand years ago finally unplugged that continental belt sander and slowly melted it away. This left behind a mish-mash of soil particles of all sizes, from the largest to the smallest: hence the nickname "boulder clay." Till soils are stony and hard to plow, but they hold water and so make for good orchards, pastures, and woodlots. There are plenty of nutrients available for perennial plants that know where to find them, down among the granite shards.[8]

Our thirty-five-acre woodlot on the hill may have always been a forest, or it may have sojourned for a time as a pasture. Perhaps it was cleared soon after the Revolutionary War and abandoned soon after the Civil War, to be reoccupied first by pine and then by oak (a common rhythm around here); perhaps not—I can't tell just by looking at it. In any case, by the time they came into our hands, its dominant oaks were a century old and two feet in diameter—a magnificent stand with great monetary value, except that the timber market had just crashed along with the rest of the economy. But we were in no great rush to liquidate this lovely asset, in any case. Mixed in with the oaks were emergent pines of even greater size, along with smaller but substantial pignut hickory, red maple, and black birch. These mid-sized hardwoods were beginning to fall behind the closing oak canopy, while the scattered pines towered above it. Here and there were pockets of mature hemlocks. The understory was dominated by hemlock saplings and mountain laurel, about the only species able to flourish in such deep shade. What a wonderful woodlot to crown our farm!

The question was, what to do with it? From a silvicultural point of view, these beautiful woods needed work. Silviculture is the art of removing some trees in order to enhance the growth of those that remain, and the abiding principle is to cut the worst first. Let me repeat that: *cut the worst first.* As an art form silviculture most resembles sculpture, because it works by subtraction—but subtraction from an expanding whole. Many of our trees—particularly the best oaks—already had significant commercial value. But this was no time to be harvesting high-grade oak—selling at the bottom of a fallen market. Besides, our woods had never been managed, so they were crowded with crooked trees. Trees that aren't straight are perfectly fine ecologically, but of little value for timber. Again, they are a natural outcome of the way a forest grows: initially packed with small trees, most of which fall behind and gradually succumb from lack of sunlight—though some of the more shade-tolerant species may find enough light to persevere and break into the canopy in time. Among the trees that survive this winnowing, some are straight, while others are crooked or fork into more than one stem, which makes them less valuable. This is less a genetic defect than a matter of chance: which way the light comes through the surrounding trees, damage from ice and wind, an insect that destroys a terminal bud. Beyond good form, some species simply have more pecuniary value than others because we prize their wood more or because they reach a larger size. The object of silviculture is to someday harvest as many outstanding specimens of the most valuable trees as possible, by removing everything else first.

Practicing good silviculture doesn't improve the ecological health of the stand in any meaningful way. You can't really "improve" upon nature. Rather, it improves the stand's ability to serve human needs without doing any appreciable ecological damage, by periodically excising low-value trees. This accelerates and concentrates growth in the trees that will be most valuable for timber, once mature. So, for our oak lot and adjoining pine woods on the hill, Lincoln Fish recommended starting with a low-grade harvest: cut the rest, leave the best. That is, remove a few hundred cords of firewood and over a hundred thousand board feet of mediocre timber and leave the most valuable trees to keep growing. With less competition around their crowns the best-formed pines, oaks, and other hardwoods could realize their full potential, to be gradually harvested in the years to come once the market for quality timber rebounded and when suitable regeneration—young trees nurtured by their mothers, if you like— was thriving underneath.

But who would do this exacting work? I had long dreamed that one day we might acquire the equipment—a small forwarder, a band mill, planers, a kiln—to harvest firewood and timber from our woods, make distinctive wood products ourselves, and supply specialty timber to other woodworkers. I still have that dream. But I am becoming reconciled that at this point in our lives, Tom and I no longer have the time or energy to devote to such an enterprise, which might have been possible when we were younger. Instead, we could at least set the stage for younger people to run such a business in the future by improving the forest and getting a road system in place. Given the acreage we have and the volume of wood that needed to be cut just to get started, even those first steps would mean timber sales to a commercial logger, larger than anything we could just nibble away at. Unlike building fence, cutting hay, or raising beef, trying to actively manage these woods in our spare time was out of our league.

If the first part of a forester's job is to meet with landowners, cruise the woods to inventory the trees, and write stewardship plans, the second part is to oversee timber harvests. Lincoln marked the trees to be cut, laid out skid roads to reach them, and put the job out to bid. Prospective loggers then viewed the site and offered so much per thousand board feet and per cord, or simply so much for the entire sale, based on their judgment of what they would be able to realize by selling the logs to a sawmill or firewood processor, minus the difficulty of getting them out of the woods. The forester's job is to evaluate the bids, write the contract, and then make sure the logger meets its specifications: cuts only the marked trees, minimizes damage to remaining trees, and leaves the skid roads and landing in good shape. The landowner is under no obligation to accept the highest bid, and it was pretty obvious who Lincoln thought would be perfect for this job: Ed Klaus.

Some years before, Susan and Lincoln (among others) had helped launch an intrepid organization called the Massachusetts Woodlands Cooperative. The MWC was a group of woodland owners, foresters, loggers, and processors such as sawyers, millworkers, and timber framers—everyone along the wood supply chain—with the common goal of promoting sustainable forest management that could help keep them all in business. The idea was to bring Forest Stewardship Council (FSC) certification to a large enough group of woodlands to consistently supply timber to a network of FSC-certified processors. The co-op aimed to develop a line of distinctive value-added wood products, including a few made from lower-grade material, such as red maple flooring—because harvesting low-grade trees is key to timber improvement. The concept was similar to organic certification in farming: a way for discerning consumers to pay a little extra for products they can trust are made sustainably and sourced locally. We were happy to support this effort, so we joined the MWC and enrolled our woodland. The forest products industry is tough, though, and the MWC experiment did not survive the long decline in home construction that followed the 2008 recession—sadly, a load of black birch flooring from our woodlot turned out to be the cooperative's final project. But in the process, we were introduced to a group of skilled woods workers and friends who ended up supplying most of the materials for our house. One of them is Ed Klaus.

We hired Ed to log our woods. Ed is a slight man a few years older than I am with wire-rimmed glasses, a long gray beard, and an old cable skidder he claims you can hear seven miles away on a cold winter morning,

Ed Klaus's cable skidder, with Maggie and Liam. An earlier pine "seed tree" cut is in the background. (Faith Rand)

which I can believe. "Ed cares more about your trees than you do," Lincoln told us, and that was true, too. He also warned us that Ed worked slowly, usually by himself, as he could find time between other jobs, so it might take a while. But that turned out to be an advantage: we were in no rush, and since Ed and his equipment were on the property while the house project unfolded, he was accommodating enough to take on a few extra jobs that weren't in the original contract, as you shall hear. Ed worked on and off for the best part of a year, summer and winter, extracting the low-grade trees without marring the timber that remained and periodically selling truckloads of firewood and sawlogs to various buyers. Some of what he cut we diverted to build our house.

Ed kept the skid roads nicely graded and provided with water bars on the steep slopes, and he kept a neat landing—the spot by the road or edge of the field where the logs are piled to await trucking. Small and crooked logs to be sold for firewood were piled to one side, larger timber logs to another, often separated by species. As he brought trees to the landing Ed would periodically buck them to log length, looking to squeeze

The landing, with hardwood sawlogs on the left and smaller-diameter firewood on the right. (Faith Rand)

out the most value by finding the longest straight sections with the fewest knots, setting the rest aside for pallet logs or firewood. At the sawmill the same exercise takes place a second time, as a sawyer with an experienced eye squeezes out the most select boards to be found in the log.

As someone who has spent a lifetime working with chainsaws and tractors, who once had a small band mill himself, and who has struggled with an innate lack of mechanical ability, I cannot exaggerate the pleasure it gives me to watch people who know how to do these things well. I need to stress this for my sophisticated urban readers: logging takes great intelligence and skill, as well as patience and endurance. You cannot do it well unless you love the work—and it is so demanding, you probably wouldn't be doing it if you didn't love it. I have been on logging sites where you could tell that the loggers didn't care what the place looked like (or had been put in a position where they couldn't afford to care), but not very many: by and large, the independent loggers I know care deeply for the woods and are among the most knowledgeable and steadfast conservationists you will ever want to meet. Ask them to meet a high standard and accept a price for your trees that is fair for such difficult work, and they will leave your woods a better place.

Ed was cutting plenty of oak and pine timber—even though it wasn't the best in the stand, it was still where most of the value was. But he was cutting just as much hemlock and black birch, which made up most of the lower-grade timber Lincoln wanted to get out of the woods at this stage. Although they fetch less in the market and don't reach the same size as pine and oak, hemlock and birch are handsome, useful woods all the same. It began to occur to us that the house could be an expression not of the grand thing the woods would become, those towering oaks and pines, but of the more pedestrian trees they were shedding now. We could try to build the best house from the poorest trees—a worst first house. It was as if Michelangelo had chiseled David out of marble and then said okay, now I will make my masterpiece from these chips. If Michelangelo had been a Yankee, that is exactly what he would have said. Faith and I wanted a house that expressed the woods: that meant we ended up using the trees we did not want growing in the woods anymore. Above all, that meant we ended up building our house out of hemlock and birch.

FOUR

Hemlock Frame

I HAVE A DEEP EMOTIONAL ATTACHMENT to eastern hemlock (*Tsuga canadensis*)—the tree, not the timber. My attachment to hemlock timber is a more recent development. My love for the tree itself goes back to Pennsylvania and my time at Todd Sanctuary, a nature reserve near Buffalo Creek in Butler County that was given to the Audubon Society of Western Pennsylvania in 1942 by W. E. Clyde Todd, a noted ornithologist. The land had once been part of his grandfather's farm.

Not far away, near the mouth of Watson's Run, Todd made his first important discovery: in 1889, at the age of fourteen, he collected a female magnolia warbler, nesting in a dense young hemlock. This record extended southward the known breeding range of a bird found mostly in boreal forests, except on migration. Unfortunately, Todd's prize specimen never made it to the taxidermist, because it got crushed (while riding in a box in his pocket) in a runaway wagon accident on its way to the post office. My friends and I used to walk that vertiginous stretch of road and marvel that young Todd himself had survived. Luckily, he had also collected the eggs, which are now at the Carnegie Museum of Natural History in Pittsburgh. The hemlocks where Todd bagged his warbler were subsequently logged off, and half a century later he acquired and then donated his old family woodlands just upstream, to protect them from the same fate. This was all part of the lore of the place that we learned at the knees of our birding elders.[1]

Todd Sanctuary encompassed a couple of hundred acres, and the heart of it was Watson's Ravine, which was heavily populated with hemlocks. Above the ravine were mature oak forests, and above them rewilding crabapple and red maple thickets that merged with the remaining upland farms. Near the head of the ravine, just where the upland started to tumble, at the edge of a small meadow, under the shade of sweet birch and oaks,

A hemlock tree in our woodlot, with its dense lower branches. Another hemlock and a white pine just behind this one were harvested, creating an opening. (Tom Chalmers)

stood a simple block and timber cabin with a great stone fireplace—no plumbing, no phone, no electricity. You reached the cabin by crossing a bouncing footbridge over Hesselgesser's Run, through the streamside hemlocks.

My friends and I went "up Todd" as often as we could throughout our high school and college years, and several of us served as summer naturalists, looking after the place and running research and educational programs for the Audubon Society. We explored the Sanctuary woods and streams at all seasons and took long birding and foraging rambles through the surrounding countryside. We learned to cook our own meals—anything from elderberry blossom pancakes and boiled day lily pods to Dinty Moore beef stew and Chips Ahoy cookies, washed down with Lemon Blennd— and in the evenings, around the fire, we engaged in impassioned discussions about the imperiled state of the planet and what we might do to save it. We fully expected industrial society to run out of oil and other resources, or at least encounter crippling limits to their extraction, within a decade or two. Fifty years later it appears we were correct in our underlying analysis, just off in our timing by approximately one generation—ours.

Todd was a place of enchantment, and it set us on our life journeys. For me, that enchantment came from more than the independent, spartan living, immersed in nature, though that by itself was pretty great. It was something about those hemlocks—especially when I stayed at the cabin alone in the fall and winter, beside the rushing stream. I did this every chance I got, being an introspective lad. The graceful, dark-green trees, usually found in cool, rugged terrain, leaning close to the water, represented something wild and northern. That was just the feeling they gave me, which I am intellectualizing in retrospect. At that age I yearned to migrate far from civilization myself, to dwell among the magnolia warblers in the forests of the frozen North.

In Weston I traded those wild dreams for a more civilized adventure in suburban farming and forestry, but hemlocks kept their special place in my imagination. They were a part of nature meant for respite, where I turned off my managerial eye. The same goes for Faith: when she was young, she spent summers in New Hampshire where her grandparents and then her parents ran a camp for boys called The Hemlocks. It featured tall pines and hemlocks along a narrow brook that ran down to the Pemigewasset River, and it had cabins with names like the Beaver and the Bobcat,

which her father, uncle, and grandfather had built. That camp later became simply a summer and fall family getaway, so hemlocks held many of
those same northerly associations of roughing it (with sketchy wiring and
plumbing) for Faith while growing up and for our children in turn.

Hemlock was also special in the conservation forests of Weston. The
species is more common in eastern Massachusetts than southwestern
Pennsylvania, but still not nearly as common as it is up-country. In Weston,
hemlock is found in secluded pockets, mostly by brooks or small ponds.
Weston has half a dozen hemlock stands of only a few acres each—they are
one of the town's links to New England at large. These hemlock groves
form soaring cathedrals, with parallel shafts of light breaking through high
windows in their dark canopies, held aloft by stately pillars. Hemlocks
often grow interspersed with white pines whose larger stems pierce the
ceiling and enhance the nave effect, their crowns out of sight somewhere
high above. Stands of hemlock, slow-growing, shade-tolerant, and long-
lived, are the crown jewels of the Weston town forest. As I helped to manage that forest through forty years, it never occurred to me to think of them
as timber or to do anything other than leave them alone—that is, until the
woolly adelgid showed up.

About the time we were searching for a farm, the hemlock woolly
adelgid arrived in Massachusetts. This tiny aphid-like insect clusters at the
base of the needles and sucks the starch out of them, often killing the tree
within a few years. The adelgid is native to Asia and has long been established in the Pacific Northwest, where the local hemlock species are more
resistant. These bugs made it to the East Coast sometime in the early
twentieth century, finding hemlocks with little or no resistance. Down
South, hemlocks in the Blue Ridge and Great Smokies have been devastated, and in recent decades the adelgid has slowly spread northward into
New England as well. By the turn of the twenty-first-century hemlocks in
Connecticut were being decimated, and we began to see the fuzzy little
beasts in Weston, causing lower foliage and then entire trees to turn brown,
and then gray. It looked as if our beloved hemlocks might meet the same
fate as Todd's magnolia warbler.

The question for the Weston conservation commission was what
(if anything) to do about it. Most of the ecologists we consulted thought
the decline of hemlock had become inevitable—the species might not be
driven to extinction but would be reduced to greatly diminished ecologi-

cal significance across much of its range. It seemed like a tragic replay of the coming of chestnut blight a century earlier, described to me in my youth by old-timers, like Land's Sake co-founder Doug Henderson, who saw it as kids themselves. Will our children be telling our grandchildren the same sad stories about hemlocks, fifty years from now? The only question is how far north the adelgid will spread, as it can be slowed by sub-zero cold snaps, but the rapidly warming climate is working against us. Seeing what was coming, some horticultural showplaces such as the Arnold Arboretum in Boston pre-emptively salvage-logged their stately hemlock groves, to get a jump on something new. But in a woodland situation like Weston's, my Harvard Forest colleagues advised allowing nature to take its course: even though the hemlock's distinctive ecological qualities would be lost, other trees such as black birch would replace it with something new.[2]

And yet we also knew that entomologists were conducting experiments by acclimating and releasing adelgid predator beetles brought from Japan and the Pacific Northwest. If we could keep our hemlocks alive for a few more years, there might be an effective biological control. We also learned about soil injections using very low doses of imidacloprid, which is taken up by the roots and confers several years of protection. But imidacloprid is a notorious neonicotinoid, possibly implicated in the global decline of pollinators and other insects. This weighed on our minds, yet the tiny amount we needed to use was dwarfed by the volumes already being routinely applied to lawns all over town, so what additional harm would we really be doing? In the end we went to town meeting for a special addition to the conservation commission budget, and we treated five hundred of the healthiest trees in our four best hemlock stands. A local arborist with a passion for conservation and hemlocks, Jonathan Bransfield, gave us an absurdly low bid—I think he must have done it at cost. I deployed Brandeis students to map and tag the trees, and we set up permanent plots to monitor how well the treatment was working.

More than a decade later, most of the hemlocks we dosed are still alive and looking much better. But so are a lot of hemlocks we didn't treat, especially if they have their feet wet. So far, the adelgid invasion hasn't wiped out Massachusetts hemlocks as fast as predicted. Why that is and what the future holds I am not sure—meanwhile, biological controls seem to be making progress and may soon be widely available, so perhaps we made the right call. Out at our farm in western Massachusetts, we haven't seen the adelgid yet, though we know it is not far away.[3]

In any case, although Faith and I knew hemlock could make service-able lumber, given our strong emotional attachment to the tree we were not predisposed to log it. Just the opposite: we were fighting to keep it alive. So why did we end up building our house with hemlock?

If you had asked me anytime in the past forty years what trees I *would* choose to build a house, I would have told you pine and oak. As hand-some as hemlock in their own way, these are trees I have also known as wood: I have their sap on my hands. I have felled hundreds of them, limbed them out, bucked them to length, sawed them into beams and boards. I know how they look, feel, and smell when they come off the mill: bright, heavy, wet, and fragrant. Oak (being harder) saws smoother; pine saws rough and ragged. Over the years we have used pine to build barn lofts, farm stands, garages, sheds, and hundreds of one-bushel apple boxes—an intersectional Yankee tree product if there ever was one (pasture pines, orchards). I feel even closer to oak thanks to cutting and splitting hun-dreds of cords of firewood, the most intimate way of knowing wood be-cause it follows the grain, but we sawed oak boards, too. We used red oak to rebuild the beds of cordwood trucks and hay wagons and to make count-less tomato stakes. Faith and I even made a few sturdy baskets of white oak splints—I rived them out, she wove them back together into new forms. We were on familiar terms with oak and pine right down to their growth rings and pitch, and now we were blessed with a woodlot conveniently full of those very trees and a house to be built. Seemed like an easy call.

White pine (*Pinus strobus*) and red oak (*Quercus rubra*) are in fact the two leading timber species of our region, foundational building blocks of American material culture. Tall and straight, white pine provided the lumber that built everything from city triple-deckers to little houses on the prairie, extracted from the southern edge of the great North Woods that stretches from Maine to Minnesota. Light and easy to work, pine is our signature softwood timber species. Oaks are the dominant trees of the central hardwood forest that runs from here to Arkansas, with white oak more prominent to the south and west and red oak more important to the north and east, where we are. Hard and heavy, with a handsome open grain, oak is the country's most valuable hardwood timber, used for mak-ing furniture, flooring, barrels, and (once upon a time) ships. Oak and pine were key drivers of the nation's rapid nineteenth-century commercial expansion, but they also have a deeper, preindustrial history in our part of the world. To build a house with pine and oak straight from our woodlot would have been a satisfying evocation of an earlier time when Americans had a closer, more enduring relationship with the local forest. To my mind, that is tightly pegged to the timber-framed method of construction.

Building a house frame out of large timbers enclosing a central hearth that burns wood—drawing both frame and fuel from the surrounding forest—is a simple pattern European settlers brought to these shores. Here it was refined to a high art. Although that art was all but lost for more than a century, it is now being rediscovered. Plenty has been written about traditional framing methods and how they differ from modern stick-built construction. I don't think enough has been said about parallel changes in the relationship between homebuilding and forests. This may be because it is now commonly assumed that the relationship of European "settler culture" to the American environment has been uniformly destructive from the get-go, but I do not think that is true.[4]

Of course, we can't forget that for thousands of years before my ancestors arrived, there were already people here who had their own ancestral relationship with the forest. The Native people of the Eastern woodlands lived in a world of abundance, which they conserved. They had the power to shape forest ecosystems by hunting and burning, and over thousands of years they had an impact on its composition and structure, though exactly how much is debated. This influence was felt mainly within a few miles of Native settlements along the coast and inland waterways, where there were often swaths of intensely managed, frequently burned open woodlands, orchards, and fields. But the great upland forests that lay between these strings of Native communities were for the most part little altered by human activity. They were visited for hunting and foraging, they were *peopled* in the sense that human beings knew them and cared for them, but there is little evidence that they were significantly transformed by human action—or needed to be. The diverse peoples of eastern North America relied on cultivated crops to varying degrees, but no more than a small percentage of this region's vast forests were ever cleared. These were primarily societies of the forest.[5]

Native wigwams and long houses were constructed of poles, bark, and reed mats; they were tight and warm, though by most accounts a mite smoky. Smaller camps were relocated frequently in response to seasonal shifts in available foods such as game, fish, fruits, and nuts, as the wigwams could be quickly moved or reconstructed. Larger settlements with their long houses (which seem to have been rare in New England but more common to the south and west) were moved less often in response to gradual depletion of planting grounds and wood supplies—an eminently sustainable way of occupying a large territory. I am of course generalizing very broadly about patterns that had great regional variation and that changed over time. Many Native people today are engaged in reconnecting with these cultural legacies of land stewardship and spiritual closeness with natural materials, the gifts of fellow creatures. This is one important strand in the broader movement for forest reengagement I am advocating here— but not the only strand.[6]

A very different, equally venerable cultural connection to trees was also alive at that time in early modern Europe. These were agrarian societies, ten times more densely populated than their eastern North American Native counterparts, that retained a much smaller but still critical woodland element. The farming and herding cultures of my Irish, Scottish, and English ancestors had their own ancient ways of integrating fields, meadows, pastures, and woodlands, also featuring tremendous regional variation— but that balance was periodically upset by population growth, which demanded increased farmland at the expense of trees, timber, and fuel. By the early seventeenth century when (not coincidentally) New England was being invaded, old England had climbed back close to its fourteenth-century demographic peak and was again feeling the pinch: land and work were scarce for young people, food was growing short, and supplies of wood and timber were being undermined. Woodlands covered less than 10 percent of the heavily cultivated English countryside, and they were hard-pressed to supply adequate material for buildings and fuel. Roger Williams, founder of Rhode Island, reported that some Native inhabitants wondered if the English had ventured to America because they had run out of firewood back home. Historians dispute whether or not acute wood scarcity had yet been reached in England, but English society was certainly headed in that direction—although it was also coming up with two connected world-beating substitutes for relying on local woodlands, namely mining coal and forging a global empire.[7]

English woodlands were patches of a few acres, tucked away here and there in the agrarian landscape, often on the least farmable ground. The genius of these ancient woods lay in their dual management to produce both lowly wood and lofty timber, with cutting rotations that overlapped in both space and time—a system of management known today as "coppicing with standards." Wood and timber should not be confused. The understory (the "wood") consisted of a dense thicket of hazel, birch, lime (linden), or, in wetlands, willow. These copses were cut clean every decade or so and then sprouted back vigorously from the stump (or "stool"), producing a heavy growth of long, flexible rods an inch or two in diameter. Standing above this underwood were scattered mature trees (the "timber") that had been allowed to grow up and form an open overstory—mostly oaks, but also other species such as beech, ash, and elm. A similar juxtaposition of closely cropped shrubbery interspersed with larger trees also flourished in hedgerows, which were metastasizing during the early modern period because of the process of enclosing common fields. Hedges were a linear version of the same dual-use concept as woodlands, providing a second important source of both wood and well-spaced timber. In either case, the larger trees were harvested on a longer cycle that spanned decades or centuries, providing heavy timbers for buildings, bridges, and ships. This system of woodland management was almost eternal—thousands of years old—and eminently sustainable.[8]

Smallwood and timber, growing side by side in hedges and woodlands, were reunited in the buildings made from them. An English frame consisted primarily of oak, though other timbers such as elm were sometimes used. Unlike the great manor houses, the timbers in a husbandman's cottage were mostly short, sometimes crooked and forked (known as "cruck" framing), and just stout enough to do the job. Whether noble or common, the timbers were worked and raised green, and they were pegged together into a sturdy frame with pretty much the same mortise and tenon joinery framers still use today. "Wattle and daub" made up the walls, filling the spaces between the timbers. A lattice of split wood (the wattle), thickly covered by clay mixed with straw (the daub), was often finished with a coat of whitewash or plaster. This style was later dubbed "half-timbered"—that is, the oak frame was left uncovered, inside and out, with striking visual effect. The exposed timbers were often carved and embellished, making the dark frame itself the main decorative element of the house, set against the plain walls that it encased. Sawn boards that might have sheathed the frame more snugly were an even dearer commodity than structural timbers in early modern England and mostly had to be imported from the Baltic, so this handsome but austere style was born of necessity. It was an economical use of scarce wood resources, found across much of northwestern Europe.[9]

When English colonists ventured to America they encountered a new world with not merely enough but (from their point of view) far too much wood: the Eastern woodlands region was at least 90 percent forested. For these yeomen farmers that abundance was a blessing and a curse, and for the next two centuries both local household economies and the emerging market economy were strongly shaped by the forest and by its steady removal—this became "America's Wooden Age." The blessing of dense, mature forest was mixed because the aspiring husbandmen had to clear it away so they could make farms. But they continued to rely on the forest even as they cleared it, and so in the end they didn't clear it all. They effectively conserved a significant part of the resulting agrarian landscape in woodlands—more than they had in England, because they needed more wood.

There are two ways of looking at this transformation, and both are true and important. It was, in many respects, manifestly destructive. The ancient American deciduous forest was reduced to less than half of the landscape, and what remained was cut repeatedly. Keystone species were extirpated—beaver, deer, cougars, wolves. The Native people were systematically dispossessed of their land, their numbers decimated by disease and violence. These human and ecological losses need to be acknowledged and, to the extent possible, put right. But at the same time, a new cultural landscape was created that deserves to be understood and appreciated in its own right, which includes its close relationship with the remaining forest. That culture of diversified farming, including managed woodlands that (at least in some areas) provided a renewable supply of wood and timber, is as much the progenitor of the landscape bequeathed to us as the Native ecological culture that preceded it, and it has as much relevance to how we forge an enduring relationship with the forest that we have all inherited.

To make farmland, you have to remove a good part of the forest, whether by fire, flint, or steel. That was the challenge facing my Yankee ancestors. Only those yeomen didn't yet have decent axes, let alone chainsaws. The edged tools the English settlers brought to the encounter were woefully inadequate for dealing with such large trees, so it was a long, hard slog—but then, being Calvinists, they fully expected their god to afflict them, and he lovingly obliged. The settlers found plenty of trees, had compelling reasons to cut them, and had many good uses for the resulting wood—but had no easy way to work them down to size. For generations, the main thing to be conserved was not wood, but labor.

New England house wrights carried on framing as they had in England, and it served them well. Using large timbers minimized cutting and sawing structural lumber. With a broadax, round trees could be hewn into square beams that were sized to the logs, chipping away as little surplus material as possible. There were plenty of trees to choose from, and so colonial houses grew larger over time. At first the carpenters preferred white oak, which reminded them of the English oak they knew so well. Oak is strong but also heavy, and they soon learned that many other American trees were suitable—particularly chestnut, which was lighter than oak but still quite strong and more durable where exposed to weather (as in barns and outbuildings). Pine also worked well, if the timbers were hewn thick enough. The trick was getting the right proportions—balancing the strength of the species, the length of the span, and the spacing between the members. This knowledge was honed by experience. There was no penalty for overbuilding, so we see some impressive timbers in these early structures—although if they were too big, they became difficult to handle. Of course, the colonial houses that survive for us to admire today represent a distilled sample of those originally built, somewhat distorting our backward gaze. All the poorly built ones have long since disappeared.[10]

The most important innovation to appear in early New England houses wasn't the structure but the sheathing. Soon after they arrived, Yankee farmers began to clothe their frames with pine boards. Boards were not cheap in New England, but they quickly became far more plentiful than in old England. Small water-powered sawmills (a fairly recent late-medieval invention) popped up on every stream. I mean this literally: just about every tiny brook I have studied in Concord or Weston had its now-vanished colonial sawmill, which could only have run a few months of the year, whereas most towns had only one or two more substantial grist mills, farther downstream. Building many small sawmills made sense, because dragging large sawlogs from the woods to the nearest mill was arduous. By the middle of the seventeenth century larger sawmills also appeared along rivers in southern New Hampshire and Maine, supplying lumber not just to local markets but also to the sugar plantations of the West Indies.[11]

What these mills were sawing, more than anything else, was the tallest, straightest tree they could find, far above anything old England had to offer: white pine. Tall pines were found towering above the oak forest, and here and there in purer stands on sandy soils where they had sprung up following windstorms and subsequent fires. Pine is lighter and softer than oak, hence easier to saw—an important consideration if you have ever watched an up-and-down sash saw (say at Old Sturbridge Village) chew its way the length of a log, slowly turning what seems like half of it into sawdust. The mills sawed some planks, but mainly they sawed more valuable one-inch boards, for interior paneling and exterior sheathing. The carpenters set ranks of upright studs (often riven, rather than sawn) between the large posts of their frames, on about a two-foot spacing. These studs helped reinforce the structure, but their main purpose was to provide a nailing surface for pine boards.[12]

To make it weather-tight, this board sheathing was itself commonly sided with clapboards, riven from clear, straight-grained pine, or even better from rot-resistant Atlantic white cedar (*Chamaecyparis thyoides*). Many early towns in eastern Massachusetts and Rhode Island had a prized cedar swamp, which you can still find today, amazing your friends (or long-suffering family): just start in the town center and follow Cedar Street until you arrive at a swamp. Although cedar has long since grown scarce in many of these wetlands and has been supplanted by red maple (*Acer rubrum*), it has not entirely disappeared, and perhaps its day will come again. Inside the outer wall sheathing, the spaces between the studs were often filled with bricks; and inside that came a finish layer of lath and plaster. This sandwich of clapboards, boards, bricks, and plaster may not have constituted what we would call a tight, well-insulated exterior wall today, but it was a notch above asking wattle and daub—mere sticks and mud—to withstand the onslaught of a New England winter. Especially during the Little Ice Age, which was then in full swing. Up on the roof, thatch was soon replaced by a layer of pine boards, covered by split shingles—which had the added virtue of being somewhat less flammable. These boards, clapboards, and shingles, mostly sawn and riven from pine, became distinctive features of American frame houses, reflecting the abundant forest.

With the house boarded on the outside the medieval half-timbered facing disappeared, but *inside* the house the frame was still exposed—

almost always in the ceilings, and sometimes in the walls, too. The frame thus remained an integral ornamental feature of the living space, as it had been in England, and it was often finished with chamfered edges and intricate carvings. The simplicity and structural clarity we sought in building our house, which we thought were matters of modern taste, actually echo ancient practical necessities that were similarly embellished. The exposed beams, the curved braces, the interplay between plaster walls and wooden posts, the ceiling that is simply the underside of the upstairs floorboards, the board and batten doors—many features of our house would turn out to be more authentic than we consciously intended, because they were derived from the same basic approach to building, using the same materials. They tie directly to the "First Period," or "late medieval" New England houses of the seventeenth century. They remind us that just as we borrowed structural ideas from our ancestors, we often made similar aesthetic choices that flowed from working directly with local wood.[13]

By the middle of the eighteenth century, that ready abundance of local wood was being tested, at least in older towns. New England had become a successful, relentlessly expanding agrarian society, driven by a population that doubled every generation—starting from a base of little more than twenty thousand immigrants and reaching one million inhabitants by the end of the colonial period, almost entirely by natural increase. Most families had at least two children (often the youngest) who settled at or near home and carried on with established farms and artisanal trades (many of them involving wood), plus five or six more who had departed for newer towns on the frontier. There were economic links between these siblings and cousins, as well—for example, in the yearly droving of dry cattle to the hill towns for fattening on new pastures being hacked from the forests there. By the late colonial period woodlands were becoming constricted in the earliest towns "down below" near Boston and along the coast, but they were still abundant up-country. Some frontier forest products, such as pine boards, shingles, and potash, could profitably travel that distance; but others such as firewood and heavy timbers were generally too bulky to pay for the trip (except to supply the largest port towns, usually going by water) and still needed to be generated locally. From these contrasting opportunities and constraints within an interconnected regional economy emerged one of America's most enduring architectural traditions: the Georgian farmhouse, and its progeny.[14]

These houses—many of which still stand—are deeply expressive of

Yankee agrarian culture and the iconic New England landscape that had
fully emerged by the early nineteenth century. Sure, we romanticize them,
but for good reason. They look great and are all the house anyone really
needs. By the mid-eighteenth century the Yankee building tradition had
entered its classical period, which lasted one hundred years. This was also
the era when New England was most intensively cleared and cultivated,
driving forest cover to its nadir. But as a result, those shrinking woodlands
became more carefully husbanded, too. This epoch was distinguished
from the "First Period" that preceded it by improved technical ability to
make full use of the trees of the region; it was distinguished from the industrial era that followed precisely by its reliance upon those local resources. With mastery of wood for building came architectural refinement
that appeared in house design and decoration, but some aspects of that
design still reflected tight dependence on local wood and timber. These
competing forces found expression in the Georgian houses of the eighteenth century and the Federal and Greek Revival houses that followed,
lasting through the first half of the nineteenth century to the Civil War.[15]

The eighteenth-century Georgian style was a departure from the
plainness of the seventeenth century, and it marked the spread of more
cultivated tastes from the urban upper crust to the sturdy yeomanry of the
New England countryside. Of course, not everyone was thriving in this
expanding society, and those who were marginalized continued to live in
smaller houses that have long since disappeared, but in each generation a
substantial part of the population, even in newly settled hill towns, gained
access to the resources to build improved houses or upgrade existing ones.
Above all, such refinement required more *boards*—not just for exterior
sheathing but increasingly for well-finished interior walls and paneling as
well. Houses were still *framed* with heavy timbers—there was not yet any
practical substitute for that. Large timbers could seldom bear the cost of
long-distance transport, so even in long-settled inland towns there had to
be enough local woodland to supply them. Sawmills were kept busy but
were not yet producing much dimensional lumber—they were still sawing
mostly boards for skin, not bones. The use of these boards brought greater
refinement to what was still a very symmetrical, boxy style of building, en-
forced by that unbending rectilinear frame.[16]

Houses tended to become larger and better appointed; they were
often two rooms deep as well as two rooms wide. By the Federal period

many added a central hall, with a more elegant staircase. The massive central chimney then became two (or, in fancier houses, even four) and moved toward the gable ends, though still symmetrically placed within the structure, to provide a fireplace in every room. As better glass, too, had become widely available (thanks in part to abundant potash), houses had more windows, which certainly made for more gracious living. But mainly there was more wood covering the walls. There was wainscoting, paneling, molding. Overhead there were drop ceilings, plastered over. The old-fashioned timber frame was still holding up the dwelling, but it had all but disappeared behind walls and decoration. Even the exposed summer beam that bisected the room's ceiling was often cased. All this required a ready supply of white pine boards, both from local sawmills and moving through the region from the frontier to the coastal cities.[17]

But the timber frame of the house, the skeleton, remained a local production—and this, together with the ubiquity of wood throughout the local economy, meant that a significant part of the landscape had to be conserved in woodland, even in the older towns. Decay-resistant white oak remained the timber of choice for sills, but the rest of the frame might be oak, pine, chestnut, or whatever was at hand—as long as it was large and sound enough and reasonably easy to work. A wide array of trees supplied especially the smaller members, such as joists and purlins. The house also needed prodigious amounts of fuel for its many fireplaces—this remained the largest demand of all. Beyond the house and barn, other requirements for local wood included fence posts and rails (oak or chestnut), carts and wagons, cooperage (oak staves, hickory hoops), grain chests, furniture, pails, tool handles (ash and hickory), on and on—right down to particularly fine charcoal needed to make gunpowder (alder and willow). Each of these products required different types of wood with the right qualities to do the job.[18]

Once the early generations of rapid land clearing were past, this continuing local demand for wood could not be allowed to deplete the forest. Conserving local woodlands required systems of management and skills of cutting that could produce a wide diversity of material ranging from slender rods to towering timber, generation after generation. New England farmers, craftsmen, and builders in the older towns solved this problem by retaining sufficient woodlands (from one quarter to one third of the landscape, in towns I have studied) and managing them in a dual system reminiscent of the practices used by their English ancestors: "sprout woods" cut every thirty years or so and taller woods of oak and pine timber allowed to stand closer to a century. Sometimes the wood and timber production even overlapped on the same woodlot, as they had in England. The sprout woods produced fuel, fencing, barrel hoops, and small timbers; the larger trees produced timbers for buildings, bridges, and ships, along with barrel staves, boards, and clapboards. I will return to this complex system and its signature tool—the American felling ax—later, when we talk about firewood. The central point here is that houses from the late colonial and Federal period featured some refined wood products, such as pine paneling, that were part of a wider regional timber economy, but they still depended primarily on materials such as the frame and fuel that came directly from surrounding woodlands. The houses were tightly bound to the careful stewardship of nearby forests.[19]

Where was hemlock in all of this? This northerly tree was uncommon near the coast, but as later generations ventured up-country in the second half of the eighteenth century—to western Massachusetts, southern Maine, New Hampshire, and Vermont—they began to encounter more hemlock. The most salient feature of hemlock lumber is that it is not pine: in many respects, it just isn't as good. Hemlock holds its lower branches and hence is full of knots. The wood is coarse and splintery and does not finish as smoothly as pine. This made it largely ineligible for high-end products such as clapboards and shingles, let alone clear boards for furniture and paneling. Consequently, hemlock did not have much market value, especially when transportation was slow and expensive.[20]

On the other hand, hemlock is a shade stronger than pine, and it is perfectly well suited for rough construction. Thus, as Yankees moved west and north, they began using hemlock locally for building their barn and house frames. Hemlock is one of the most common framing materials found in eighteenth- and nineteenth-century buildings that are still standing in western Massachusetts, for example. Roughly the same thing was happening in New York and Pennsylvania, after the Revolution: having once again broken the Native strength on the frontier, white settlers were pressing from the crowded coastal plain and piedmont onto (and beyond) the Appalachian plateau, encountering hemlock, and building with it. And in moving from Weston to the Connecticut River valley, Faith and I were about to make the same discovery about hemlock ourselves.[21]

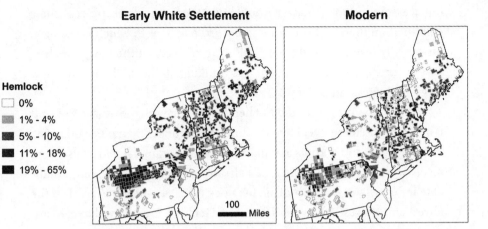

Maps of the Northeastern forest showing the relative abundance of hemlock. Information about the time of white settlement comes from "witness trees" on early township surveys; the modern map is based on U.S. Forest Service "Forest Inventory Analysis" plots in the same townships. Areas outside the townships that are outlined lack survey data. You can see the sharp decline in hemlock in Pennsylvania and the Catskills region of New York, with less change in central New England. (Data from Jonathan R. Thompson et al., "Four Centuries of Change in Northeastern Forests," *PLOS One* 8 [2013]; revised map by Brian Hall)

» » « «

With Ed Klaus steadily cutting and skidding the trees Lincoln Fish had marked, it was time for us to get serious about designing our house and figuring out who would build it. We needed architectural drawings to get a building permit, and we needed a site plan to get an approved septic system design and to file a Notice of Intent with the local conservation commission, since part of the construction was going to fall within the wetland buffer zone. Getting started hinged on somebody drawing us a house plan.

To design the house we engaged Tom, our farm partner, who is conveniently also an architect. Tom had never tackled a timber frame house before, so he was stoked to try. But to design it, he needed not only the usual information such as what kind of floor plan and how many bathrooms we wanted; he also needed to know what kind of wood we were planning to use for the frame. Without that knowledge he couldn't calculate the loads, size the timbers, and apply his coveted engineer's stamp certifying that the house wouldn't keel over in a light summer breeze. Our initial assumption was that we would build the frame of oak, pine, or some combination thereof. I was leaning toward oak myself, which is stronger, historically resonant, and (to me) more attractive. But the low-grade harvest occurring in our woodlot got us thinking about the house in a new way—or, I guess, an older way.

Ed was cutting a good bit of hemlock along with the other trees, and it began to catch our eye. Hemlock timber is stronger than pine and richer in color, with redder knots and more interesting grain. Hemlock also went nicely with black birch, which had already emerged as the leading candidate for our floor. But best of all, hemlock is just about *worthless*. It is the lowest and slowest of low-grade lumber. Hemlock is a beloved tree, of undoubted ecological and aesthetic value, and we wanted to protect it along the river if we could. But hemlock in a working woodlot is a commercial black hole from which nothing of pecuniary value can ever escape, and you don't want it taking over—which it appeared to be stealthily accomplishing on our shady, unmanaged hillside. To make matters worse, the invasion of the woolly adelgid might soon render all our standing hemlock really and truly dead and worthless—so we were in trouble either way. We might fight to save the hemlocks by the river, but now was a perfect time to get them out of the woods on the hill.

Why is hemlock worth so little money? From a structural point of view, hemlock and pine are almost interchangeable, and they often grow closely together in the forest. But hemlock is white pine's lowly stepsister— the Cinderella of softwood. This hasn't changed much since colonial times—hemlock's fairy godmother has yet to appear. It all comes from the two trees' different ways of growing and their response to light. White pine is only moderately shade tolerant. Our tallest eastern tree, it is lofty and emerges above the canopy, its distinctive top branches sweeping upward in search of the sun. Most of its life is in its high open crown—its lower branches die off and gradually disappear. Hemlock is just the opposite: slow-growing, compact, and shade tolerant, it tends to hold its dense lower branches, making it knotty—a knot in a board is nothing but a round (or worse, oblique) slice through a branch that the trunk of the tree enclosed as it grew outward. Thus, besides taking longer to reach a smaller size than white pine, the outer growth of even a big old hemlock yields fewer clear, knot-free, high-grade boards, which is where the money is.

Hemlock is also prone to "ring shake" (separation between the annular rings), which can render its dimensional lumber useless. Two-bys sawn from shaky hemlock devolve into jagged spars even as they come off the saw—a melancholy sight to behold. Between ring shake and rampant knots, a truckload of hemlock logs is likely to yield much less profit for a sawmill than a comparable load of white pine. Consequently, where pine is worth in the vicinity of $100 per thousand board feet on the stump (and oak several times that), hemlock is worth something like $25 per thousand. And yet, for building a frame, a sound hemlock beam is better than a similar beam of pine. Used for heavy timbers, hemlock really comes into its own: both stronger and prettier than pine. For a couple of old Yankees, this amounted to an irresistible formula: sell the pine to pay for the harvest, keep the hemlock to build the house. And a fundamental truth of building with slow wood dawned on us: in the right hands, low-grade wood can make a high-grade house. Hemlock is the slow-braised brisket of the timber world, and we had loads of hemlock.

Now the house plan began to take shape. With hemlock selected for the frame, Tom could size the beams and finish the drawings, and we got our approvals. Lincoln Fish went back into the woods and marked a few more hemlock trees to make sure there would be enough for the frame. We took all the hemlock out of the sale and engaged Ed to cut and yard it for us on the side, at a rate that was a better deal for him. Meanwhile we had hired Dave Bowman (and his then-partner Neil Godden) as our framer, based on his solid reputation but also on his eagerness to work with timber from the property. Dave is a well-known timber framer whom I had met a few years earlier, one of the early stalwarts of the Massachusetts Woodlands Cooperative. He went over the frame design with Tom, making suggestions regarding timber sizes and placement of braces. We took a walk on the hill with Dave to make sure that the marked trees were suitable for the major elements in the frame, which they were. Once Ed had cut and skidded them to the landing, Dave selected logs for the big timbers— the two-story gunstock posts, top plates, and tie beams—and we had them trucked to his shop, where he sawed them on his band mill. Luckily, none of them turned out to be prohibitively shaky. By spring 2011, our house project was rolling.

One of the delights of this "woods to house" project was working with a group of artists who were predisposed to cooperate, starting with the forester, the logger, the architect, and the framer. This is a long way

Ed Klaus yarding hemlock sawlogs. (Faith Rand)

from the world of Ayn Rand and her tiresome acolytes, in which a lone genius creates and all others bow to his oracular specifications. Instead, we built our house by engaging the collaborative vision of craftspeople who understood trees, wood, and buildings from different angles, informing and correcting one another all along the way, in a tolerant and good-humored manner. It was, in every sense, a warm, organic, and sociable way to build. It also makes a somewhat humdrum story because no insufferable egos clashed and nothing went badly wrong, but to sustain interest I will interject all the minor mishaps I can muster.

To saw the bulk of the frame we engaged Michael Idoine, a man from a nearby hill town who presented as half well-seasoned local planning activist and half retired wood industry technician. I had actually met Michael years earlier when he attended a talk I gave at the library in his town, and I vividly remembered him sitting there in the front row with an unwavering gaze, asking searching questions. Exactly the sort of man you want sawing timbers for your house, and now here he was. Michael had an old band mill that looked like something assembled from spare parts

Michael Idoine sawing hemlock beams. (Faith Rand)

picked up over a lifetime attending machine shop bankruptcy sales, fes-
tooned with furlongs of looping hydraulic hose. He leveled his mill on the
pasture behind our barn and began sawing timbers from hemlock Ed
carted down from the hill—the numerous shorter beams, posts, and joists
we would need, everything but the largest members that Dave was sawing
himself.

Michael was in no great rush, but worked with care and precision.
As he got into the job, which lasted from late spring into summer, he asked
another searching question: What did we want him to saw? Obviously, he
was sawing the frame, but to do that he had to remove other material. The
beams consisted of the center "box" that was left after wood was sawed
from the outside—first rounded slab and then one-inch boards, typically.

Then there were all the top logs that Michael would render into smaller joists, along with any combination of boards and dimensional lumber we wanted. But I had no idea what we wanted—I hadn't thought too far past the frame. What else goes into a house, anyway?

Another version of the same question was posed by Toby Briggs. Toby is the local carpenter we engaged to handle the construction of our house, once the frame was up; he was also helping Tom fix up his own place at the time. One day when we were going over the plans, Toby asked what we were thinking about for ceilings. I wasn't thinking about anything for ceilings—ceilings hadn't crossed my mind. I had forgotten that ceilings even existed. We were going to use black birch for flooring, that much we knew; Ed had piled the birch sawlogs to one side of the landing, and we had them trucked to another local mill where they were sawed into one-inch stock. Now they were drying at the kiln, waiting to be milled into floorboards.

But from the room below, you wouldn't see the bottom of that birch—you would see whatever was beneath it. Toby reminded us that the finish flooring normally runs over something, to stiffen it and take the nails—usually chipboard. Not exactly what you want to look up at between your exposed hemlock joists; it would need to be covered by some kind of ceiling. Toby thought maybe a simple sheetrock ceiling between the joists, painted white, would look nice. That would brighten up the rooms below, and if we dropped it a few inches, we could run the wiring and plumbing above it, too. But honestly, we didn't want to cover the joists at all—we wanted to see them in full. They were handsome four-by-eight hemlock timbers—they were part of the *frame*. Gazing up at the ceiling in Tom's kitchen, I realized Toby might have just handed me the answer to Michael's question about what he was supposed to saw.

"Could we maybe make that subflooring out of hemlock two-bys?" I ventured, pretty much expecting to be patiently told why that would be a bad idea.

But Tom and Toby both thought that might look good. We'd just need to have the rough hemlock planed, milled tongue-and-groove, and kilned. We had already engaged Tony Mason, a custom millworker who had also been associated with the Woodlands Cooperative, to mill the birch finish flooring for us. So maybe we could truck a few loads of hemlock two-bys down to Tony and have him mill those, too.

Toby suggested Tony could cut V-notches in them, while he was at it. I had no idea what a V-notch was then, but I do now, and I see it in lots of similar ceilings—that little groove on the underside where the boards meet does add a nice, understated decorative touch. It also neatly disguises any slight irregularities in the thickness of the two adjoining boards, because the *notches* meet perfectly. The ceiling and the subfloor could become two sides of the same thing: tongue and groove hemlock. We would just need to figure out somewhere else to run the utilities, which we solved with a couple of closets and a single strategically placed dropped ceiling in the front hall. With that settled, Tom worked up a tally of a few thousand feet of two-bys for Michael to saw from the hemlock top logs, in five-, six-, and seven-inch widths. He sawed enough for the second floor and the attic, and because you always allow for a healthy surplus, we ended up with enough to make the porch roofs, too. That patient, shade-tolerant, unshaken hemlock was slowly taking over our house.

At this point I began to fully comprehend what we were up to. We had given at least some thought to a few prominent features of the house: the frame, the floor, the kitchen cabinets, the stairs, the masonry heater. But there were many other elements we hadn't yet considered—the ceilings, the siding, the trim, the doors—that might also come from our woodlot. The right materials might simply present themselves, as useful by-products derived from making something else. Now I saw the principle involved: everything flows from sawing the frame. In a conventional house, the structure disappears. It is made of bland, uniform industrial materials that may have their origins in the forest but that are robbed of their distinctive organic character: plywood, chipboard, nominal two-by studs. These do their jobs well enough, but they look like crap. So they get hidden behind drywall, paneling, drop ceilings, tile, linoleum, carpet. In your typical house, structure is one thing, finish is another.

But with a timber frame, the structure itself is ornamental. The timbers are robust and attractive and can be planed and oiled to bring out the grain: the central decorative strategy is simply to showcase the frame. Now I saw that principle might be extended, if there were other home-grown materials that we wanted to put on display simply doing their job. Not to the point of uncovering *everything* that was functional, although something approaching that aesthetic was a possibility. You often see it (in an industrial style) in old mill buildings that have been rehabbed into artist studios or brew pubs, for example, where steel beams, pipes, and ducts are left exposed, tidied up a bit, and double as decoration. That can look good in the right setting, but not our house. Yet without celebrating every wastepipe and conduit we could still strip down the design and find more places to fashion a comely face directly from form and function.

This simple principle, as applied to hemlock, reached its ultimate expression in the doors. We had found a home in the ceiling for the two-bys sawed from the top logs, but we had yet to find a place for the burgeoning piles of one-inch boards that Michael and Dave were sawing from the faces of the beams. At worst, we figured we could use them around the farm for years to come, for new cow pens and barn repairs, which in fact we have. For example, that fall we had Tony Mason mill us a load of hemlock boards tongue and groove so we could build new runway doors for the barn, using a simple Z-frame backing to stiffen them. Those barn doors were easy to make and looked sharp, which got me thinking maybe I could make all the interior doors for our house the same way.

I picked through the piles and got Tony to kiln, plane, and mill about a thousand feet of our nicest hemlock boards. At his suggestion, this time he cut not just a groove but a little bead behind the tongue to make them meet up a bit fancier. I set up a square jig on a table in Tom's basement shop to bang the boards together and screw them in place with two wide hemlock battens, top and bottom—just about the simplest door you can make. I am a sub-par carpenter at best, because I lack the requisite steady hand and patience, but making those doors, I couldn't do much damage. Luckily, as I have said, hemlock boards are cheap, and there's always a need for kindling if you screw up. When you heat with wood, even your carpentry mistakes can at least start your morning fire and brew your tea.

Over the next year I made twenty-six doors, as work on the house progressed. It kept me out of trouble. From the plain bedroom and bathroom swinging doors I graduated to sliding closet doors with slightly more elaborate frames, as it seemed like they needed to be sturdier and also as my door-making skills had marginally improved. Then we have three interior windows that look out onto the living room from other rooms and so, feeling ambitious, for those openings I made sliders that were double thick (to dampen noise) with inlaid herringbone panels on the back. All were made of the same hemlock but now running diagonally, so it was a good use for leftover short pieces. Plus, I got to use a router. It's a good thing I

Toby Briggs framing a bathroom door. Toby and his partner Chris Krezmien built the house. (Faith Rand)

ran out of doorways to close, so I could move on to other amusements—
such as installing birch shelves and hanger rods in the closets—before
making hemlock doors (as Thoreau once remarked about hoeing beans)
could become a dissipation.

    While he was milling the hemlock boards for our doors, Tony Mason
asked me what I was thinking about for hardware. Again, I had no idea—I
had forgotten that doors needed hardware. Tony recommended a couple
of blacksmiths he knew, but when we checked out their web sites we saw
that custom colonial hinges would cost us more than the doors themselves, which didn't seem right. Mass-produced "mild steel" reproduction
colonial hardware, by contrast, was less expensive but still not as cheap as
it looked. We weren't sure what to do, until one Fourth of July I was searching for a bungee cord in the shop up at Faith's family camp in New Hampshire and stumbled on two buckets in a corner packed with, packed with,

hmmm, what have we here . . . packed with a few dozen wrought-iron strap hinges and pulls. Well hey, genuine colonial door hardware: the very thing we're looking for.

When I asked Faith's mother what these hinges were doing up in the shop, she told me matter-of-factly that they were from her parents' summer place over in Temple, New Hampshire, that burned to the ground in 1950. Hinges, pulls, and antique dresser handles were all that was salvaged from the ashes in the cellar. They had been sitting in various crates and buckets for sixty-two years, moving from one family barn or garage to the next, patiently waiting for us—the Yankee way of building. We cleaned them up with a wire brush, hit them with some Helmsman spar varnish, and they were good as new—just the right number for our doors, needless to say. That Temple house had been a handsome Georgian, built about 1780. Quite by accident, our house is now directly linked to the very building tradition it evokes, by its hinges.

But something still bothered me: those hinges were all different, many of them distinctly *seventeenth* century in style (as I learned from the standard works on the subject—I previously knew nothing about hinges). What were they doing way up there in New Hampshire, in 1780? Being a colonial historian, I decided to trace the family that built that house, thinking perhaps they had brought their hinges with them from Massachusetts, perhaps after some earlier fire. I thought that would make a good story: hinges migrating across the evolving New England landscape; domestic stability punctuated by calamity. And it is a good story: the Richardsons' Temple house had been built by the descendants of John Cragin, who was captured by Oliver Cromwell at the Battle of Dunbar in 1650. That was part of a well-known New England story: many of those Scottish prisoners of war were sent as indentured servants to the Saugus Iron Works. There is no evidence that Cragin was in Saugus, but he did turn up in Woburn, Massachusetts, after working off his indenture, and assimilated into Puritan society. His grandson, also John Cragin, a blacksmith, became a solid citizen of nearby Acton, which split off from Concord in 1735. Now that corner of the world is familiar to me, so I dug into the Acton town records. After his wife, Judith, died, John pulled up stakes and moved (at the age of sixty-three) with three of his sons and their families (others having already gone off to Maine) to the New Hampshire hills on the northwestern horizon, in 1764. This made perfect sense to me. There the Cragin family became leading citizens in the new town of Temple, into the mid-nineteenth century. John's youngest son, Francis, who settled nearby, was a master builder; John's oldest son, Deacon John Cragin, is thought to have built the Georgian house on the homeplace about 1780.[22]

The Cragins' story exemplifies the relentless agrarian expansion of colonial New England I sketched earlier, and it resembles the migratory patterns of Faith's family and my own. It was like finding yet another Yankee clan lurking among our ancestors, or at least in the lineage of our hinges. Once again, I was struck by the ability of these middling yeomen to build such substantial farmhouses within a decade or two of arriving in a heavily forested, rocky hill town that would later be judged barely marginal for agriculture. Yet they quickly filled it with handsome homes that would cost a pretty penny today. How did they do it? A large part of their prosperity was derived not so much from farming but from the forest they were clearing: pine shingles and potash to sell, abundant local timber to build those houses and barns. But this got me no closer to understanding where those hinges actually came from. The smaller house the Cragins left behind in Acton hadn't burned down—after they left, it apparently got dragged a few miles across town and attached to the Faulkner House, which has since become a museum, so you can still visit it today. Whatever hinges it had, it presumably kept.

Then I looked more closely at Faith's grandfather, Charles O. Richardson. Temple is just a few miles up the road from his grandfather's farm in Pepperell, Massachusetts, where he had spent many weekends as a boy in the late nineteenth century, cycling out from Boston. Richardson subsequently rose from office boy to vice-president of a textile merchanting firm and made his home in Weston. After buying the Temple house for a summer place in 1920, Richardson engaged the noted colonial revival architect Joseph Everett Chandler to renovate it. Chandler and Richardson really went to town. They raised the roofline and blew out the back to create a complicated salt box complete with a long dormer, excavated the filled-in fireplaces, and attached an outbuilding to form an off-kilter ell the children christened Askew Hall (with the accent on the first syllable), in honor of a local carpenter who objected "But, it's all ass-kew!" Then they built a second askew ell to match, planted an enclosed colonial garden between them, and tricked out all the rooms with loads of colonial gear—wide pine floorboards, paneling, andirons, spinning wheels, antique furniture, hinges, delph. And where did they get all this stuff? From auctions and dealers. There was a flourishing trade in colonial artifacts at the time, as many older houses were being demolished while a chosen few were being lovingly restored—or *more* than restored, as in this case. Our hinges didn't come from a particular colonial house after all: they came from *many* colonial houses, scattered all across the region. They evoked not just colonial New England itself, but also an early twentieth-century wave of nostalgia for colonial New England. History is a complicated beast.[23]

Those old hinges still work fine, in any case. It was a challenge hanging them on their massive pintles, but Toby found a way. They look great. But I sometimes wonder where they are going next, and *when?* They seem happy enough where they are at the moment, but I know they have other plans. They are both a reminder and a portent—they have indeed been through the fire.

It took a few years, and no one planned it ahead of time, but once hemlock was established as the main timber in our house it worked out its full story in three stages, derived from different parts of the tree: frame, subflooring, and doors. It's satisfying to look around the house today and see every part of those hemlock trees expressed from top to bottom and from pith to bark, if you know where to look. The main timbers are made from the centers of the trunk, and because they are rectangular members sawed from round logs they tend to have tight edge grain at the corners, widening to a strip of broader face grain down the middle. The largest timbers barely fit inside the logs so they are often waney at the corners, providing relief from perfect squareness and reminding us that these were once trees. The eight gunstock posts that rise two stories flare at the top to carry first the top plate and, above that, the tie beams athwart the plate. Complicating the posts simplifies the joinery. Since our living room is open above to the attic subfloor—our only nod to useless empty space— you can follow two of these posts all the way up to the plate. Of course, tree trunks do not naturally widen as they go up, so these posts are actually standing upside-down from the way they grew in the woods, with the butt flare at the top—which you can also tell because the oblique knots slant down instead of up, opposite the way the branches grew. These posts were a key design element added by Dave Bowman, as it is how timber framers have done it, time out of mind.

Looking at the smaller hemlock members, more is revealed. Many of

Hemlock door with genuine colonial hardware, in our own
Askew Hall—a.k.a. the mudroom. The trim is black birch.
(Faith Rand)

the four-by-eight floor joists were derived from a perfectly centered eight-
by-eight box that Michael then sliced in half, so the final saw cut exposed
two faces where the slender knots curve out in opposite directions from
a wavering line down the middle. This provides an intimate look at the
yearning heart of the tree, the tip advancing toward the sun and throwing
out branches as it grew. I love the way those knots get *larger* as they go
from the center to the edge of the joist, making them somewhat leaf-like
in appearance, because the branches were also growing as the tree grew
around them—they look almost as if they have stems. You can sit by the
fire with your glass of wine, gaze up at an attic joist, and see which way that
tree was once growing. Somewhere in the house, if you can find it, on some
other joist is a bookmatch to that face, with everything reversed. Sometimes after dinner we wander around in search of these matching faces, but

we seldom find them, because it is hard to visualize the flipped pattern you are looking for—or if we do, we soon forget where they are, so we have to search again some other night.

The subflooring, running at right angles over the joists, is plain sawn from the top logs and shows a variety of grain patterns, dominated by narrow edge grain. It is also lighter in color, because we did not oil those boards—but they will darken, over time, and some future occupant may want to take measures to correct that. The doors, on the other hand, are made of boards sawed from the outside of the beams, so they feature broad and handsome face grain. There are six to eight vertical boards in each door, and many of them are also waney-edged, so irregular strips of the rich brown and purple-tinged inner bark of hemlock are often embedded here and there along the joints.

All in all, the house presents quite a diverse and dashing display of character from a modest bunch of hemlock trees. If you have a sufficiently nurturing imagination, you can sit in the living room and put the trees from which the house was made back together in your mind, from pith to bark and from butt to crown. Even on the darkest winter night you can see from the house back into the forest, without even looking out the window. The biggest open window to the woods is the house itself.

Cherry Braces

FOR YEARS, I DIDN'T HAVE MUCH respect for black cherry (*Prunus serotina*). I just couldn't take it seriously as a tree. Everywhere I have lived, black cherries were scrubby upstarts in old fields and rough edges. We used to climb them as kids, back in suburbs of Pittsburgh. They were strange little trees—they started up scraggly and then just sort of petered out, seemingly. The trunk and limbs were often marred by scabby "black knot" infections, which exuded a sticky jelly that reminded us of the Blob, and we used it as such on our unsuspecting foes. Black cherry is lovely in bloom, with its racemes of tiny white flowers, but the small black fruits barely coat a hard seed: vaguely edible, but not really palatable. The crushed leaves and scraped bark have the bitter smell of cyanide—in fact, the wilting foliage from a fallen cherry limb can sicken livestock, as Faith and I learned when we had sheep.

In Weston, we cut black cherry while clearing pastures or pushing back field edges. The wood is very pretty, in resinous, black-speckled shades of yellow and red, especially when freshly cut. It splits easily and makes decent firewood, roughly equal in heat value to red maple. We rarely encountered it in the Weston town forest, and when we did it was crooked and suppressed or, as foresters say, subdominant. And yet I knew that somewhere up on the Allegheny Plateau of Pennsylvania, not that far from where I was born, cherry grew tall and straight enough to make highly prized hardwood lumber. But when I saw furniture made from cherry, for some reason I still didn't like it. It always struck me as too showy, like some exotic hardwood—not something I could get from virtuous local sources, anyway. To my eye, it lacked the familiar, robust honesty of oak or the straightforward simplicity of pine and hemlock.

So, like hemlock but for different reasons, cherry was one of the last trees you would have expected to find in our house made of local wood. And yet it ended up playing a defining role. How did that happen?

Three old black cherry trees in the fence line between us and the farm to the north.
(Tom Chalmers)

The same question might be asked of how black cherry got to be a
premium hardwood in northern Pennsylvania in the first place—and that
story, curiously, is also tied to the history of hemlock. It flows from the
larger story of how Americans lost their connection to local forests in the
nineteenth century, as both logging and construction were industrialized
with the invention of the two-by-four.

Our farm has a classic mid-nineteenth-century New England barn—one
of the fading few, although to slow that long slide into oblivion we gave
ours a fresh coat of red paint as soon as we bought the place. It sits next
to Tom and Joan's house, which is a classic-looking white New England
farmhouse. The house and barn are in line, though not quite connected—

altogether, a classic nineteenth-century New England pattern. These buildings replaced the original colonial homestead across the road, now marked
only by two dimples in the pasture and a few grand old sugar maples.

The existing house and barn were built together soon after the Civil
War, yet their methods of construction were strikingly different. The barn
is old school, composed of massive hemlock timbers. The forty-two-foot
tie beams are continuous—no scarf joints connecting those babies! But the
house represents something new: it is a stick-built "balloon frame," made
entirely of two-by-fours. The lumber itself appears to be hemlock and
probably came from a local sawmill, as was often still true in rural areas;
but the framing *method* was an innovation that was sweeping the country,
using materials that in most cases were anything but local. They were part
of an emerging national economy of rapid resource extraction that ultimately devastated the Eastern forest.

Through the colonial era and into the early decades of the New Republic, houses were still built primarily with local wood, and farmers' winter work in the forest supplied materials and energy primarily for the local
economy. Primarily, but not entirely: as we have seen, American farmers
had always made some value-added commercial wood products such as
pine shingles and oak barrel staves, earning them a little cash to purchase
goods from the emerging world of global trade—English pewter, Barba-
dos rum, Indian calico. The rural economy was dominated by household
production and local exchange but also had links to the larger market
economy, and forest products exemplified that duality.[1]

As the new country rapidly expanded during the early decades of the
nineteenth century, that balance began to shift decisively. The flow of wood
products from the frontier increased, feeding into a growing national market economy. Every spring, flotillas of flatboats and rafts made from half-
squared white pine logs descended the great rivers of the East—the Connecticut, Hudson, Delaware, Susquehanna, and Allegheny—bound for the
burgeoning port cities. The rafts themselves were fungible and provided
beams for city halls and mills, while their decks were piled with boards,
shingles, staves, and barrels of potash (potassium carbonate)—an industrial alkali used to make glass and soap and to clean and bleach cloth. For
decades, potash was one of the young nation's leading exports. It was
produced by thousands of frontiersmen clearing and burning millions of
hardwood trees, leaching the ashes to yield lye, and boiling it down in

shallow iron kettles. Forest products such as these financed the purchase and improvement of many a farm—indeed, in rugged highland regions, clearing the land often proved more lucrative than farming it ever would. Even frontier households began devoting more of their production to the cash economy and purchasing more of what they consumed—a transformation historians call the Market Revolution. But by the middle of the nineteenth century, those home-grown rafts were being swamped by a new interloper: mammoth log drives heading for the booms of industrial sawmills.[2]

The industrialization of American lumbering took shape by 1840, with Maine, New York, and Pennsylvania leading the way. The work itself employed mostly the same old methods: men with axes, crosscut saws (those were new), and teams of oxen and horses cutting, skidding, and sledding pine logs out of the woods. But these "shanty boys" had become wage laborers in large, well-organized crews, rather than farmers finding winter work in their own woodlots. Commercial lumbering was undertaken on an enormous new scale and with breathtaking speed. Large capitalists acquired vast timberlands where the lofty pines prevailed, in back-country regions not yet heavily settled by white farmers—northern New England, the Adirondacks, northern Pennsylvania, and finally northern Michigan, Wisconsin, and Minnesota: the mother lode. Few objected, because many Americans believed the lumber barons were doing the nation a favor: "letting light into the swamp," opening more land for the independent yeomen who were manifestly destined to follow. The pine industry grew explosively and swept west, making boom towns out of places like Bangor, Glens Falls, Williamsport, and Saginaw, to which millions of logs were flushed downriver on the spring drives to be sawed into boards and planks. In 1850, the United States produced about 5 billion board feet of lumber—not a shabby number. By 1900, it was producing 35 billion feet, a figure that has fluctuated surprisingly little ever since.[3]

Cutting lumber on such a grand scale relied on water in all its phases—it only really worked in the frozen north country of the United States and Canada. The logs were cut and sledded on snow in the winter to ice-covered streams, and then floated downriver on the rushing meltwater of the spring drives. But after that the prime mover became gaseous: steam to power the new circular saws (and then bandsaws) that drove a quantum leap in production; steam to drive the locomotives that delivered

the sawn lumber not only to the booming cities but back out into the settled eastern countryside and westward onto the plains, where little local
timber was to be found. Prairie pioneers soon graduated from a "sod"
house to a "sawed" house, as the saying goes. Back east, when Henry
Thoreau watched railroad cars loaded with pine lumber from the Maine
woods rattle past Walden Pond they were headed *up* from Boston to country customers, not down. By the time of the Civil War, mass-produced
lumber was available everywhere—and there was usually nothing local
about it.

And these were not just one-inch pine boards to clothe the house
frame, inside and out—they now included dimensional lumber (that is,
two-by-fours) to *build* that frame. The logging boom was tied to a parallel
revolution in construction: stud wall, or stick framing. It was known as
"balloon framing" when the studs ran two or more stories from sill to
plate; by the twentieth century that largely gave way to the story-by-story
"platform framing" still widely used today. Either way, abundant materials
and machine power replaced more exacting skilled labor: frames made of
heavy timbers with intricate joinery gave way to frames made of many light
studs, quickly nailed together. The transformation that had begun with
hiding the frame inside the walls was complete.

Stick framing required another mechanical innovation to clinch it: the
lowly nail. In colonial times nails were hand made by blacksmiths, or sometimes by farmers (or their children, or their slaves) in odd hours: heating
nail rod in the forge, beating one end to a point on the anvil, striking the
nail off the rod, and beating the other end to a head. A good nailer could
make you one in a just a minute or two—in other words, nails were expensive. By 1830, that all changed—machines cut thousands of nails per hour,
making them plentiful and cheap. Frames could be nailed up in no time
using many light pine studs and joists spaced close together, doing away
with the painstaking craft of cutting mortises and tenons and raising heavy
timbers. With industrial power it became cheaper to cut big trees into little
pieces, ship them hundreds of miles, and pound them back together into
the frames of buildings than to wrestle with them nearly whole.[4]

Two-by-four pine studs and machine-cut nails built much of nineteenth-century America, filling the cities with wooden frame triple-deckers
to house the growing urban workforce, along with bungalows and four-
squares in the surrounding streetcar suburbs that subsequently bloomed

for the white-collar middle class. The new framing method spread into the countryside as well, because it was fast and cheap. Eventually it even conquered barns: by the early twentieth century you could go down to the depot and pick up a gambrel-roof barn kit from Sears, milled from southern yellow pine and bald cypress, and shipped anywhere in the country. No heavy timbers involved. I have encountered exactly the same barn in Weston, Massachusetts, and in Matfield Green, Kansas—wherever I go, one seems to find me. Honestly, it is a darned good design. Sears and other companies sold house kits, too. In the space of half a century, both lumbering and building were nationalized and industrialized, and the connection between homes and the local forest was broken.[5]

Along with that lost connection went any effective economic framework for conserving forest, at least for a while. Even long-settled New England farm towns such as Weston and Concord, which for generations had been holding at least a quarter of the landscape in woodlands to supply local wood, sank to only 10 percent forest cover by 1850—the degraded landscape where Henry Thoreau had to beat the huckleberry bushes in search of any sprig of remaining wildness. With Pennsylvania coal for heat and Maine lumber for housing there was no real need for local forest anymore—in fact, much of the rampant timber cutting that Thoreau observed around Walden Pond was as much to supply commercial markets outside Concord as for home use. But mainly, most remaining Concord woodlands were cleared and converted to pastures for milk cows, so that farmers could wade deeper into the market economy, as both producers and consumers. The same drives swept the nation as a whole, on a mammoth scale. And as the new industrial economy really took off between the Civil War and World War I, the entire Eastern forest was abruptly laid waste.[6]

The Eastern logging boom took place in a series of increasingly destructive waves. The first cut was often fairly "selective," in that the tall white pines were frequently scattered across a more diverse forest. Once that initial high-grading moved west to the next pinery, the remaining trees were subjected to successive rounds of cutting that were usually more intensive, especially as new harvesting technologies came into play. The details of this surge of industrial extraction varied from place to place, but nothing illustrates it better than hemlock.

Hemlock lumber may not have been prized, but hemlock bark was:

it is rich in tannin and makes strong leather with a dark, reddish-brown color. In the colonial era, tanning had been mostly a local affair—every town had at least one tannery, with a small mill to grind black oak and chestnut bark for soaking the hides. Leather for shoes, gloves, shop aprons, and a hundred other uses was a key material in the artisanal economy, combining a wood by-product with the local raising and slaughter of cattle. But like everything else, with the nineteenth-century rise of cities and an integrated market economy, tanning was pursued on a much larger scale. Leather became one of the nation's leading industries, supplying the material for factories that made shoes, harnesses for horses and mules (which were rapidly replacing stolid oxen for both farm work and hauling freight), and belts to drive the new machinery in textile and a thousand other kinds of mills. The tanning industry soon migrated to the margin of the great highland hemlock forests: it takes many tons of bark to tan a single ton of leather, so it was cheaper to ship the hides to the trees. Hemlocks were felled in the spring and summer when the bark could be most easily stripped, using a long-handled tool called a "spud." In the early days the timber itself was often just left to rot.[7]

The tanning industry flourished in New York's Catskill and Taconic mountains, convenient to the Hudson, through the first half of the nineteenth century. By the time of the Civil War the Catskill hemlocks were played out and the industry had moved on to more remote parts: the Adirondacks, eastern Maine, Wisconsin. But the hemlock mother lode was the "Black Forest" of northern Pennsylvania, which was supplying half of the nation's tanbark by 1900. This boom was made possible by another new technology: the logging railroad. These temporary narrow-gauge lines allowed timber cutting to reach into every corner of the highlands, not just those within a few miles of a stream that could float logs. They enabled cutting in all seasons and of all species—including hardwoods that did not so readily float.[8]

Logging railroads facilitated and in fact demanded clear-cutting, as they were costly to build. At least now hemlocks were sawed for rough construction lumber, after the bark was stripped—but the northern hardwoods, beech and sugar maple growing alongside the hemlocks, were soon being cut as well. Some of these hardwoods made furniture, but most went to feed the chemical wood industry—a successor to the potash industry of old, now in the hands not of legions of farmers but of larger enterprises systematically denuding thousands of square miles of rugged terrain. Until the mid-twentieth-century advent of petrochemicals, wood distillation supplied key industrial chemicals such as acetate of lime and methanol that were used to make acetone, formaldehyde, rubber, dye, paint, and early plastics. Elsewhere across the East, suddenly accessible hardwood forests in highland regions were clear-cut for railroad ties, charcoal (also a by-product of distilling chemicals), and pit-props for coal mines. By the early decades of the twentieth century, the magnificent Eastern forest was laid low, flat-out gone: well and truly devastated.[9]

Scourging slash fires followed everywhere in the wake of logging. In 1871, a conflagration centered on Peshtigo, Wisconsin, burned a million acres and killed thousands of people—carnage an order of magnitude greater than the Chicago Fire that ignited on the same windy day, in case anyone missed the point. Across the lake in Michigan, another few million acres caught fire. The Chicago Fire fed on balloon-frame structures made of Wisconsin and Michigan pine; while the city of sawn lumber burned, the dried tops of the same trees did too, back in the land of stumps. The decades that followed saw an enormous spike in wildfire throughout the East—not only in the dry pine forests of the Great Lakes and South, where fire had been a regular part of the pre-European landscape, but even in the more mesic northern hardwood-hemlock forest stretching from Pennsylvania to Nova Scotia, where fire had once been rare. Not any more: those forests were now laid bare to the sun, strewn with combustible logging debris, and susceptible to new ignition sources such as sparks from locomotives. In dry years, they burned—often catastrophically. This surge in fires lasted until after World War I, when the recovery of the forest and more effective firefighting (thanks to gasoline-powered trucks) brought them under control.[10]

It would be hard to exaggerate the abject prostration of the Eastern forest a century ago. Today it is difficult to even imagine. The early conservationists who beheld this ruined landscape were afraid that the forest might be permanently destroyed and replaced by scrub, like the Mediterranean, and that the nation would soon be facing a timber famine. These were entirely rational fears. Yet in retrospect we know that the forest *did* grow back and a national timber famine did *not* materialize. This outcome owed as much to dumb luck as to deliberate conservation, but nevertheless it raises a question: if the worst fears of the conservationists did not come to pass, can we, with the benefit of hindsight, still condemn what the lumbermen wrought? We can, for two reasons: they cut everything, and they cut it all at once.

They cut everything: only small pieces of the pre-European forest escaped clearing for farmland or heavy logging, in spite of decades of growing calls to preserve at least a few wild places for posterity. Even New York's "forever wild" Adirondack Park, established in 1892, included only about 10 percent unlogged "old growth." The rest had already been cut over. For the Eastern Forest region as a whole the amount of old growth forest that has never been cut is much lower, probably less than half a percent. Most of these scraps escaped because they were tucked away in especially inaccessible terrain, and they are hardly representative of the diverse forest that once flourished. And *they cut it all at once:* there was no serious attempt, at any meaningful scale, to harvest trees in a measured way that might have initiated long rotations while preserving the ecological benefits of a diverse forest of mixed ages and the economic benefits of a steady local and regional wood supply. Again, this was in spite of calls for just such an approach since the early nineteenth century and despite some nascent examples of sustainable management in older regions (though these were not widely recognized). Instead, an orgy of untrammeled industrial extraction took everything in the span of a few decades, concentrating the environmental impact: the loss of habitat for species that require mature forest, the degradation of waterways and disruption of hydrological cycles, the brutalized landscape left behind. It was devastation, sure enough, for those who had to live through it.[11]

Was the forest diminished in the long run? That is a more complicated question. Surely, in some obvious ways it has been—for example, the passenger pigeon, a powerful ecological force for thousands of years, is gone forever, and many other species remain much depleted. Yet the natural world is full of disturbances and deeply resilient, and given enough time it establishes new working conditions that become the next natural order and deliver much the same benefits as before. But a century later we are only partway there. The fate of the "second growth" forest that has sprung back up across the East remains in our hands: it cannot become the same forest that it once was, but it is the forest that we have been granted, and it could become equally magnificent, in its own way. The challenge is the same as ever: we are still a large industrial society that needs to consume

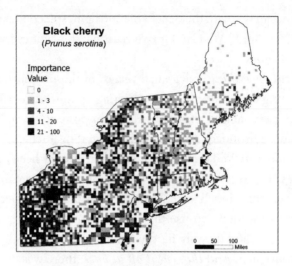

Black cherry "Importance Value," a measure that combines relative abundance and basal area of the species in U.S. Forest Service "Forest Inventory Analysis" plots. The concentration of black cherry in western Pennsylvania is especially heavy. (M. P. Peters, A. M. Prasad, S. N. Matthews, and L. R. Iverson, *Climate Change Tree Atlas*, Version 4, 2020 [Delaware, Ohio: USDA Forest Service, Northern Research Station and Northern Institute of Applied Climate Science])

millions of cubic feet of wood to prosper, yet we also have a responsibility to nurture the larger benefits of a healthy standing forest, at which we utterly failed the first time.

This much is certain: the forest has been changed, sometimes radically, in terms of which trees dominate. One of the most striking examples is the hemlock and northern hardwoods forest that once prevailed across northern Pennsylvania but was clear-cut by the early twentieth century: it has grown back as a new forest type called "Allegheny hardwoods," featuring a leading role for none other than black cherry. The turn-of-the-century removal of hemlock, sugar maple, and beech gave rise to a resurgence of shade-intolerant, early successional species such as red maple, tulip poplar, and cherry. By the second half of the twentieth century cherry had emerged as a particularly valuable timber, and so the recovering forest of the region came to be widely managed to grow more cherry rather than allowed to succeed entirely to slower-growing, more shade-tolerant species. There is more to that story, but we will come to that. The gist of it is that the destruction of the northern Pennsylvania "Black Forest" for tanbark and wood chemicals gave rise to the unusually black cherry–rich forest of the region today. The mystery of how that distinctive cherry timber region originated, which had puzzled me for so long, has been solved.[12]

But that didn't happen to the forest where we live. As I have said, our black cherries grew up in old fields and are mostly small, crooked, and pretty much worthless for timber. Or so I thought.

Once we had hemlock selected for the beams of our house, we needed something complementary for the braces. Braces are short timbers that fit diagonally in the corners between posts and beams to give the frame the rigidity it needs to resist racking in the wind. Hemlock itself makes perfectly good braces, and we did use some hemlock; but Dave Bowman thought that a darker-colored wood, such as red oak or black cherry, would make a nice accent. We might even find something curved.

So one pleasant February afternoon Dave and I snowshoed around the farm, looking for brace material. This was my kind of quest—scouring the woods for just the right tree to serve a special purpose, looking into nature with a different eye. In the small woodlot next to the beaver meadow, we found what we were seeking. This middle-aged woods is composed of red and sugar maple, white pine, shagbark hickory, and black cherry—an unusual mix of species. The soil is rich and moist, and the trees had been making rapid growth. The cherries among them were unusually tall but still mostly crooked, as cherry around here tends to be. Crooked trees are ripe for removal, silviculturally speaking, but generally only good for firewood. But also, it turns out, perfect for curved braces. Ah ha: it's not a bug, it's a feature. Another golden opportunity for low grading.

Dave and I marked half a dozen of the crookedest cherries we could find, and later I found a few more in a nearby hedgerow, crowding young sugar maples that would be superb for tapping in another few decades, once they spread their crowns. A week later I drove out to the farm with my saws, because this was a job I could just about handle—the trees were no more than sixteen inches in diameter, just challenging enough to make life interesting. Plus, Ed Klaus was busy up on the hill felling hemlock for the frame, so if I could get this cherry on the ground and ready to go it would be quick work to bring his skidder down and pull it out while the swamp was still frozen.

It had snowed again since my last visit, and the morning was cold.

The February snow cover was a layer cake composed of alternating icy meringue and sugary powder two feet deep, a record of a long winter of snows and thaws I had already forgotten; the temperature was in the teens as I stomped out on snowshoes about a quarter mile from the gate by the road, towing my gear behind me in a little red plastic toboggan borrowed from the kids. Perfect woods weather, once you get out of that stiff north wind. Building your house from your own trees should come with a little adventure, such as risking your life contesting the finer points of the law of gravity with a few tons of twisted lignin. You want to have skin in the game.

First, I had to shovel to the base of the trees. I didn't want to leave any timber on the stump. Next, I had to be on my best felling behavior to avoid splitting the butt log. Though they weren't that big, these trees presented difficulties precisely because they were crooked, and the stand was crowded. Low-grade logging requires high-grade logging skills. I relied on the bore cut.

Since I began working in the woods forty years ago, the art of cutting down trees has been transformed by a Swedish training course known as the "Game of Logging"—a set of precise felling techniques designed to put a tree on the ground in a safe, controlled manner. You start by making a steep, shallow "open face" kerf in the exact direction you want the tree to fall. Well, no, actually you start by looking up in the crowns of the trees to see what might go wrong—a dead or broken branch that could fall on your head, a vine tying back to another tree, or any place your tree could get hung up on its way to the ground.[13]

Generally, you have a series of trees you want to fell in the course of a day's work, so you scope out an order by which each fallen tree makes an opening for the next in line. Sometimes adequate gaps are hard to find, especially if the trunk has any sweep or you need to fell it at an angle to its lean, which gives it a wider and more awkward descending profile. You need to visualize where each part of the crown will pass as the tree goes over. Then you need to be deadly accurate with your directional felling.

All right, so you look up and make sure nothing is likely to kill you right away and then decide where you are going to drop your tree. You plan an escape route (back at a 45-degree angle) by which you are going to walk away as the tree starts to fall, and you clear anything that might trip you up. You line up your saw and make your kerf.

So far, this is pretty much how we would have done it back in the day. Next, we would have made the back cut to fell the tree—sawing in from the back side just a shade higher than the base of the kerf. That is still the easiest way to dump a small tree that poses no difficulties. But once you got past the middle of a larger tree it might sit back on your saw if you misjudged its lean, which is especially easy to do if it is multi-stemmed or crooked—like these cherries, for instance. You could have tapped in a plastic felling wedge behind the saw if you saw that coming—always a good precaution—but sometimes you got lazy and didn't, or the tree might tip to the side far enough to grab the nose of your saw anyway. A pinched saw is a headache, so I always bring two saws: even though the smaller one is mostly for limbing, it has helped me free my big saw in a pinch—or rather, my saw bar, because you always remove the more vulnerable and expensive body of the saw if you can, before freeing the pinched bar and chain by dropping the tree.

Most difficult and dangerous of all, paradoxically, is a big tree that is already leaning so heavily that it can only fall one way. It may look straightforward, but, with all that weight, once the back cut gets past the center the whole tree can come crashing down prematurely and totally out of control, splitting far up the trunk. This is known as "barber-chairing" because of the tall, jagged stump it leaves as a memorial to the sawyer who made it. I have seen this happen twice with monster red oaks, once when a friend was cutting and once when I was. That is a sight and sound you won't soon forget, if you survive. When the butt end of a giant tree abruptly flips up ten feet with a great ripping crack and then comes smashing back down in an instant, you are either still standing there dumbfounded with your saw idling in your hand, or you aren't.

There ought to be a safer way, and now there is. Although big machines surely come with dangers of their own, the safest way of all, frankly, is to use a feller-buncher to cut the tree, while you sit in the well-armored cab, listening to Bach cantatas. A logger who cares about the woods can do beautiful work with such a machine—but of course they are expensive, and in the way of capitalism they often drive their owners to press hard and cut corners for the sake of making payments. The pricey cutting head can be damaged by grappling with a really heavy tree; I once saw a logger who was cutting good-sized pine pause the music, climb out of his secure steel cocoon, and grab a chainsaw to fell a giant oak (which weighs much more than pine), just to protect his *machine*. Talk about irony. If you are going to fell by hand and put your body on the line for the sake of your iron, you better use the bore cut (he did).

To make the bore cut, first you make your felling kerf as just described. But then you do not finish the job by cutting in from the back, hoping for the best. Instead, you rev the saw up as high as it will go and plunge the tip straight through the tree, somewhere near the back. This is a great trick for impressing your friends—or better yet, your tree-hugging students. Then you cut forward to just behind the felling notch (keeping everything as even and level as you can), pull your saw out of the tree, and there it stands. You have left two small, critical strips of wood still attaching the tree to its forthcoming stump. The first, at the front of the tree just behind the kerf, is called the hinge. It is an inch or two thick, depending on the size of the tree, and runs the width of the bole from side to side. Its job is to swing the tree down gracefully and keep it from going sideways. The second, in tension at the back of the tree, is a piece of holding wood called the trigger. The tree can't go anywhere until the trigger is cut. If the tree has any sideways or backward lean, you can now drive your plastic felling wedges into the cut on either or both sides to keep it from tipping the wrong way when you cut the trigger.

This method of felling has two advantages. The second is to preserve the quality of the sawlog. The first is to preserve the life of the logger, along with any innocent bystanders who might happen by. With the trigger to hold it and the hinge to guide it, the tree cannot fall out of control. The feller can take the saw out of the cut, tap in wedges, examine the hinge to make sure it is even and correct, and look around the woods to see that all is well before bringing the tree down with a quick final cut. With a routine tree leaning in the right direction and not requiring wedges you might dispense with withdrawing the saw after finishing the bore cut and creating the hinge and pause just long enough to look around and make sure Bambi isn't coming down the trail before you run the saw out the back of the tree, and over it goes. In situations where more care is required, especially involving wedges, once all is prepared you cut the trigger properly, from the back. When you hear the pop of the last fibers of holding wood separating or see the back cut widen as the tree starts to fall, you turn and walk briskly away, trusting that gravity is now your friend.

Once you have gone four or five calm but expeditious steps you can safely turn around and see how well you have done. If you are trying to fell the tree against its natural lean, it may not go over at once but instead sit back on the wedges, as provided for. The side wedges hold the cut open so you can now drive in a larger wedge from the back, making it possible to topple a tree at a considerable angle from where it wants to go and put it where you want it instead. This is your closing argument, and the hinge and wedges provide the only hard evidence you can adduce, unless you have a skidder handy. Felling more than a few degrees against the lean, however, is an advanced piece of gravitational jurisprudence, which should be litigated only by those with advanced logging degrees. In other words, not me, and probably not you.

By using this sensible Scandinavian method you gain control over the direction the tree falls, finding a clear path to the ground even in a crowded stand. This keeps it from striking another tree and kicking back off the stump, which is dangerous (and why you walk away somewhat to the side); or getting hung up in another tree, which is dangerous, difficult, and time-consuming; or damaging another tree on the way down by breaking its branches and scraping its bark. If you have judged the angles and executed the cuts correctly, you will also avoid splitting the butt log, which usually has the most valuable timber because the knots are buried deep inside by clear wood; the narrow hinge will snap near the end of the fall.

A mistake I often make is leaving the hinge too thick (because I am cautious) so that the base of the tree splits a little as it goes over, but that isn't the end of the world if I'm just cutting firewood. Alternatively, I some-times get my angles screwed up or overcut part of my hinge (because I get cocky) so that it is too thin on one side, tears out, and the tree goes more with its natural lean, ignores my careful instructions, and sure enough gets hung up after all. Again, if I am cutting firewood this just means I will have to cut a series of 32- or 48-inch bolts from the butt of the tree with the top of the bar to bring it down piece by piece, which is a pain in the ass but no big deal. But on this cold morning I was cutting sawlogs to make fancy braces for the *house,* so none of those errors were permissible. I needed good, clean falls.

When cutting firewood I usually measure up and fell the tree sixteen inches above the ground—that is a comfortable working height and gets me above the butt flare so it is easier to make the cuts. Once the tree is down, I just flush the stump to get that bottom piece of firewood. But this being timber, I had to fell at the base so as not to waste any, which meant shoveling more snow to reach the ground and make room to work and then cutting away shoulders on the sides to get a manageable hinge. That also makes it easier to do the bore cut—although one of the beauties of the bore cut is that on a big tree you can do it from both sides. The two cuts don't even have to meet exactly; they just have to pass one above the other so that all the vertical fibers are severed. That way you can fell a tree well over two feet in diameter with an eighteen-inch bar, should you care to.

This cold morning I had four trees lined up before lunch. The first was little more than a foot in diameter and had a ready-made hole to fall through. It went down into the snow with a serene and contented swish. It is always good to get warmed up with a relatively safe and easy tree if you can. I had taken off my snowshoes once the saw was in my hands, of course, so I was wallowing thigh deep. But one useful thing I have learned is that once you start limbing a downed tree, the severed branches form a buoyant mat upon which you can stand on top of the snow as you work your way up the trunk. I limbed the cherry trees all the way to a six-inch top—much smaller than could be sawn for lumber, but since Ed was going to drag them out tree-length I figured he might as well take along as much firewood as possible, too—no sense just leaving it in the woods. I also cut three-quarters of the way through the base of the upper forks so they would fold in and drag more compactly, a trick I learned thirty years earlier while logging with Hercules the mule and was pleased to recall this snowy morning.

The second cherry was a little bigger and a lot crookeder, but it went neatly through the hole in the canopy the first one had opened. Things were going well. I looked the third tree over for a long time: it was bigger still and split into two twisting stems about ten feet up. Dave had been particularly enthusiastic about this tree. Those crooked stems were perfect for curved braces and we had to have them, but the more I looked the more I saw that the odds of getting that tree hung up were high, verging on a dead certainty, and then I would have no way of getting it down without ruining the butt log. I decided to leave that one until Ed was there with his skidder. That way I could see how a real logger did it.

I moved on to the fourth tree, which was the biggest and crookedest of them all. It was back in the stand away from the others and also split into two stems, with the bigger one on the south side away from the meadow, the way I wanted it to fall. And it had room—the only thing it might damage was a similarly gnarly old wolf pine with zero commercial value. But the north stem was also pretty big, and it had a heavy back branch on it that was almost a third stem, so the weight and lean were a little hard to judge. Still, it looked like something I could manage with my wedges, and I didn't want to be defeated by a difficult challenge twice in a row, so this time I ventured a try.

The tree was about sixteen inches in diameter at breast height, so maybe two feet at the butt. After making the felling notch I cut away the shoulder on the far side so I could get my saw tip all the way through from the near side. I made the bore cut and created my hinge; then I started cutting backward out of the tree to drop it. I was confident the tree would go over the way it should, but as a precaution I stopped and drove in wedges on either side once I had room behind the hinge, in case it didn't. Then I finished my cut out the back. That was a mistake: I should have pulled the saw out, set my wedges farther back, and then cut the trigger from behind, the right way. But that is what I mean about getting a little cocky, after felling the first two expertly. This tree didn't fall—it settled back on the wedges and beyond the wedges. I was lucky to have gotten my saw out of the tree, because my wedges were too far forward and the tree leaned back and closed the kerf good and tight.

So, there I was. The tree was all cut except for the hinge but still standing up straight, with no easy way to drive a wedge from the back now. If I had left my hinge a little thick I might have risked shaving it a hair on the front side to see if that would do the trick, but from the way the tree sat back I was afraid I had misjudged its weight so badly that if I tried this the tree might go all the way over backward, totally out of control—it would be like turning the hinge into the trigger. I stomped out to my sled, fuming at my own carelessness, and got a spare plastic wedge. It was still cold and windy out there in the beaver meadow, but my blood was up and I wasn't feeling it now.

Back in the shelter of the woods, I tried driving that third wedge in just behind one of my side wedges, hoping to free the first wedge and leapfrog them back on both sides, gradually reopening the cut far enough to drive my big wedge from the back. This never works, but I tried it anyway. It didn't work—I got my first wedge out but that tree was firmly settled and was not accepting any more wedges after that. My bag of tricks was just about empty. Maybe I was going to have to leave it there until Ed came down next week to push it over with the dozer blade on his skidder—but I really, really didn't want to do that. Leaving a cut tree hung up or standing is extremely bad form, patently dangerous, and the worst possible way to introduce Ed to my supposed logging prowess.

I decided to go back to Tom's house for lunch and look in the barn for one or two big steel wedges and a sledge to drive them. Maybe I could cut a little kerf into the closed back cut and drive a heavy metal wedge in where the plastic ones refused to go. I have in fact extricated myself from similar sticky situations that way before (and since), but I had my doubts this time. After that, I might be looking at rope, trying to pull it over—a dubious prospect without a tractor. What you always do in these cases is start with the things that are easiest but don't work and progress doggedly toward the things that are more of a pain but actually do work. You never, ever cut straight to the thing that will do the trick—that just isn't allowed. Always see if the half-assed will suffice, is my motto—but then, almost never settle for it.

I had only gone a few steps when I heard a soft whispering sound behind me. I turned and discovered that miraculously my tree had toppled over into the snow exactly where it was supposed to go. A big gust of north wind at the top had done with ease what a little wedge at the bottom was incapable of doing. I was grateful that my problem had been solved by nature and that the basic mechanics of how I aimed the tree had been sound, but I was also appalled that the tree had gone down with my back to it, totally out of my control. It was not hard to imagine an only slightly changed set of circumstances that would have left me walking away directly underneath where the wind blew that tree. People die that way.

I had lunch back at the house in the warm kitchen of Kathy and Ivan, the tenants in the farmhouse ell that Tom had already renovated. They are kindly folks and offered to come help, but I declined. There was actually nothing useful they could have done, and the last thing you want wandering around on a logging site is inexperienced people. It was bad enough having *me* on a logging site—the next to last thing you want. After lunch, I headed back out on my own. The wind abated and it became a pleasant afternoon, still well below freezing so things stayed nice and dry. I limbed out my big tree and brought down a few more without incident—all in all, a good day in the woods that ended on a high note.

Like most things we do, logging is probably no more dangerous than

A black cherry stump, with Brian standing on the hinge and
Maggie on the trigger. (Faith Rand)

driving your truck to get there, but you really do need to take every precaution you can to spread out the odds of enough things going wrong si-
multaneously. There is even a name for this in safety theory: it is called the
Swiss cheese model, the idea that with enough overlapping safety slices, the
remaining holes of danger in each will never all line up perfectly. Well—
hardly ever. It is another name for redundancy, in which I am a firm and
fervent believer. Most loggers are alive today only because that one time
when four things incredibly all did go wrong at the same time, there was
that fifth thing that didn't.

The following week Ed brought his skidder down and we finished
felling on a lovely day at the end of February, just below freezing. I let Ed fell
the double-stemmed cherry I had passed on before and watched carefully:

Cherry sawlogs. The curved sections have already been removed, and the odds and ends bucked for firewood. (Faith Rand)

he promptly hung it up and then just pulled it down with the skidder. So that is how real loggers do it, just as I suspected. We twitched the cherry logs out of the woods to the frozen meadow—a throwback to the old days of setting choker chain for me. There Ed made up bigger hitches and pulled them through the pasture gate and down to a corner of the field by the road. Dave Bowman came by with a flatbed trailer a week or two after that, and we cut out the curved sections so he could take them back to his shop to make braces.

I drove out to Dave's place in Cummington to spend a March morning helping him saw slabs for the braces. I was invested in these cherry logs now and wanted to see the process through. With a band mill like Dave's the log is dogged to the carriage and the bandsaw blade rolls over it, taking a horizontal slice off the top. Typically, the log is then turned— either by hydraulic dogs or (on starter models for penurious but persevering young sawyers such as I once was) by hand, with peaveys—and the process is repeated until the log is squared. This "cant" is then either completely sawed into boards and dimensional lumber or shaved down board

Dave Bowman sawing black cherry into slabs to make braces. (Brian Donahue)

by board on all sides until a central beam remains, depending on what is desired. The sawyer or an assistant carries away each board to stack it or places it on tractor forks to stack it someplace else.

Sawing the cherry braces was a bit simpler than that, actually. We dogged the six-foot logs to the mill with the curve lying sideways, and we sawed them straight through into three-inch slabs—no turning involved. In these crooked sections Dave would look for braces that were particularly attractive and structurally sound. He would rough them out with a chainsaw and then plane and smooth them. The braces follow the curve of the tree—cutting curves across the grain would make them prone to splitting and much weaker, not exactly what you want in a brace.

Dave and Neil were able to make several book-matched pairs of braces from opposite sides of the same saw cut, which were later mounted side by side in the frame, curving away from and mirroring each other. Some of these braces have a pronounced curly figure, which is just a surface manifestation of waves in the grain produced by tension in the curving trunk, so they tell their own stories. All of the braces are longer than strictly necessary, meeting the timbers three feet from the joint, lending a spreading, tree-like quality to the posts. They became one of the most dramatic features in the house.

Back at the farm, the rest of the cherry logs did not go to waste. Between the sweeping curves were straighter sections that Michael sawed for porch posts, as black cherry heartwood is durable and weather-resistant. The odds and ends I bucked up for firewood. In the course of sawing the posts, Michael generated almost a thousand feet of beautiful one-inch cherry boards. That fall I trucked most of them down to Tony Mason to be kilned, to give Toby something besides birch to work with for the finish carpentry. Just as with hemlock for the frame, with black cherry what started as a simple quest for a few good braces ended up supplying material for the porch frame, stairs, window sills, stove bench, and decorative floor banding. Oh yes, and shelves in the medicine cabinets. The extravagance of using fancy cherry for porch posts scandalized some of the carpenters, but in fact those timbers were just leftover straight box centers from crooked trees of little commercial value. Again, the secret is finding high-grade uses for low-grade trees—or in the case of the porch posts, a low-grade residue of high-grade timber cut from low-grade specimens of a high-grade species.

Best-quality black cherry is for sure a high-grade species—top of the line, worth as much on the stump as red oak. It is presently out of style and down in price, I am told, but surely that will pass. If hemlock is brisket, cherry is rib-eye steak. The scrappy cherries I know best may be low-grade, but, it turns out, they have great artistic potential when you seek it craftily enough. It is amazing how just a handful of these commercially worthless trees contained within them the material, in the right hands, to transform our house into something extraordinary. And to transform my churlish disdain toward cherry into friendship and admiration.

We made many trips to Dave's shop that spring and summer, as work on the frame progressed. We didn't participate in the actual joinery—cutting mortises and tenons would have involved learning a whole new set of skills for which I didn't have the time or patience. What I did have the talent for, once I was free of the spring term and starting a year of sabbatical, was trucking. Every few weeks I hauled rough timbers over to the framers as Michael sawed them out. While there I loaded hemlock boards Dave had slabbed from the outside of the big posts and tie beams, which I brought back to the farm or over to Tony Mason's to be kilned and planed (I always look for a back haul). The framers power-planed the visible faces of the timbers for a smooth finish and cut the joints using augers, chisels, and saws—some electric, some hand-powered. Sometimes after delivering timbers we stayed for a few hours to oil the finished beams, joists, and braces, using a mixture of linseed and tung oil. The oil protects the wood, gives it a warm red-yellow tone, and makes the grain pop visually. The timbers were left exposed for a few days to turn golden in the sun and then covered to prevent them from weathering gray. Keeping them in the shade also kept them from drying too quickly, which could cause excessive twisting and checking.

Timbers are traditionally worked and raised green before they twist, but you have to accept some harmless radial checking afterward, as they shrink. Once the frame is up and pegged, they can all season together in place and do what they please. Typically, long months will pass as roofing, siding, and rough interior framing proceeds on the house, so the worst of the frame movement is over by the time the more finicky finish work such as drywall and trim gets started. Still, the largest timbers will continue to shrug and shrink for years. Loud cracks will be heard at night, and new gaps in the joints and seams will appear in the morning. If that isn't something you can tolerate, stop reading now. Go directly to conventional framing. Do not build a timber frame house from local wood.

Timber framers employ a few tricks to make sure the joints stay good. First, the faces where the beams and braces meet the posts are let in half an inch so that there is a shoulder upon which the full timber is supported, and there is some room for the post to shrink without putting all the downward load on the tenon. This is known as "housing" the joint. Second, the hole in the mortise is slightly offset from the hole in the tenon, so that the peg pulls the joint tightly together when driven through. This is known as the draw bore.

About those wooden pegs: according to Dave there are 101 of them in the frame, holding it securely in place. Well, possibly only one hundred, because one joint never got pegged, as you shall soon hear. No nails were used—of course, plenty of metal fasteners were employed afterward to attach other parts of the house to the frame and to each other. But to secure the frame itself, wooden pegs are enough. They have been holding up magnificent barns for centuries, not to mention cathedrals.

Our pegs are an extravagant fifteen inches long—long enough to be driven through an eight-inch timber and protrude three and a half inches on either side, or a full seven inches when driven all the way in from outside. Some peg ends are in the way and have to be sawn flush, of course, but mostly we could choose whether to cut them off or not. From what you have already learned about us, you will have guessed that we left most of ours sticking out. I rounded the points to keep them from stabbing anybody and to placate the old feng-shui. Most are up too high to pose any danger, and they are handy for hanging things such as towels, nightgowns, work pants, binoculars, old conference name tags, and mistletoe.

To make good pegs you need a straight, even-grained block of hardwood. Some of the pegs in our house are red oak, but most are black locust (*Robinia pseudoacacia*)—one of my favorite trees. Locust is hard, heavy, and eternally rot resistant. Because of these qualities it was preferred for pegging ships such as Old Ironsides, whose planks are made from Southern live oak but whose indestructible trunnels (tree nails) are black locust. Dave had some clear locust bolts that he cut from a tree on his father's property, which he split into one-inch square blanks with a froe. To finish the peg you shave the corners with a drawknife, rendering it roughly octagonal, and taper one end. Now you have a somewhat square peg to drive through a perfectly round hole, which it will grip tightly forever. Not to put too fine a point on it: putting a square peg in a round hole is a *good* thing. Only an industrial mind would fail to grasp that. On one of our trips to Cummington we found that Dave had been making pegs, and all the tools and blanks were sitting out in his shop, so I sat down at the shaving horse and shaped one of them, just so I could say I did it. He had invited me to shave as many as I wanted. That peg is somewhere in the frame, but I have no idea where. Any one of them could be mine.

By late summer all the sawing was done and the joinery was nearly complete, so we scheduled our raising for the last Saturday in August and invited all our friends. The basement had been dug, the foundation poured and insulated, and a conventional deck built to underlie the first floor and hold up the frame. We assembled the food for a big lunch, ordered a keg of local brew for the after-raising party, even gussied up the swimming hole with new hemlock steps cut into the bank. A few days before the raising, Dave and Neil brought over the big gunstock posts and crossbeams, and with Tom and Liam we pre-assembled the bents on the deck. Bents are the

Shaving my black locust peg, using a drawknife. (Liam Donahue)

main structural units that run across a building, and we have four of them, dividing the house into three bays. They are pegged together ahead of time, and at a raising they are the first thing to go up; then the other pieces of the frame are fitted into place.

All was prepared. We had such a stellar crew coming that we were planning to raise the bents the old-time way, with pike poles, though we had hired a small crane for the upper timbers. We had friends who were planning to camp out. My brother Neil and family brought our mother up from Pittsburgh, although by then she scarcely knew where she was, sadly. Then an uninvited guest named Irene crashed the party. The hurricane wasn't due until Monday, but we all needed the weekend to tie down our lumber piles and prepare for the blow. We postponed the raising and re-treated to Weston to ride out the storm, which brought devastating rain and flooding across western Massachusetts and Vermont, although our little river stayed within its banks, mostly. It did wash away all but one of our new swimming hole steps. We returned and raised the frame on Thursday, the first of September, with a smaller crew of stalwarts.

Liam pegging a cherry brace. (Faith Rand)

The day went well, though it had its share of urgency because we wanted to get the frame up by nightfall to avoid paying the crane operator for a second day. Showers were predicted for late afternoon, which if heavy enough would have made work on the upper floors slippery and dangerous, bringing everything to a halt. We donned our hard hats, and Dave gave us a pep talk concerning proper safety and etiquette for a raising—never leave a hammer or tape measure sitting on a beam or a ladder where it could fall on somebody's head, that sort of thing. The crane hoisted the first bent, and it was slotted into tiny mortises in the corners of the chipboard deck, plumbed, and tacked in place with temporary braces. Then the next three bents were raised in turn and attached one to the next with girts along the sides of the frame and a few pegged joists in the middle to hold everything together. Once the bents were all up and trued, with a customary twenty-dollar gold piece (thoughtfully provided by Faith's brother-in-law Paul MacDonald—I was hoping to get away with a quarter, but Paul wouldn't hear of it) slipped beneath the southwest corner for good luck, we started dropping in the rest of the second-floor joists. Some

Dropping in joists with a crane, as the crew, family, and friends help out. The tops of the gunstock posts have tenons at right angles for both the plate and the tie beam. (Faith Rand)

were flown in by crane; others were carried up onto the deck by teams of two, muscled up stepladders, and pounded home. Most of the joists were not pegged but simply snugged into pockets in the crossbeams. By the time we had a late lunch the joists for the second floor were all in place, and it was starting to look like a frame.

After lunch we spread planks and sheets of plywood across the joists so we could move about and work on the top floor. First came the big timbers that hold the frame together and support the roof: the top plates and tie beams. Running longitudinally along both sides are the plates—massive eight-by-ten timbers that sit on the shoulders of the posts and carry the rafters. Ideally the plate should be a single member, but continuous hemlock forty-footers (like those in our barn) are hard to find. This gave Dave and Neil an opportunity to practice one of the masterpieces of the timber framer's art: the scarf joint. Or more precisely, the stop-splayed, under-squinted, tabled-and-wedged scarf joint—a fancy diagonal way of splicing two timbers that is about a million times stronger than a simple half-lap. What framer wouldn't want to make one of those, or, actually, two of them?

The two parts of the plate are not equal in length, because you don't want the splice midway between two posts—that is the point of maximum bending stress. You also don't want the scarf joint sitting right on top of the post, although that seems intuitively like the best place to put it: that is the point of maximum shear. Old framers knew this because they could see where old frames had failed. The right place for the joint is about one quarter of the way across the span, which is a compromise spot where both bending and shear stress are relatively low. Given a typical twelve-foot span this also places the visually arresting zig-zag scarf joint directly on top of a brace, which is of little or no structural significance but looks terrific.

I was either helping clean up after lunch or driving pegs on the first floor, so I missed the placement of the first plate on the east side. Although I did not make most of the pegs in the house, I did *drive* most of them. That is because I enjoy pounding things, and also because I like to come along behind and make sure that nothing has been missed, leaving the job of pressing ahead to more competent and ambitious individuals. (However, I might note that a canoe is best steered from the stern, with light strokes.)

But by the time the crane lowered the first piece of the plate for the *west* side of the house onto its posts, I was up on the deck holding one of the three braces that had to be fitted as the plate came down. It was at this moment that Brian Hall, who had just guided a similar plate onto its tenon on the east side, called out that something didn't look right.

Brian is the GIS mapper at Harvard Forest and a blacksmith on the side, so he has well-developed spatial awareness. Everything stopped, while Neil Godden ran from post to post with a tape measure. Something definitely was not right: on the second post on the west side, the shoulder supporting the plate had been cut two inches too low.

"Uh-oh," I said, uncertainly.

In fact, for the framers it was a very big uh-oh. They were mortified. They take great pride in cutting joints to exacting tolerances. For them, being off two inches might as well have been two miles—it was an astronomical error. I am only publishing this because I have heard Dave himself tell the story in public and because it became central to the identity of the house. In the end it reflects well on all concerned and illustrates something about vernacular building.

Neil Godden, Brian, and Brian Hall discussing the short post dilemma. (Faith Rand)

There we stood, discussing what to do: Neil and I up above, by the offending post, looking down, Dave and Faith on the ground, looking up. And everybody else, waiting to see what would happen next. Tom, the architect, wasn't there to offer an opinion: he had another appointment that day and so missed the raising entirely, thanks to Irene.

The framers said they would make it good. They could cut a new post from a hemlock tree back at Dave's place.

"God," I said. "How long would that take? We'd have to get the crane back again, and everything, wouldn't we?" We'd also have to take everything apart. It was unthinkable.

Dave and Neil insisted that was on them. It was a ludicrous offer, but they felt obliged to make it.

"Geez," I said, after another minute's contemplation. "Couldn't we just make, you know, like, some kind of little block, to sit on top of the shoulder?"

This was the obvious solution, which had in fact already occurred to everyone else. They just had to wait for the right person to suggest it, the one who would have to live with it: the owner, steering lightly from the rear.

The framers (figuratively) slapped their foreheads. Make a two-inch block instead of another eighteen-foot post: What a great idea! Why didn't they think of that?

"We have a nice piece of cherry in the barn," I said. I remembered picking up a load of hemlock boards at Dave's a month earlier, when he urged me to take the leftover pieces of cherry slab, too—they might be useful for something, someday. That day had arrived, and this time my suggestion was a real contribution: it meant that rather than trying to hide this mistake, we were going to flaunt it as if we had planned it that way. And right next to that showy scarf joint, too. A cherry block on the second west post: that's just an old Franklin County framing tradition, isn't it?

We got the slab, and Dave and Neil quickly cut a nice cherry bolster (and oiled it) to fit over the shoulder tenon on the post and raise the plate up where it belonged. They also had to raise the mortises for the braces and stick cherry blocks under those, too. The plate could not be pegged to the post, since there was not enough relish left on top of the tenon for a new hole, so that accounts for the one unused peg I mentioned earlier. But that didn't matter much, as the plate continued over the post and got sandwiched in there by the tie beam on top, so it wasn't going anywhere.

That cherry block ended up defining our house. From then on, through the whole project, whenever something didn't quite fit right or some other mistake was made, we just threw in a cherry block. I could show you a dozen or more of them around the house, or you could look for yourself, like an Easter egg hunt where you find a jelly bean from last year. They range in size from three-quarter by three-quarter inches to seven by twenty-seven. Many of them are neatly beveled, just like their grandmother, as if we meant it that way. It sort of depends on what you want to count, as some of these fixes were planned, and others weren't. I'm sure there will be more cherry blocks to come, as there are things we are still working on, and I am not through making mistakes. But I am also not out of cherry.

With the post error fixed and the scarf joint wedged, the second plate was made secure and we drove on through the rest of the raising. The massive tie beams had to be lowered into place atop the gunstock posts at right angles to the plates, running across the top of the bents. Then the crane flew in a whole second flight of joists for the attic floor and we pounded those home, one by one. As the afternoon wore on Faith and the children departed for Weston, as we had pulled them out of school for the day and

Neil pinning a scarf joint, which he has already wedged with op-
posing wedges driven from either side. You can see the cherry
block at the top of the post and temporary blocks under the
braces. (Faith Rand)

were already in trouble with the authorities, so they couldn't be up late.
We had taken them out once before back in June, to watch Dave Barnard
pour the foundation, because that is an often overlooked part of building
a house we didn't want them to miss.

As darkness closed in and the last joists were dropping into place,
light rain began to fall. Toby and Chris, the carpenters who had built the
deck and were going to be building the rest of the house, had been on hand
at the beginning of the day to watch the first bent go up but then made
themselves scarce, as they had other business. Now they magically reap-
peared, helping piece together the ridge beam assembly by truck headlights

The frame from beyond the pasture gate, with the hill woodlot behind it. (Brian Donahue)

on the far side of the frame. We nailed a hemlock sapling to the top corner of the ridge, hoisted it into place, trued it up with temporary bracing, and we were finished. It was a damp and diminished crew that assembled for pizza and beer in Tom's garage, out of the drizzling rain. Not quite the triumphant feast we had once planned, but still a fitting conclusion to a satisfying day.

The next day dawned cool and clear. I was alone at the farm, after all the activity. There was still mist in the hollow when I emerged from my tent, but the new frame was etched against the blue sky, catching the morning sun as it made its way over the nearby ridge of the woodlot. There is something magical about a frame for those few days before you close it in: it is elemental and unadorned, a simple but magnificent piece of sculpture. You see it open and exposed in a way you will (hopefully) never see it again but will always remember. I made the rounds and photographed the frame from every conceivable angle—over stacks of boards, nestled against the woods on the hill, over pasture gates. I had plenty of chainsaw work to do along the fence line, after all, cleaning up after Irene. I got enough screen savers that morning to last a lifetime.

Scarf joint and cherry blocks in the finished house.
(Michael Lovett, courtesy of Brandeis University)

It is a handsome frame and would be so even if it were all made of hemlock. But most people who have seen it agree that it is lifted out of the ordinary and into the realm of uncommon beauty by those curved cherry braces—especially where they rise at the top of the posts in the two-story living room, beneath the top plate with its energetic scarf joint and enigmatic cherry block (which no one ever notices unless we point it out). Today, when you sit on the cherry bench by the masonry heater, the posts and braces frame a long view down the pasture and over the beaver meadow to the woodlot where the braces were cut in the deep February snow. I am particularly fond of this view when I reflect that those braces once had an excellent chance to kill me but passed it up for a lifetime of service.

Eastern hemlock and black cherry tell an interesting story, both locally and nationally. They became specialized wood products, one following the other, on the Allegheny Plateau of Pennsylvania in the nineteenth and twentieth centuries. In that way, reduced to commodities, they stand for the way Americans' use of wood became divorced from our local forests. On our farm, though, they are contrasting elements in a diverse and changing woodland. It is nice to see them pegged back together in the frame of our house.

Birch Floor

BLACK, OR SWEET, BIRCH *(Betula lenta)* is another tree I never took too seriously, although I always gave it more love than black cherry. The two species look very similar when young, but they *smell* different: break a black birch twig or scratch its bark and instead of bitter cyanide you will detect pleasant wintergreen (methyl salicylate). This is a reliable trick to play when you lead walks, to get the people in your group to engage nature with all their senses. Even better is casually chomping the first fiery red and black Allegheny Mound Ant you come upon (formic acid—tastes like a Sweetart). You learn these things on your first day of Todd Sanctuary junior naturalist spring training and carry them with you for life.

Black birch typically grows straighter than black cherry, and it is slightly more shade tolerant. But its response to light is shifty. Black birch moves stealthily through the woods, and it crept into our house on the floor and around the corners, like a cat. The medium-sized tree is widespread throughout the oak forest region of the Northeast, but never dominant— mostly overlooked and unheralded. If hemlock is brisket and cherry is steak, black birch is more like lean, grass-fed lamb: appreciated by slow foodies but pretty much unknown to the average diner.

Every few years, black birch catkins produce a multitude of tiny, scaly seeds. Released in late fall and on into winter, the seeds can scoot forever over the snow, forming a ubiquitous blanket of birch fecundity that covers square miles of woods and fields by spring. White birch is similarly dispersed but needs mineral soil and strong light to get established, so it only takes hold in an old plowed field or after a fire. Black birch seedlings demand nothing and can grow anyplace, or no place: on downed logs, in the moss on granite boulders, in uncleaned gutters, high in the crotches of forked trees, waving triumphantly. When you discover a tree perched on top of a ten-foot-high glacial erratic, with a long root snaking down the side

A mature black birch. This tree is about sixteen inches in diameter and stands beneath the oak and hemlock canopy. (Tom Chalmers)

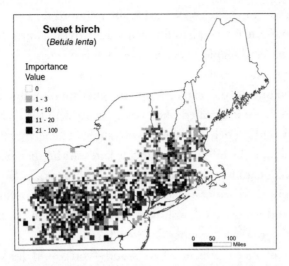

Black birch "Importance Value" map. Sweet birch and black birch are both used as the common name for this species. Black birch is found mostly in the southern part of the region; to the north it is replaced by yellow birch. (M. P. Peters, A. M. Prasad, S. N. Matthews, and L. R. Iverson, *Climate Change Tree Atlas*, Version 4, 2020 [Delaware, Ohio: USDA Forest Service, Northern Research Station and Northern Institute of Applied Climate Science])

of the rock to reach the ground, more often than not that tree is a black birch. Smell a twig and see if I am right.

Sweet birch can tolerate deep shade as a seedling, but it is poised to exploit any opening that might present itself. Once established, it responds to sunlight with great vigor. When the woods are disturbed—by chestnut blight, spongy moths, the 1938 hurricane, hemlock woolly adelgids, a logging job, or an ice storm—black birch springs up to fill the gap. But after racing ahead for a few decades, by the time it reaches a century it has seldom exceeded sixty or at most eighty feet, and it has been overtopped by slower-growing but larger trees such as oak and hemlock, and so it fades from the canopy until the next disturbance.

At Todd, black birch was found most often in openings among the hemlocks but was scattered across the upland forest as well, mixed with oak, hickory, and cherry. In Weston, we treated it as firewood, not potential timber. The black birch in the town forest was small, often afflicted with disfiguring *Nectria* canker, so we generally removed it in favor of oak. It does make first-rate firewood: unlike white birch (which burns brightly but even faster than red maple or cherry), black birch is hard and heavy, and it rivals oak for slow, steady heat. If the grain has any twist (as trees thinned for cordwood often do), it can be tough to split. But once opened up, it is quite beautiful. Tight-grained like maple, its sapwood is creamy yellow and its heartwood is a rich reddish-brown—similar to cherry at first, though not as intense, and the bright color quickly fades. As lumber, black birch is indistinguishable from yellow birch (*Betula alleghenesis*), its larger, slower-growing, more shade-tolerant northern cousin. Just to confuse matters, both black and yellow birch are often called "red birch" in the lumber trade, but most red birch lumber is yellow birch.

Nice color, nice figure, nice hard wood—you would think that while splitting all that birch it would have occurred to me long ago that it might be nice to have some of it in our house. But it didn't. I guess the black birch I had encountered always seemed too small to make sawlogs, and I had never seen it in a house, that I knew of. Compared with oak, maple, and cherry, birch is just a tiny sliver of the hardwood market—a percent or two at most. But once again, the low-grade timber harvest on our hill showed me the error of my ways, and now birch is found on almost every surface of our house, second only to hemlock. Similarly, it looks as though black birch is gaining a more prominent foothold in the Eastern forest of the twenty-first century. To understand why, we need to return to the story of that ever changing forest—and its miraculous recovery.[1]

Incredibly, in the course of the twentieth century the flattened Eastern forest got back on its feet and began to spread itself around again—reclaiming some seventy million acres, although that recovery has pla-teaued since about 1970. Considering that forests worldwide suffered a stark decline over the same period, as they were cleared to feed and cut to shelter a surging global population and a gluttonous global market, the simultaneous rebound of the world's greatest temperate deciduous forest, in the heart of one of its most industrialized regions, is indeed something of a miracle: it has been celebrated as an "explosion of green." The Pro-gressive conservation movement had a hand in this resurrection, but only a minor one. Instead, it was mostly the unintended consequence of a set of broad shifts in American extraction and consumption of natural resources, which were both still skyrocketing, even as the forest grew back. It is great to have our forest again, but the accidental way we got it has left us more disconnected than ever from local woodlands and subject to worsening global environmental degradation as its price. It was a miracle that came with a heavy deferred cost, now coming due.[2]

Three closely related developments enabled the recovery of the Eastern forest and shaped its new face. Regional agricultural production first concentrated and then outright shrank, allowing millions of acres to revert to trees. Within the forest industry, a parallel shift to new products, along with a turn to other regions for lumber, meant that even as the forest grew back, it was cut differently. Finally, new building materials, particularly steel and concrete, truncated the expected rise in demand for timber. All of these changes were tied to the spectacular growth of a modern, energy-intensive consumer economy—an explosion not only of green, but of greenhouse gas emissions.

The reversion of Eastern farmland to forest took place in two phases. The first, which corresponded with the age of coal, got rolling after the Civil War, with the accelerating spread of farming and ranching beyond the Mississippi. A continental rail network flooded Eastern markets with Western meat and grain. This caused the region's agriculture not to collapse but to consolidate onto its best land, as Eastern farmers concentrated on higher-value crops such as milk, fruits, vegetables, and eggs. There was also unflagging demand for hay, as long as horsepower ruled the fields and the roads—that last mile home from the depot. This era saw widespread abandonment of the most marginal uplands in the East, especially in New England. Cheap Midwestern feed grain enabled farmers to keep more cows and produce more milk, without needing all their exhausted pastures. The value of farm production in the Northeast actually *increased* into the early twentieth century, and it stayed high through World War II—but at the same time, millions of redundant acres were recolonized by pines and early successional hardwoods such as aspen, tulip poplar, birch, cherry, ash, and red maple. This recovery of the Eastern forest was indeed a wonderful thing—if you are willing to overlook the monumental loss of prairie and erosion of prime soil out West that enabled it. You might say without too much exaggeration that we sacrificed one precious biome to enable the recovery of another.[3]

The second wave of farm contraction that came in the decades following World War II was more severe, and it has allowed Eastern reforestation to continue to this day. The twentieth century saw the rise of intensive industrial agriculture across the nation, driven by abundant oil and natural gas and new technologies that flowed from them: chemical fertilizer, pesticides, large-scale irrigation, farm machinery, rapid long-distance transportation by plane and truck. The drive to make "every farm a factory" was launched by 1920 and took off after 1945. The resulting surge in national agricultural production was staggering and transformed land use everywhere. Milk output in the eastern United States continued to rise but consolidated on still fewer farms on even less acreage—a harsh winnowing with no end in sight. Hayfields grew up to red cedar and crabapple as horses were replaced by tractors and trucks. Across the South, millions of acres of cottoned-out red clay reverted to pine—much of it planted by big timber companies that snapped up the old sharecropper holdings. Out West, massive federal irrigation projects rationalized the hydrology of millions more acres of fertile but arid land in places like the Central Valley of California and the Columbia River basin in Washington, undercutting once-prosperous Eastern truck farms and orchards. Faced with this mass onslaught of not just grain and meat but virtually everything it could grow, Eastern agriculture went into steep decline.[4]

These were the invisible forces that created the scruffy rewilding landscape where I grew up in western Pennsylvania in the 1960s. Some farmland nearest to cities was lost to suburban sprawl, but more reverted to forest. Again, there is a positive note of ecological healing in all this. But this time more than marginal farmland was being lost: the East jettisoned a large part of its proven capacity to grow high-value crops on perfectly good land. Feeding ourselves from local farms still cannot compete with a national (now global) system of energy-intensive agricultural extraction that pays no penalty for its creation of dead zones in the Gulf of Mexico and similar estuaries worldwide or its major contributions to global warming. When we celebrate our reincarnated Eastern forest, we need to look behind the green curtain of its resurrection and pay attention to these dark, menacing shadows as well.

Much the same story unfolded in the recovering forest itself: narrowing to more specialized production, while turning to other regions to meet the bulk of the demand. As the twentieth century began, conservation-minded foresters foresaw a desperate race to find enough trees to supply the nation's rapidly expanding economy—a looming "timber famine." Their fears seemed justified at the time, but, in retrospect, they misapprehended both supply and demand. As to supply, there were more trees in other regions than the conservationists initially supposed. After stripping the standing forests of the Northeast and the Great Lakes the timber industry moved on to the sandy pinelands of the South—the soils too poor to have been cleared for cotton—that were opened by logging railroads. The South led the nation in timber production for a few decades until 1920. But the twentieth-century mother lode for timber was the Pacific Northwest. Those temperate rainforests were relatively small in area but stupendous in volume. Redwood, western hemlock, western red cedar, and Douglas fir are magnificent trees, two to three times larger than an eastern white pine in both height and girth (do the math, and don't forget to square the radius). It turned out there was more than enough domestic timber to provide the nation's building needs through most of the booming twentieth century.[5]

In recent decades the expanded pine plantations of the South have come into their own, surpassing the West in production. The national woodshed has grown to include substantial softwood imports from Canada, as well, but not because adequate timberland in the United States is lacking. All in all, the annual U.S. lumber harvest has remained about where it was at the beginning of the twentieth century: fluctuating between thirty and fifty billion cubic feet, with about three quarters of that softwood and the rest hardwood. The nation did not run out of timber. But surprisingly little has come from the regrown forests of the Great Lakes and the Northeast—perhaps 15 percent of all timber and a mere 5 percent of softwood construction lumber. Just as it relies on other parts of the country for most of its food (which is at least understandable), this heavily reforested region now imports most of its wood, too. The recovered Eastern forest didn't just re-expand in acreage—it has also steadily increased in volume and maturity, because on the whole we don't cut it as fast as it grows.[6]

Domestic timber supply was not as strapped as the foresters thought it would be, but that was not the biggest surprise: *demand* for timber did not rise as much as they expected, either. In the course of the twentieth century the American population doubled, then tripled, just as predicted. Cities grew enormously, both up and out; but they grew without requiring as much wood. Much of this new urban structure was built with modern materials: steel and concrete bones, glass and aluminum skin. The nation was consuming more timber at the end of the century than at the outset, but not that much more—about a 50 percent increase overall (a large *decline* per capita), but nowhere near a doubling or tripling. Wood, which embodies nothing more than sunlight, water, carbon dioxide, and a trace of minerals, was replaced by heavy, energy-intensive earth materials that must be mined, smelted, and forged, to build skyscrapers, apartment buildings, warehouses, and shopping malls.

Much of the still impressive amount of lumber that was cut went into postwar suburban sprawl. To this day, American single-family houses are built primarily with wood. Softwood two-bys nailed into stud walls and roof trusses provide the structure, which is now sheathed not with boards but with another new hybrid material that adds rigidity: plywood. Plywood (along with its chipboard cousins) is composed of thin layers of peeled or chipped logs, glued and pressed back together using resins made from formaldehyde, which is now synthesized mostly from natural gas. That points to another big change in the forest: the chemical wood industry has all but disappeared, supplanted by petrochemicals derived from gas and oil. Plastics—such as laminated paneling and countertops, carpets, and the glue in plywood—have augmented or replaced wood products throughout the built environment and in consumer goods and packaging. This material revolution comes with toxic side effects that have afflicted workers, communities, ecosystems, and homes (especially when they burn). Wood, often in these new forms, remains a vital part of the modern economy; but wood consumption did not expand in lockstep with the spectacular twentieth-century growth of that economy, particularly in the realm of construction. All these changes mark the transition from an industrializing economy in the paleotechnic age of coal to a fully industrialized world in the more powerful and supple neotechnic age of oil.[7]

As part of this new economy, harvesting from the Northeastern forest has become more specialized and more limited. The focus of that production depends not only on where you stand but on who owns the ground beneath your feet. Forest ownership can be divided into three major categories: corporations, families and non-profit organizations, and the public—plus tribal lands, a category that remains inexcusably minor (Table 6.1). The public sector marks the rise of conservation: the twentieth century saw the reemergence of the government as a long-term landowner, in the form of national, state, and municipal forests, wildlife areas, and parks. In the West, national forests were created simply by withholding a large part

Table 6.1. U.S. Forest Ownership

REGION	FOREST AREA (MILLIONS OF ACRES)	CORPORATE (%)	FAMILY FOREST/ NON-PROFIT (%)	PUBLIC (%)	TRIBAL (%)
NORTH	175	18	54	27	1
SOUTH	266	29	58	13	0
WEST	263	11	14	70	6
UNITED STATES	704	19	40	38	2

Source: Brett J. Butler et al., "Family Forest Ownerships of the United States, 2018: Results from the USDA Forest Service, National Woodlands Survey," USDA Forest Service, 2021.
Notes: "North" is all states north and east of (and including) Delaware, Maryland, West Virginia, Ohio, Indiana, Illinois, Missouri, Iowa, and Minnesota.
"South" is all states south and east of (and including) Virginia, Kentucky, Arkansas, Oklahoma, and Texas.
"West" is all remaining states except interior Alaska.

of the public domain from settlement—an astounding 180-degree reversal for a laissez-faire nation in love with private property. In the East that revolution required an even greater turn: land that had been expropriated from the Native people and privatized by white colonists centuries earlier was repurchased by the government. This was an even more amazing turn of events—though we haven't quite gotten around yet to returning very much of that land to its original owners. At least we are moving in the right direction, you might say. In 1911, the Weeks Act enabled the U.S. Forest Service to reacquire private land, starting with the White Mountain National Forest in New Hampshire and the Pisgah National Forest in North Carolina. Soon many state governments (especially in the North) were following suit and buying millions of acres of land themselves to create state forests, in a campaign that lasted through the New Deal.[8]

These were the "lands no one wanted"—either clear-cut and cast aside by the logging industry or too rugged and marginal to remain viable for small farmers, at least in the eyes of well-educated and powerful conservationists. Today, public lands make up about an eighth of the forest across the South, about a quarter of the northern part of the Eastern forest, and nearly three quarters of Western forests. Federal and state agencies initially withheld or reacquired these forests to protect waterways and to

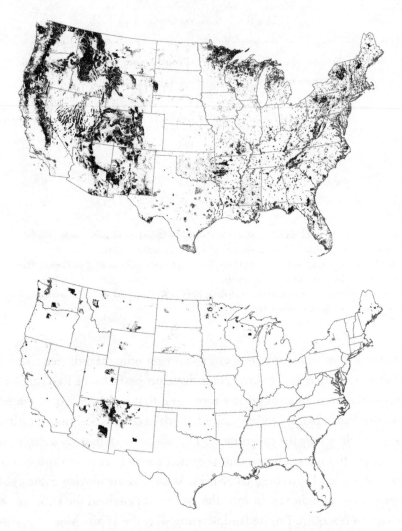

Forests in the United States under public (federal, state, and local) ownership, a total of 266 million acres, *top;* and tribal ownership, 17 million acres, *bottom.* (Emma M. Sass, Brett J. Butler, and Marla A. Markowski-Lindsay, *Forest Ownership in the Conterminous United States Circa 2017: Geospatial Dataset* [Fort Collins, Colo.: USDA Forest Service Research Data Archive, 2020; doi.org /10.2737/RDS-2020-0044])

guarantee future timber supplies—both noble purposes. Since World War II they have come to be valued as much for recreation and for their broader ecological benefits. The challenge of reconciling these conflicting "multiple uses" has led to a dramatic decline in harvesting on all public

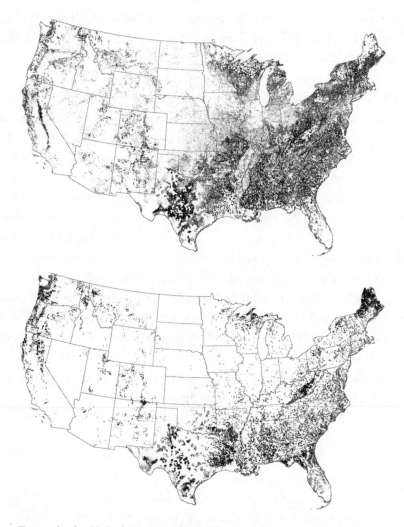

Forests in the United States under family and other private (mostly non-profit) ownership, 283 million acres, *top;* and corporate ownership (including timber investment management organizations and real estate investment trusts), 137 million acres, *bottom.* (Emma M. Sass, Brett J. Butler, and Marla A. Markowski-Lindsay, *Forest Ownership in the Conterminous United States Circa 2017: Geospatial Dataset* [Fort Collins, Colo.: USDA Forest Service Research Data Archive, 2020; doi.org/10.2737/RDS-2020-0044])

forests since 1990, following a tremendous half-century surge from the 1940s through the 1980s, during which the national forests, primarily in the West, supplied the suburban housing boom.[9]

The majority of the Eastern forest belongs to "non-industrial private forest owners," or NIPF-ers, as they were once known in forestry circles. They are now called "family forest owners," or FFOs, a more empathetic monicker. These woodland owners, whether they know it or not, have inherited most of the deserted nineteenth-century agrarian landscape of small farms and woodlots, which is now held in a few million pieces by a diverse range of farmers, grandchildren of farmers, old family camps, and vacation homeowners (I have lumped non-profits such as the Nature Conservancy, Audubon societies, and local land trusts in with these FFOs because their behavior is similar—and they only add a few percent). Foresters have been trying for more than a century to convince these small private owners to manage their woodlands according to accepted silvicultural principles, with near total lack of success. Family forest land is harvested infrequently, and when it is cut, it is often high-graded with no more guiding principle than a need for cash, coinciding with a knock on the door by a logger who promises to cut "selectively." The disinclination of family owners to carefully manage their forests, together with the propensity of corporate owners in northern regions to manage primarily for pulp rather than quality sawlogs, helps explain why the regrown woodlands of the Great Lakes and the Northeast, which account for 25 percent of the nation's forest, cut only 15 percent of its timber.

Wood production in the Eastern forest today comes mostly from land owned by large timber companies. This is particularly true in the South, which now produces over half of the nation's timber, along with more than three quarters of its pulp. In the North, a smaller portion of the forest lies in corporate ownership, mostly in regions where it has been passed down from the timber barons of the nineteenth century to their modern successors, bearing names like TIMOs (Timber Investment Management Organizations) and REITs (Real Estate Investment Trusts) that bespeak more love of money than trees. These lumbering giants stalk the North Woods of the Great Lakes, the Northern Forest from the Adirondacks across northern New England to Maine, and the Appalachian Highlands stretching from southern New York through Pennsylvania to West Virginia, always searching for the highest possible return on their investment: fast wood.

By the beginning of the twentieth century, many of the heavily cutover northern regions had shifted to a new product, cutting pulp to manufacture paper. Pulp comes mostly from early successional trees such as aspen, birch, red maple, and fir, harvested on short rotations to maximize

Table 6.2. U.S. Timber Production, 2017

REGION	U.S. FOREST AREA (%)	HARDWOOD SAWLOGS (8 BILLION BOARD FEET, %)	SOFTWOOD SAWLOGS (34 BILLION BOARD FEET, %)	TOTAL SAWLOGS (42 BILLION BOARD FEET, %)	PULPWOOD (91 MILLION CORDS, %)
NORTH	25	60	5	15	13
SOUTH	38	40	54	51	80
WEST	37	0	41	34	7

Sources: James L. Howard and Shaobo Liang, "U.S. Timber Production, Trade, Consumption, and Price Statistics, 1965–2017," USDA Forest Service, Forest Products Laboratory, 2019; Butler et al., "Family Forest Ownerships of the United States, 2018."
Notes: "North" is all states north and east of (and including) Delaware, Maryland, West Virginia, Ohio, Indiana, Illinois, Missouri, Iowa, and Minnesota.
"South" is all states south and east of (and including) Virginia, Kentucky, Arkansas, Oklahoma, and Texas.
"West" is all remaining states (except interior Alaska as regards forest area).

profit. Other logged-out regions, such as northern Pennsylvania, have been allowed to regrow a bit more to specialize in higher-quality second-growth hardwood such as oak and cherry, used for furniture and flooring. Only a tiny fraction of our softwood construction lumber now comes from the Northeastern forest, which once built a younger nation (Table 6.2).[10]

This continual remaking of the Eastern forest is epitomized by the black cherry region of northern Pennsylvania, which has even been labeled the "forest of unintended consequences" in a recent scientific paper. After the white pine had been selectively logged out, the Black Forest of the nineteenth century was clear-cut to extract hemlock bark and wood chemicals. Stripped of its trees and its value, the forest was left to grow back with early successional species such as tulip poplar, red maple, and black cherry. By the mid-twentieth century, cherry had emerged as one of the most valuable hardwood species in the nation, and foresters employed silvicultural methods aimed at regenerating cherry when it was harvested— namely, patch clear-cuts or shelterwood harvests that supplied ample sunlight to favor shade-intolerant species and those that sprout vigorously. These efforts were largely successful, at least in the short run, and supported a thriving hardwood timber industry in the region until the 2008 recession, with stylish black cherry leading the way. Because these mixed hardwoods were grown to a reasonably mature age (compared with pulp) and were not all harvested at once, and because cherry is a prolific producer of "soft mast" (those little black fruits), this profitable forest also provided multiple benefits for a wide range of wildlife. All seemed reasonably well.[11]

However, cherry's extraordinary success on the Allegheny Plateau may have been driven partly by other, more problematic forces. One was the amazing twentieth-century rebound of white-tail deer, which by 1900 had been almost completely extirpated by farmers and market hunters. This comeback was a triumph for early conservationists, who changed how deer were being hunted from a free-for-all to a tightly regulated recreational system that encouraged rapid reproduction—something deer are extremely good at. The recently denuded landscape, becoming crowded with early successional regrowth, provided splendid habitat, which quickly supported far more deer than the old-growth hemlock and northern hardwoods forest had ever dreamed of. This provided an extra boost for black cherry, with its twigs protected from deer browsing by those toxic cyanogenic glycosides I mentioned earlier, at least compared with other more palatable species such as oak and maple. Deer recovered only too well, with high populations decimating many spring ephemeral wildflowers and inhibiting regeneration of several important tree species, including oak. By contrast, less-preferred black cherry prospered.[12]

But black cherry may have been aided by an even stranger secret agent than deer: air pollution. For most of the late twentieth century, the Allegheny Plateau was bathed in nitrogen and sulfur deposition (better known as smog and acid rain), spewing from automobile tailpipes and coal-burning power plants that supplied the industrial cities just to the west—Pittsburgh, Cleveland, Detroit, Chicago. For some beloved trees such as sugar maple and red spruce, acid rain was a looming disaster, and it was growing steadily worse as taller smokestacks dispersed pollutants away from the cities and into the Appalachian Mountains downwind. But for other species like fast-growing black cherries, nitrate deposition was just catnip, to which they responded with increased rates of growth. That puzzling success of black cherry in northern Pennsylvania was more directly the result of profligate fossil fuel combustion than I could ever have guessed: we were fertilizing them. Then the passage of the Clean Air Act Amendments of 1990 dramatically reduced nitrogen deposition, which was a good thing, of course. But maybe not so good for black cherry, for its reproductive success and growth rates have since markedly declined, at least in some parts of the Allegheny Plateau. The golden era of black cherry may be fading into the past, just like hemlock before it, though for different reasons. And one species that seems poised to replace cherry, a species deer also detest, is none other than black birch.[13]

We got the Eastern forest back thanks to a couple of lucky breaks—the departure of both food and wood production to other regions that have fallen willy-nilly into intensive industrial farming and forestry. But those breaks were not so lucky for many of the rural citizens and other creatures who live in those dubiously blessed regions of extraction, or for the planet as a whole. Simply leaving our forest to grow unmolested, and celebrating its recovery, does not address that larger planetary damage. We must do a better job of harmonizing our need to obtain food and wood with our responsibility to safeguard all the ecological values that dwell in our forests and in other ecosystems around the world, difficult and uncertain as that may be. Right now, we are hardly even trying; we are just letting the market rule.

Most of the woods we love today are, to some degree, forests of unintended consequences. This heritage of centuries of ongoing change—and the difficulty of controlling it to serve human ends—is nicely illustrated by the ascending bands of pine and oak woods on our own Massachusetts hillside. These woods trace the arc of rapid agricultural clearing followed by reversion to forest that is so typical of New England. This is easy to see in the pine stands on our gravel bench, simply by counting tree rings. The rings tell us that the southern section of the bench (ST-5 in the forest stand map shown in Chapter 3) had once been pasture, abandoned around 1940. The northern part (ST-7) seems to have transitioned from pasture to pines a couple of decades before that, about 1920. By contrast, our big woodlot at the top of the hill (ST-6) is dominated by large oaks, a few of which we cut in our first low-grade harvest. Tree rings tell us those oaks started growing around 1900. But it isn't as easy to say what had been there *before* the oaks. In this part of the world, a stand of solid white pine (at least in a farm setting like ours) is almost always the successor to an abandoned pasture. A stand dominated by oaks, with a few towering pines mixed in, has antecedents that are harder to decipher.

It may be that the top of the hill always served as the farm's woodlot and so was never fully cleared and converted to pasture, but only periodically cut for firewood and timber. But if that were true, I would expect to see multi-stemmed oaks and hickories that curve away from their (often vanished) siblings, the legacy of the sprout wood that once was. Such old woodlots are familiar to me, but I am not seeing one here. Instead, all the oaks, hickories, and birches appear to be single stems grown up straight from seed, so they seem to tell a different story, also quite common in our region: first clearing for pasture, followed by reversion to pine, and then transition to the hardwood stand dominated by oak (with scattered pine) that we see today.

On our farm, clearing probably started from the bottom and worked its way up, only to be abandoned in reverse order. The relatively flat plowlands and meadows on the valley floor and lower benches surrounding the homestead were opened first, soon after our town was resettled by white farmers in the late colonial period. Those, we still farm today. The Bascoms likely cleared the upper benches next, adding to their acreage of pasture and upland hay. If that final steep slope at the top was ever cleared, as I suspect it may have been, it would most likely have happened in the early part of the nineteenth century, when the commercial drive to expand grazing of sheep for wool or cows for butter and cheese was at its farthest reach. The farmers who laboriously cleared that hillside, perhaps burning its hardwoods for potash to pay their way, no doubt intended for it to remain in pasture forever. Instead, it lasted scarcely a generation before the process of clearing went into reverse. In the decades following the Civil War the pines took the highest land back first, on behalf of the other trees that would follow: cows did not care to eat pine seedlings, which became a strapping pine forest as soon as the farmer turned his back. In New England, more often than not, juniper, red cedar, and white pine actively drove the cows out of the pastures, rather than waiting politely for them to leave. That upstart pasture pine was then logged off in the early twentieth century, probably to make box boards, as was the common practice at the time. After the pine was cut, the hillside grew up to what became the magnificent stand of oak, mixed with pine, hemlock, black birch, and hickory, that came into our possession a century later.[14]

That last transition from pine to oak is telling, because if the foresters had had their way, it never would have happened. It is unlikely that a professional forester oversaw the logging of our woods a century ago, but a few towns away, in Petersham, they were striving mightily to manage for more pine, and better pine. In 1900, the freshly minted forestry profession was on a mission to stave off an anticipated timber famine. Young foresters such as Richard Fisher, a recent graduate of Gifford Pinchot's Yale Forest School who became the first director of the Harvard Forest, were confronted by a landscape of dense low-quality pine stands growing in abandoned pastures and even less promising crooked sprout hardwoods that crowded old farm woodlots. In their eyes, well over half the landscape was a sorry mess, a legacy of benighted ignorance and blind neglect. They were determined to plant pine wherever they could and to upgrade the existing pasture pine stands by cutting the worst trees for box boards (or if too gnarly to be used, just strangling them) and letting the best grow for timber, meanwhile establishing a new crop of pine seedlings underneath, which they could then systematically release and manage properly, according to silvicultural principles.[15]

But nature did not always cooperate with their earnest plans, and neither did the timber market. On rich, moist glacial till soils, like our upper hill, pine proved harder to regenerate than expected. Instead, its harvest often released young oaks and other hardwoods that had been surreptitiously planted by squirrels or the wind. This is a deep lesson of forest ecology: the trees that are on top now are not always the ones that will grow back most profusely next time—and there is no simple successional sequence back to them that will always prevail. Mother trees often fail to reestablish their own progeny, and foresters frequently do no better. Pine does have an advantage on sandy soils, and some sandier pasture pine stands *did* rebound to pine again after disturbances such as box board logging or the hurricane of 1938. But in general, in spite of the foresters' best efforts, the twentieth-century forest of central New England ended up much fuller of *oak* than they anticipated or desired. Much of the oak forest we cherish today is not the straightforward return of an ancient oak forest but the result of a more complicated, contingent sequence of events that often ran from the original mixed forest to open pasture, from pasture to pine, and from pine to oak—each time, in defiance of human expectations. The Native people certainly had no wish to see pastures, the white farmers who opened those pastures hardly intended to grow pine, and the foresters who inherited the pasture pine did not mean to grow oak—but ultimately, that is what they got, and what we have now.[16]

Which was not such a bad thing, as it turned out: by the late twentieth

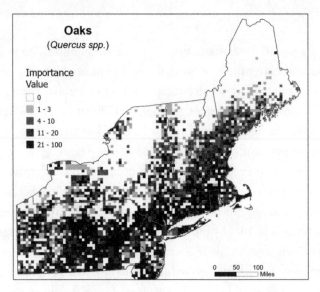

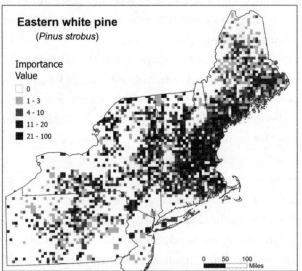

Oak and pine "Importance Value" maps. The upper map combines red oak, white oak, and all other oak species. Oak remains a dominant tree across much of the southern part of the region. The lower map shows the strength of white pine recovery across central New England and parts of New York. Pine has not rebounded as strongly in central Pennsylvania, where it was once a leading timber species. (M. P. Peters, A. M. Prasad, S. N. Matthews, and L. R. Iverson, *Climate Change Tree Atlas,* Version 4, 2020 [Delaware, Ohio: USDA Forest Service, Northern Research Station and Northern Institute of Applied Climate Science])

century, oak had become a more valuable timber species than pine: worth twice as much, if not more, for quality trees. To be fair, an acre of pine is likely to yield more salable timber than an acre of oak—there is nothing wrong with growing pine, if you can. Still, it takes a long time for trees to grow, and neither nature nor markets can be trusted to do what you expect. Chastened foresters today tend not to favor a single species but instead strive to maintain diversity and work with whatever nature seems to be prompting at the moment. That lesson was already being absorbed by the 1930s, and it is conveyed by the dioramas at Harvard Forest's Fisher Museum—completed just before the hurricane of 1938 swept most of their carefully managed pine trees away. By that time, Fisher and his colleagues had learned to embrace hardwoods as well as pine, depending on the site. The dioramas are filled with exquisite little trees and tiny woodsmen, demonstrating the recommended management sequence in either case. Many of the methods on display in the museum are still considered good silvicultural practice today. It is well worth a visit.[17]

A century later history is repeating itself; only this time it is oak that is struggling to stay on top. Oak will surely continue to be a valuable timber species, a bountiful tree for wildlife, and a beloved tree for emotional reasons—to me, much as I love other trees, oak just epitomizes what a forest ought to be. Where foresters find a beautiful stand of mature oak, like the one on our hill, they can be forgiven for trying to convince it to grow oak again. But getting oak seedlings to flourish under oak trees is not as simple as it sounds. The acorn may not fall far from the tree, but whether it will *grow* there is another question. Why? It could be that more cautious cutting today does not create the kind of light conditions that favored oaks in the past—ruder disturbances like clear-cuts, fires, or even periodic roosting by millions of passenger pigeons may be better for young oaks. Or it could be that white-tail deer are hell on oak and wipe out the seedlings as quickly as they appear; and we do have a high population of deer these days—though whether we have *more* now than in the pre-European forest, which had plenty of oak nonetheless, is anybody's guess. By contrast, deer don't like black birch any better than they like black cherry—wintergreen oil was presumably invented to repel browsers, not to flavor toothpaste. In any case, in the last few decades the regenerating understory beneath oak, pine, and hemlock woods in our part of the world has been dominated not by oak, not by pine, not by hemlock, and not even by ubiquitous red maple, but by black birch. Young oaks just keep getting harder to find.[18]

Our forester, Lincoln Fish, loves oak, and he has a few tricks to try to encourage it. Lincoln doesn't believe that oak is *always* the best tree—it's just that other species like black birch seem to be doing fine on their own, while oak appears to be struggling, so why not help it along where we can? I tend to agree with him, because I love oak, too. At any rate, there is no harm trying, because the price of failure is just ending up with some other perfectly good forest. Lincoln likes to harvest oak stands after "mast years" when the ground is littered with acorns, creating openings that are just big enough to give the oak seedlings enough light to get established and shoot up quickly to sapling size. If that works, the plan is to gradually enlarge those openings with subsequent harvests. He tries to persuade loggers like Ed Klaus to leave their slash (tree tops and large branches) high, making it harder for deer to devour all the infant oaks. That makes a god-awful mess that offends good loggers, but the hope is that at least a few oak seedlings will grow beyond the reach of deer by the time the slash breaks down. This has worked for Lincoln on a few sites, and we have tried it on our hill. But so far, I have to say, the only thriving regeneration I can find, beneath the mother oaks, is a nice thick carpet of upstart black birch. Deer and birch seem to be winning, in spite of Lincoln's prescriptions and despite our neighbors who hunt the property.

Meanwhile, as those mother oaks were growing up starting about 1910, reversion of pasture to pine continued to march on down our hill through the twentieth century. On the sandy bench where the cows were withdrawn around 1940, history is again repeating itself—but with a new twist. The resulting sixty-year-old pasture pine was heavily harvested in 2005, just before we bought the property, leaving a dozen or two of the straightest "seed trees" standing on every acre. That achieved its silvicultural purpose: thanks to the flood of light, a heavy crop of healthy pine seedlings soon shot up through the brambles. Success: pine regeneration under pine. More than a decade later we harvested the remaining pine timber, as prescribed. But before that, shooting up alongside our lusty little pines and quickly overtopping them, there came an even more vigorous crop of black birch. What to do? Lincoln helped us secure an NRCS "timber stand improvement" grant to knock back the birch and let the young pines forge back into the lead.

Now I felt as if I had stepped inside one of those Harvard Forest dioramas, joining the crew of sturdy woodsmen a century ago, stubbing

Natural white pine regeneration after black birch saplings were cut back. The large
residual "seed tree" pines were harvested some years later. (Brian Donahue)

birch in a young pine stand. Only they were swinging brush hooks, poor
saps, whereas I was sporting my bright orange Husqvarna brush cutter
with a circular saw blade capable of slicing through a two-inch sapling with
ease or even taking out a four-inch pole. That was good fun, and, with the
harness and the long, well-balanced cutting arm, not as taxing or dangerous as it sounds. Still, fifteen acres was more than I had time or stamina to
complete. To finish the job we hired a young neighbor named Rhys Hatch,
who had also helped Michael Idoine saw the hemlock timbers for our
house. After Rhys cut the birch saplings (carefully sparing the occasional
young cherry and oak) everything looked good: the young pines shot
ahead again, tall and thick. But then, incredibly, within three years the
birch sprouted back from the cut stumps and overtook many of the pines
for a second time. These days, for whatever reason, the woods just seem
to be in the mood to grow birch.

But here's the funny thing: mixed in among those throngs of young
pines and birches are a fair number of thrifty *oak* saplings, safely beyond the
reach of the deer. Most are red oaks; a few are the white oaks that Lincoln

and I love best. Over the years, squirrels and blue jays must have carried acorns down the hill and planted them under the pines, even as birch seeds skated in over the snow. After the tall pines were harvested, the unpalatable birch seedlings came up so thick and fast the deer couldn't find all the tasty little oak seedlings hidden among them, and they, too, have grown well. In a century or so, if all goes according to plan (their plan, now ours by default) at least a few of them will catch up and overtop the birch. So we may be growing oak for the future after all, just not where we meant to (but exactly where Henry Thoreau and his farmer neighbors would have told us to look): under the pines, not under the oaks.

In other words, the rampant birch on the clear-cut pine terrace has accomplished what all our well-meaning efforts on the selectively cut oak hillside could not: fostering young oaks. To sum up, in different parts of our woods we experimented with the prevailing silvicultural objective of a century ago, regenerating white pine, and the prevailing silvicultural objective of our own time, regenerating red oak. We achieved better results with pine than oak, but we discovered that a sizeable chunk of the future may belong just as much to another species—black birch. You can see this for yourself by driving around southern New England in early May when the new leaves are just emerging from their buds. The mature oaks and maples in the canopy are a soft pastel green, tinged with red, and the pine is as dark green as ever. But the understory of both pine and oak woods has frequently turned the brilliant emerald green of black birch. In that color contrast, you may be glimpsing which species will dominate the region's next forest. Still, the young pines have not entirely disappeared from that future, and neither have the oaks.

Who knows? Perhaps a century from now, foresters will be laboring to regenerate that beloved and valuable timber species black birch, finding it harder than they expected. By then, nature may have something else entirely in mind. In forestry, you can't always get what you want—but, if you are patient and adaptable, you might get what you need.

Black birch is mostly used for flooring, although it isn't generally as highly regarded as oak, maple, or cherry. But when Faith and I started scrolling through online galleries of timber frame houses, we chanced upon a few pictures of a nice hemlock frame that had birch floors and kitchen cabinets. We liked the look of that birch, it paired beautifully with the hemlock, and we had lots of it in our woodlot. Indeed, the older generation of birch on the hill had mostly reached full size and been overtaken by the slow-poke oaks, so it was time for a large part of it to be removed. Lincoln had marked almost fifteen thousand feet of black birch as part of our first low-grade harvest. Deciding on birch for our floors was actually the first house decision we made, and discovering that it went nicely with hemlock rein-forced our inclination to use hemlock for the frame. Black birch goes just as well with black cherry—in fact, it is a perfect bridge in tone between cherry and hemlock—but we hadn't discovered that yet.

Fifteen thousand feet of birch was way more than we needed, so we struck a deal with the Massachusetts Woodland Cooperative, which we had joined to get Forest Stewardship Council certification. In the fall of 2010, we trucked all the birch sawlogs that Ed Klaus had cut to David Lashway of Highland Community Lumber, to be custom sawed for flooring. This was our first real step toward generating materials for the house, before anything else was built or even designed, and it set the tone for what was to follow. It was exciting to visit David's mill and see those stacks of fresh, rough birch boards, before they went off to the kiln. It made us feel like the house was really going to happen. We then sold the best of that birch to the co-op and kept the worst for our own floor. Same old low-grade Yankee logic. Step one: cut the worst first. Step two: sell the best of what you cut, keep the rest to build your house. This meant we sold the selects with the fewest knots and held on to the more colorful "character wood," appro-priately enough because as Yankees we believe that frugality builds char-acter. What better place to flaunt your parsimony than underfoot?

Even after the sale to the co-op we had more birch than we needed for floorboards. We had the roughcut birch trucked from the kiln to Tony Mason the following year, who milled most of it for our flooring and set the rest aside. I hauled it all home. The finish flooring went straight to the house, which by then had its frame and sheathing up, its roof on, and its hemlock subflooring down. The unmilled rough birch we stacked in the barn to wait and see what would happen next. That winter, once the floors were all laid, the interior walls built, and the drywall up and painted, we decided to use the extra birch for baseboard and trim. Toby picked through the pile and worked up what he liked best in his shop. He fitted particu-larly interesting pieces of trim where their colors and grain echoed the figure of adjacent cherry braces, and then he waited for us to notice. We did—or at least assured him we had once he dropped a hint. The oiled birch is a warm brown, shading on the sapwood side toward yellow and on the heartwood side toward red—more muted in tone than the brighter polyurethaned birch floor. Toby used richer, redder cherry for the window sills, including the three large inside openings with sliding hemlock doors that look out onto the living room on both floors. Those wide cherry sills are among the prettiest boards in the house, set off by hemlock and birch.

I don't remember Toby mentioning these ideas to us beforehand, although he might have. In my memory, the cherry sills just magically appeared when the trim went up. So the house worked out its final form as the plans and frame passed from Tom (the architect) and Dave (the framer) to Toby and his crew to be filled in, an interplay among hemlock, cherry, and black birch—with a small walk-on part for sugar maple, which will be coming up next. As I said, this was not a project where a single mastermind drew up the plans and called out all the details for mute craftsmen to execute with their subservient hands. Instead, many creative minds and hands built the house piece by piece, adding interesting features along the way, much as the forest itself grows and presents its gifts to us.

From early on, we had in mind that we could use birch for kitchen and bathroom cabinets. Toby started that project but then suggested we hire Bryan Dolan, a carpenter on his crew who ran a woodworking business on the side. What Bryan did with that black birch was something to behold. All the cabinet doors have panels that are book-matched, often with dark red knots surrounded by swirling grain—a doubling that makes it look as if a dozen rather skeptical owls are peering out from their burrows over the refrigerator and under the counters. The largest, eye-level cupboard doors have long, twisting rivers of fine grain with subtle back eddies—who knew such intricate figure was hidden inside the rough birch boards squirreled away in our barn?

Sometimes when I look at the work these guys did, I think it's as if they used exotic tropical hardwoods rather than our own birch, cherry, and maple. But in truth, this hidden beauty is in the woods all around us, if we know where to look for it and how to reveal it. It is the internal manifestation of the lives of trees that have been standing in the sun and wind and have developed the character to show for it. We can harvest those trees to showcase it, and the woods will keep growing more for us, until the end of time. That is the other, less celebrated miracle that could come from our

Bookmatched rivers of swirling grain in our birch kitchen cabinets. (Tom Chalmers)

vaunted "explosion of green"—the restoration of local artistic traditions that were once commonly practiced and enjoyed.

Black birch came into our house on the floor, just as its seeds carpet the forest in the spring. From there it popped up as the baseboard against every wall, like solid ranks of tiny seedlings. Then, when we gave it room to grow, birch shot up around the doorways and leapt from there to the windows. It climbed the walls and reached its fullest expression as a sub-canopy codominant, in the form of cabinets that almost touch the kitchen ceiling. That sweet birch is one unassuming but opportunistic little species. There is more of it lurking out there in the woods than you might think, and that is a good thing.

SEVEN

Maple Stairs

THE FIRST TIME I SNOWSHOED our farm with Dick French and John O'Keefe, what most fired my imagination were the sugar maples (*Acer saccharum*). I had always dreamed of living among real maples, not just the ubiquitous red maples that swarm every hill and dale from Pittsburgh to Boston and beyond, to the edge of the known world. I like those soft maples well enough, but their most salient feature is that they're not sugar maples. There were hard maples here and there in the oak forests of southwestern Pennsylvania, but not many. I encountered more when I moved to New England, where the oak, hickory, and pine "central hardwoods" forest of my childhood rubs up against the maple, beech, and hemlock "northern hardwoods" forest of my dreams.

My first real taste of sugar maple came early in 1972, when I was a high school junior in Newton, Massachusetts. My father had a sabbatical year at Harvard and we rented a nice old Federal-style house with a half dozen venerable maples in the front yard, along the sidewalk. Being sixteen years old and an acolyte of Euell Gibbons, that spring I tapped those old trees using spiles made of sumac (which has a hollow pith) hung with plastic milk jugs to collect the sap. I boiled the sap behind the garage over a cinder-block fireplace and iron grate in a large enamel vessel I found in the basement—I now realize it was probably an old diaper pail. I finished the syrup inside on the kitchen stove and made maple candy, too. That was a stirring success.[1]

A mere four years later (having returned to attend Brandeis University, before dropping out to join Green Power Farm in neighboring Weston), I found myself boiling the sap from not fifteen but fifteen *hundred* buckets over a roaring five-by-fourteen twin-pan Leader evaporator, in a rustic sugar house constructed of local white pine. We made hundreds of gallons of maple syrup, some of it Fancy grade. A visionary named Bill

A venerable maple along our river. (Tom Chalmers)

McElwain with the same idea as mine had executed it on a larger scale: the maple trees were found along the roads and in people's front yards throughout town, and the sap was collected and boiled by roving bands of Weston middle schoolers. This was to my liking, so I kept at it for about fifteen years and soon found myself running the program. We expanded the maple project until we ran out of accessible trees to tap. In later years our own children participated in the program, so again Faith and I helped hang buckets. Having become a Brandeis professor in the meantime, I took my forest class to Weston every spring to help collect and boil sap, bringing my maple tapping full circle.[2]

All very well, but where did those maple trees come from? That question began to nag at me as I became a historian, and it still does. At first it seemed obvious: this is New England so naturally there are lots of sugar maples; but as a matter of fact, until recently there weren't *that* many. In Weston the grand maples were found almost entirely along the roads, not back in the woods. Apparently, they were not left over from colonial farmers clearing the local forest. It turns out sugar maple is a relative newcomer to most places in eastern Massachusetts, perhaps because in Native times it had been less able than its red maple cousin to shelter in swamps from periodic fires or perhaps just because of the warmer coastal climate. You have to travel fifty miles west and north of Boston and reach the hills before you start to find more than a few tiny pockets of indigenous sugar maple.

So where *did* those Weston maples come from? That turns out to have a simple answer: Faith's grandparents and their fellow townspeople of that era planted them. The maples started appearing along the roads after the Civil War and especially in the early twentieth century, because those old Yankees wanted their town to look the way they thought a classic New England town should. Accordingly, they conjured up a lovely town green and planted sugar maples throughout town. They brought nineteenth-century up-country New England down to older colonial towns around Boston and reproduced it—the Robert Frost moment in our history. Faith's Aunt Mabel, for example, remembered digging up a rock maple seedling from the family's summer place in Temple, New Hampshire, to plant at their Weston house as late as the 1930s. Planting sugar maples along roads and by the house was already a Yankee habit up-country, where hard maples in the woods *are* common. This wasn't a new concept—it just got extended from central to southern New England, often by people who had a foot in each part of the region, moving back and forth over the generations.[3]

Taking full advantage of this rather unusual long-distance dispersal mechanism, sugar maple then took off from its roadside salient by its normal means—seeds that can sail a few hundred feet on the wind. There are places where maples are now two or three generations out from the road, quietly transforming Weston's oak woods into a more shade-tolerant northern hardwood forest. Many plants use bright colors, sweet nectar, and tasty fruit to travel long distances (enticing insects to move their pollen, and birds and mammals to move their seeds), but these maples have taken that strategy to another level, not relying solely on flowers and fruit but on leaves and sap as well. Human-set landscape fire may have kept hard maples out of southern New England for thousands of years, but then other people came along and planted them throughout the region for the sake of their sugar and the autumn fire in their leaves.

This Yankee maple makeover of Weston succeeded—though in a more complicated way than its architects probably envisioned. Their grandchildren did indeed start tapping those roadside maples to make syrup, half a century later; whether they intended that outcome or not, they certainly enabled it. But now those grand trees are gone: their time on earth was tragically brief. Unfortunately, the same people who planted them also fell in love with the automobile, which killed their maple trees not long after they passed away themselves. Yet even as the old maples die from road salt, we have shifted our taps to their maturing offspring in the shelter of the woods. Today most of the three hundred or so buckets that are still hung in Weston are far back from the roads, the program marching steadily into the forest, following the trees.

As a result, for the past half century *my* relationship with sugar maples has been an odd mixture of grieving over their decline and delighting in their spread, at the same time, in the same place. The streets of Weston are no longer lined with grand maples as I remember them from when I came to town and met Faith; but the *woods* of Weston are slowly filling with maples as future inhabitants may come to know them and think it only natural. Few of those people will have any idea where the maples came from, because the key roadside link will be missing. Most will likely just assume sugar maples are ancient Weston town forest denizens, not some recent interloper. We see the forest we grow up with as the one that naturally belongs, when it is often just another chapter in an ongoing story, sometimes with crucial pages from earlier chapters torn out and lost to memory.

Still, being mistaken for deeply native would be a happier fate than disappearing altogether, which is also a possibility: warming climate (that human fire again) may reverse this transformation, eventually driving sugar maple back out of southern New England all over again. With all this in the back of my mind, when Dick and John showed me around the farm for the first time, I was pleased to find myself in cooler western Massachusetts where sugar maple has long been an established part of the forest and where its prospects for the future are somewhat brighter, though far from assured.

Even on that first spring visit, the maple-ness of our farm was hard to miss. Both the white farmhouse and the cellar hole of the original Bascom homestead across the road were surrounded by towering sugar maples, just as a New England farmstead should be. Those trees looked not just one hundred but closer to two hundred years old, dating back to the start of the love affair between Yankees and sugar maples that later inspired Faith's grandparents to take a few seedlings from their Temple place back to Weston. There were big old maples all up and down the road, mixed with equally grand shagbark hickories and white oaks—a tension between the tides of the cool north and the warm south, tugging on our little corner of the planet. At the western edge of the fields stood a long row of venerable maples four feet in diameter, along the top of the old river bank—their great gnarly root buttresses reminded me of the maples I first met along the sidewalk in Newton, though these were probably even older. It appeared that these maples also might have been planted, or simply allowed to stand, in the earliest days of the farm. I have since confirmed their two-century age.

At some point the little river shifted course a hundred feet to the west, creating a lower terrace that soon filled with maple seedlings. Those younger maples are now anywhere from one to two feet in diameter—an odd place for hard maples, but a potential sugar bush all the same. And there were more: as we trudged over the spring snow that bright, shining day, we passed hedgerows and wood edges thick with younger maples, often mixed with crooked black cherry they were beginning to overtop. I was looking at enough sugar maples for a few hundred taps, an exciting prospect. We had been looking for the perfect country place for thirty years, and those maple trees sealed the deal in thirty minutes.

More than a decade later, we've yet to boil syrup at our farm. That project may have to await our full retirement or a new generation of farmers.

We would stubbornly hang buckets rather than run tubing; buckets are traditional and look nicer, but they make harder work of collecting the sap, and a good sap run can mean late night boils—all in all, a young person's game. It would also mean putting up a few more cords of sugar wood on top of what we already cut to heat the houses. But if we haven't made maple sugar here yet, we have cut maple timber. Faith and I knew we wanted maple to be represented in our house, since we would have a grand view of it across the fields and since we had shared a long romance with it. Sugar maple is a beautiful hardwood, close behind oak and cherry in value, widely used for cabinetry, furniture, and flooring. It is a tough, tight-grained wood—harder than sweet birch, with deeper luster, though a bit cooler in tone, too. But we didn't have much maple to play with, so we had to use it sparingly. There was no way we could harvest enough maple for flooring without overcutting our future sugar bush, and, besides, we already had black birch lined up for that job. So it occurred to us that a good place to feature sugar maple might be the stairs.

The tall, thrifty maples on the river terrace were too crowded for optimal sap production, and the smaller ones among them were suppressed: straight, but with minimal tops barely reaching the canopy. Several had maple canker splitting the bark on their trunks, making it likely that they would snap and fall before fully maturing anyway. This stand was ripe for thinning from the bottom: favoring the largest trees not for their timber potential in this case but for their sugar, making sure they had plenty of room to spread their crowns to increase sap flow. And maybe garnering some small diameter sugar maple timber in the process.

One afternoon in late March, four years after that first walk, once the snow was gone but before the trout lilies appeared, I felled a dozen or more of these subdominant trees, a little over a foot in girth, and bucked them to twelve-foot lengths. This was easy low-grading, with none of the challenges of dropping that crooked cherry. From a logging perspective these straight trees were halfway down even while standing, their tops already mostly beneath the canopy that might have hung them up. I did hang a couple of them anyway, just for old time's sake. Ed Klaus brought over his forwarding cart (a small log trailer equipped with a boom loader), collected my maple logs, and rolled them out to the corner of the pasture, where he stacked them neatly alongside the jumble of twisted cherry we had skidded there in the deep snow a month before. Most of this slender maple was only fit for firewood, but a few of the butt logs were big enough for Michael Idoine to saw into narrow one-inch boards, four, five, and six inches wide. That fall I took a trailer load of rough-sawn maple and cherry to Tony Mason to be kilned, and then into the dark barn they went, along-side the birch, to await their place in the house.

Maple was the hardest wood we had, and we didn't have very much, so it made sense to use it for the stairs. Stairs get concentrated pounding. First, Toby made three slick little rock maple ship ladders to reach the attic lofts from the kids' bedrooms and my study, but that was just to warm up. His masterpiece was the stairway that sits behind the masonry heater, at the center of the house. We thought maple treads with cherry risers would make a nice combination, and Toby added cherry stringers and newel posts, picking up the color of the braces and window sills. The cherry risers are single boards; the maple treads are glued up from two or three pieces, just that little bit harder and brighter than the birch flooring. Because the sawlogs were so small and suppressed, the maple boards have just a few strips of warmer brown heartwood mixed in and a tight, lively figure—again, so similar to the birch it is hard to tell the difference, except for that maple luster. The bright maple and dark cherry make a lovely con-trast, and a suggestive one, to those who know the farm.

You can sit on the cherry bench by the warm stove at the foot of the stairs and see, out the window and across the bottom field a quarter mile away, the two woodlots where those stairs originated: the cherry on your left and the maple on your right. Delineating the elevated field between them, along the steep edge of an older river bench that winds down the center of the farm, is a shapely hedgerow that alternates between cherry and maple, just as the stairs do. There is a similar hedgerow just behind the house, giving you a handy reference to identify what you are seeing far away, at any time of year. These hedgerows are neat binary examples of succession—gangly cherry forging ahead, overtaken in time by slow and stately sugar maple, growing straight up past the cherry.

Funny that their woods go together so well. For me it is an especially pleasing vista, because those stairs are made of the only trees in the house that I felled myself, so the view bears the memory of that work—the final realization of the intention behind the first felling notch that directed them to the ground.

The stairs needed something else, to be safe and legal—bannisters and balusters. A narrow walkway crosses above the masonry heater, open to the stairwell on one side and to the living room on the other, demanding more balusters and hand rails. Securing those hazardous edges presented another creative opportunity. I wanted to try making balusters from peeled poles, leaving them round and naked. When young trees are cut in late spring and early summer you can peel the bark off, because it slips at the cambium layer where the tree is forming a new growth ring. I discovered this by chance years ago with sugar maple saplings, and it works just as well for many other species.

Beech peels smoothly; black birch is more tedious but leaves attractive brown streaks of inner bark. Both of these species have the added virtue of growing straight. I haven't had much luck peeling oak or cherry, but I'm still trying—in truth, it's hard to find thrifty oak saplings anymore, so I don't really know about oak. Elm bark peels easily in long, fibrous strips that feel tough and useful; hickory peels beautifully though the bark is thick and unbending, like hickory itself. I have read that elm and hickory were among the barks most commonly used by the Native people of this region to sheath their wigwams, while poles formed the structure. Now I know why. It was good to connect with an even more deeply rooted local building tradition, if only by this small gesture.

I frequently cut small trees while pushing back field edges or clearing truck roads in the woods, so when I happened to be doing that work in May or June, I took some time to peel poles. Once I learned to recognize which trees peel best, I set aside a few of those jobs for that season every year. This was pleasant work for a May morning, with the spring term grades submitted and the summer before me, the trees just leafing out, and the little river rushing merrily along. Dropping a few of these small trees— just three or four inches at the butt—took only a minute, after which it was quiet, contemplative work, snipping away the small branches with the Felco pruners, leaning the pole against the tailgate of the truck, slipping a knife along beneath the bark and lifting it away in long strips. I sometimes kept the bark for tinder or, in the case of hickory, for adding a spicy zest to grilled steaks by throwing a little on the coals. The peeled poles went into the dark barn to season slowly so they wouldn't check (too badly) or lose their fresh, bright, creamy color.

The character of the wood surface beneath the bark varies from species to species—that, I did not anticipate. Maple is smooth but has stimulating knobs and pimples from twigs and branches and, if it had can-ker, irregular indented patches, which add visual and sensual appeal. Maple poles sometimes have little streaks of brown inner bark that adhere—this is partly a matter of how easily the bark is peeling and partly a matter of how persnickety the peeler is feeling. Beech is smoother than maple and feels more polished to the touch, with a hint of rose tinting the grain. Hickory has fine striations that communicate suppleness to the eye and strength to the hand, as you might expect. The longest hand rails are hickory, which is strong and straight—I'm glad hickory found a place in the house, too. It is one of my favorite trees, and favorite woods, but we didn't have enough of it to produce lumber.

Elm has coarser grooves and twists more than the others—elm is never straight. Ironwood (also called muscle wood, or blue beech) hardly peels at all—you would want to use a drawknife and scrape the bark off, for any quantity. I tried only one pole and then gave up, so there are only four ironwood balusters—though the dark gray streaks on their tortured surfaces make a handsome contrast with all the other, creamier poles. I used maple, beech, elm, and hickory for hand rails so you can feel the changes one-by-one as you go up and around—this is one of the only places in the house where you commonly have reason to *touch* the wood, so it was pleasant to build in a tactile cadence, as well as a visual one. I plan to fashion more hand rails in the future and periodically swap them out. Once you get started peeling poles, it is not easy to stop.

We cut the balusters to length, washed them, beveled the ends on Tom's drum sander, oiled them, and positioned them with rubber bands for Toby to affix to the rails with little steel sleeves and screws. Liam had gone from middle school to high school by the time we were building the stairs, so it was nice to have a job he could participate in more fully. The sheet of sandpaper on the drum sander was old and gummed up, so it burnished the bevels—one of those artistic touches you can't really plan. It was a discarded homemade sander Tom found at the dump, I believe. Once Tom noticed the sandpaper was grimy he replaced it with a fresh sheet, so the last few bevels we made are mysteriously unburnished.

Because the balusters are of different thicknesses, we arranged them in waltz time (3/4) on the stairs and in double jigs and slip jigs (6/8 and 9/8, respectively) upstairs, using heavier pieces for the downbeats. It was just a convenient way to divide up the space between the posts, using repeated patterns that had some kind of internal rhythm. I wouldn't expect many people to notice—at least, not consciously. I haven't really noticed myself whether the balusters keep time when jigs are played, or if the different species produce distinct resonant tones, but I trust that they do and that there are people who can hear it—just as there are people who can actually taste that whiff of hickory smoke on the steaks I just mentioned. I am not one of those people, but I like to keep them in mind in case they ever show up.

The balusters are blind screwed from behind, top and bottom, to two parallel rails made of black channel iron, so they float between the floor below and the wooden hand rails above. This design was Tom's idea, realized by Toby—who added cherry rails inside the iron channels to hide the heads of the screws. These pole balusters add youthful energy and whimsy to the house, as they are not timber sawed from trees, but young trees themselves, still in the round. Although they are screwed in place straight up and down, aside from those two points of connection they are not entirely straight and smooth, but crooked and knobby. Along with the curved braces they soften the relentlessly foursquare timber frame, floors, and doors. You don't want too much Yankee rectitude: throw in a few Irish twists to lighten things up.

Peeled birch poles made good hanger rods, too, for the closets. We haven't yet finished the lofts or porches, so there are more hazardous edges to be railed. But there are more peeled poles accumulating in the barn, and the woods are always growing a fresh crop, especially along the field edges where we most often encounter them. The young poles are cut from outside edges, to make inside edges. These balusters are thus, in origin, in purpose, and in effect, a little edgy—something every squared-away timber frame needs.

Faith and I love sugar maple. That is a Yankee obligation, as I have confessed. We bought our farm partly for the maples, we like our syrup Fancy grade, and we put hard maple stairs in our house.[4]

But when we say that Yankees love sugar maple, what does that really mean? What difference does our affection for maples make for the forest? A big difference, it turns out. We love this farm partly because there are maples. But the maples are also here, at least in part, because we love them. Love sustains the forest just as hope (and maple syrup) sustains the farmer.

From my study window I look west a quarter mile across the fields to that line of giant sugar maples that I admired on my first visit, standing on the old bank of the river. Beyond those maples, across the stream, is the steep slope of mature maples and oaks that we "own" but will never cut, rising perhaps one hundred feet to the sharp rim of the valley. Above that again is a rounded line of white pines crowning a small hill half a mile away. At this distance these three ranks of trees have no more depth than three layers of paint on the western wall that encloses my view. They constitute, as it were, a single "wall of green."

Wherever we go, nature surrounds us like that wall of green. If you do not know the trees by name, a two-dimensional wall is all you will ever know of nature. It may be pretty, but that is about all. It will be the backdrop to your life, and no more. But nature desperately needs more from us than such flat appreciation.

In that first line of maples, there is one tree I know particularly well. Like many large maples it was formed of two trunks growing close together, and naturally the front side leaning into the field grew heavier than the back side leaning toward the woods. And like many of us, it became progressively top-heavy and less steady with age. The front half fell in one summer, a few years ago—not even during a windstorm, just one rainy night, from sheer resignation, I expect. Slowly spreading heart rot.

Of all the trees that have fallen on our fence, this was the largest—though there will be more to follow, as other mothers lean the same fateful way. The base of its trunk was four feet in diameter, sprawled smack across our farm truck road, mashing the fence flat and extending another sixty feet into the field. Tom, Liam, and I sawed it into sixteen-inch rounds, starting from the top, cutting each limb back to the trunk and then cutting the trunk piece by piece until we crossed the fence to free the wires, which sprang back into place.

That maple yielded three full cords of firewood, and we didn't even bother with the bottom fifteen feet lying outside the fence—another cord right there, but beyond our means to salvage. You can't cut anything larger than three feet with an eighteen-inch bar, and it gets to be a pain to split, so we just pushed the butt log over the old river bank with the tractor bucket and left it in peace. For years, especially in the morning light, the second trunk that still stood made a stark gray skeleton interrupting the wall of green, especially in full summer, because all its remaining branches

Two-hundred-year-old good maple still standing after its front half fell
into the field. (Brian Donahue)

and leaves were on the back side. It was as if a secret window in the wall of
green had been opened.

Behind that window is the grove of younger maples on the lower river
terrace, the offspring of that old tree and her sisters. The grove is mostly
composed of sugar maple, but there are a few other species mixed in: red
maple, a hickory or two, a few beech, a handful of towering oaks and pines,
some basswood and ash, a couple of large snags girdled by beaver. Some of
these species I can recognize even at this distance, by their shape or shade
of green, others I can't—but I know they are there. I know that in April the

yellow trout lilies, with their speckled leaves, will carpet the ground once more. We tell students in our field courses that when you learn to recognize plants and call them by name, you have opened a window in the wall of green. Nature begins to disclose itself for you and to become three dimensional. Even viewed from a distance, the woods have more depth. You can see into them. The wall has expanded into a room.

But the insight that comes from seeing into nature with more familiarity is nothing compared to the insight that comes from working with it. Those big maples have dropped pieces of themselves that we have laboriously turned into fuel, and I can see and *feel* where those pieces are missing. Behind them is the grove where I cut the maple for the stairs. Cutting firewood in that stand, I taught Liam safe felling: the hinge, the bore cut, the trigger. The young maples were small and straight, and nothing much could go wrong. With work, the window becomes a door.

Looking from the house at the end of a day's work thinning a hedgerow or woodlot, the edge of the woods seems to have drawn closer, and the remaining trees look larger and better defined. Our fields and woods cover a large area, much of which is in view from our windows, but we don't really know all of it yet. A farm of 170 acres offers a lot to explore at the level of detail, let alone take care of. There are patches of woods we have barely set foot in, and others where we have walked but never worked. We see them, but we don't really see into them yet.

But once we pick up a saw and go to work, the view is transformed. Now what we see we also know physically by having worked across it at a deliberate, slogging pace, moving back and forth—selecting trees to remove, felling them through gaps to avoid hanging them up, hanging them up anyway and working them down, cutting the slash to lie low, tripping over that slash, bucking the firewood to length, splitting and tossing it in the truck, stacking it back at the house. A part of the view has come home with us, leaving a changed view behind. The depth and shape of the woods moves into our muscle memory—each new opening among the trees, every slight rise and fall in the ground. We don't just see it now: we feel it after dinner, with a pleasant lingering ache.

We feel it the next morning with a stiffness that is less pleasant and more a portent of our own mortality and consanguinity with the trees we have laid low. We, too, are destined to lean too far one day and fall on the fence. The remaining trees stand not only by natural selection but also by

Back half of the good maple fallen into the woods, a few years later. The top has been cut for firewood. (Brian Donahue)

virtue of choices we have made that will long outlive us. Through work, the woods become fully three dimensional and visible in a way they had not been before. We have stepped through the door, and into the woods.

One of Aldo Leopold's best-loved essays is "Good Oak," in which he and his family fell a thirty-inch oak tree and work it up for firewood, using ax, maul, wedges, and a two-man crosscut saw. Chainsaws were not yet widely available in 1945, and they are not convivial for a family outing anyway. This essay famously begins by stating that there are two "spiritual dangers" in not owning a farm: one is not knowing where your food comes from, and the other is not knowing where your heat comes from. It is worth recalling that Leopold wrote this at a time when most Americans had been born on the farm but most were no longer living on the farm. The spiritual nature of work at the Leopolds' Wisconsin "shack" (a converted chicken coop) is well aligned with what goes on at our place, which is no surprise. I started reading Leopold in high school, about the same time I started learning how to cut and split wood.[5]

Leopold's good oak was a black oak, eighty years old, dating back to the Civil War. Like our good maple, his oak yielded three full cords of firewood after being struck by lightning and left standing, sparing Leopold from killing it himself. For that time and place, it was an unusually large and venerable tree; it had sprung up along the roadside, survived repeated nibbling by rabbits, and been left by farmers to provide road and pasture shade in those pioneer days.

Leopold used the sawing of his good oak, ring by ring, mostly to chronicle *loss*—the extinction of species and erosion of soil that had been afflicting Wisconsin since white settlement. A "declension narrative" is what we environmental historians would call his oak story today. There is little that was redeeming in that history, aside from the stubborn growth of the tree itself against all odds. There was a nod near the middle of the saw's run through the kerf (cutting the oldest, innermost ring) to John Muir and the novel idea of creating sanctuary for nature. Muir, born in Scotland, grew up not far away from what became the Leopold farm. Redemption was to be found only in the larger work in which the "good oak" essay is embedded, *A Sand County Almanac:* the Leopold family's work of replanting trees and restoring their worn-out place, and the urgent societal task of developing a "land ethic," as propounded in the book.

In Leopold's telling, conservation was a novel idea, struggling to take root since about the time of Muir's coming to America as a boy. The invasion of Wisconsin by European farmers, recorded metaphorically in the rings of the good oak, had been a near total rout for nature up to that point. As we consider the impact of the rapid expansion of colonialist resource extraction across the continent in the nineteenth and twentieth centuries, as exemplified by industrial farming and logging, it is hard to dispute Leopold's assessment. His countervailing idea of a land ethic that could heal that loss was presented as something new in human affairs, part of a much-needed progressive evolution of ethical conduct in Western culture: the acceptance by man of plain "membership" in the biological community, rather than dominion; the extension of binding love and respect beyond members of human society, to embrace the entire land community.

The land ethic is, indeed, a noble idea—but Leopold's telling leaves a few things out. Quite painfully, it ignores the attitudes toward nature of the people who inhabited Wisconsin *before* the European marauders arrived and who continue to inhabit it to this day. Was their conduct not ethical, but only fit to be dismissed as too primitive to be truly progressive? That is what Leopold's omission implies. That was bad enough, but I think he also ignored something important in the attitudes of plain white farmers, the much-maligned "settler culture," as well. The European agrarian tradition is often cast as the villain in conservationist thinking, without questioning whether the problem lies in the supposed heedlessness (or flat-out antipathy) of that culture toward nature or in the market economy in which it still finds itself ensnared.[6]

Our good maple tells a different story. I counted not 80 but 170 rings across the last saw cut I made, which was fifteen feet up the fallen trunk. Young sugar maples grow slowly, so I would venture that this tree and its sisters are nearly two hundred years old and date back to the early days of our farm, which was settled by Moses Bascom just before the Revolutionary War. The white pioneer era here in western Massachusetts lies deeper in the past than it does on Leopold's Wisconsin farm, yet this tree was still able to span almost every season of it. When the *parents* of the big maples along the river were young seedlings, no white settlers had yet arrived in this Abenaki homeland.

Yes, the settlers cleared forest to make farmland, but that does not mean they were hostile toward trees, especially sugar maples. Evidently our good maples were planted along the bank by the Bascoms or were simply allowed to grow unmolested when the work of clearing plowland and pasture reached them. This is not surprising—shade trees are needed for livestock—but there may have been more to it than that. In southeastern New England, grand, spreading shade trees in fence rows were usually oak or elm, but northern and western New Englanders came to love their rock maple for shade, for beauty, and for sugar. This was a love that had long-term consequences for the landscape—and unlike Leopold's good oak, it is not all a story of loss.

The modern ascendancy of sugar maple across our hills is only partly natural. Sugar maple has been present in the forests of up-country New England for thousands of years, but its rise to pre-eminence in today's post-agricultural landscape is just as much an expression of culture. We have two lines of scientific evidence with which to discern the native forest: the record of pollen deposited in sediments beneath bogs and ponds, and analysis of "witness trees" recorded by early surveyors in laying out new townships across the Northeast. Both show clearly that before European

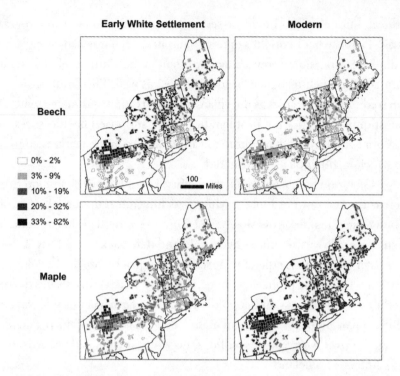

Early White Settlement   **Modern**

Beech

- ☐ 0% - 2%
- ▨ 3% - 9%
- ▦ 10% - 19%
- ▩ 20% - 32%
- ■ 33% - 82%

100 Miles

Maple

Beech and maple relative abundance maps. Beech and maple have undergone a switch in relative abundance since pre-European times. A large part of the increase in maple is early successional red maple, but some of it, particularly in the north, is sugar maple as well. (Data from Jonathan R. Thompson et al., "Four Centuries of Change in Northeastern Forests," *PLOS One* 8 [2013]; revised map by Brian Hall.)

settlement *beech,* not maple, was the dominant northern hardwood species. This seems surprising, because current forest inventory data confirm that the opposite is now true. In the forest that has grown back over the past century, beech has ebbed, while maple has surged. There may be several reasons for this remarkable turnaround, including trouble for beech: the arrival of a debilitating bark disease and the loss of the passenger pigeon, which played a key role in dispersing its seeds. But it was also partly a matter of taste, and the mystery is solved right in the tree's name: *Acer saccharum.* Sugar maple.[7]

Before the Civil War, maples were an important source of sugar in the northern backcountry, partly for economic reasons and partly for moral ones: maple sugar was not made by slaves. Sugar maples were the trees most often spared as farmland was cleared and woodlots were cut. By the end of the nineteenth century, maple sugar could no longer compete with cane and beet sugar for everyday use, but then maple *syrup* arose in its place, finding a new market among summer people (such as Faith's grandparents) and fall leaf peepers. To this day, city people flock north by the busload every autumn to see the foliage and buy the syrup. Thanks to its sweetness and its beauty, sugar maple held its place in New England hill towns through the depths of deforestation: mature trees were protected in woodlots and fence rows, and young trees were widely planted in yards and along roadsides—just as they would be down in Weston, a generation later.

This put sugar maple in a commanding position to repossess up-country pastures as they were abandoned, the seeds floating on the wind and growing up more slowly among the pioneering pine, spruce, cedar, and cherry. Beech had been depleted and was less able to disperse its heavier seeds, because most of the animals that could perform that service, such as passenger pigeons and turkeys, were gone. Two slightly different sets of ecological and economic characteristics, interacting with a complex series of human choices regarding not just the trees themselves but other species with whom their reproductive lives were entwined, left beech poised for decline and maple set to flourish as northern farmland reverted to forest.[8]

The beloved oak and chestnut woodlands of the Northeast, which now may be fading into the past themselves, were at least partly shaped by Native burning and colonial woodlot management: they flourished because of their ability first to tolerate fire and next to sprout back from the stump after repeated cutting. The equally beloved sugar maple forest of the hill country of northern New England is also not simply a gift of nature: it is partly an invention of culture. We are not merely blessed by accidental "rewilding"; we are also blessed with a forest that we have shaped by our own dreams of what we wanted the land to become.

In short, the maples are here among us today in such brilliant profusion because we love them, not just the other way around. My white settler ancestors are not often credited with loving trees, yet that love is standing right there for anyone to see. The four-centuries-deep Yankee relationship with the New England landscape is complicated, and surely not all of it was good, but it was not all pure degradation and loss, either. The recovery of the forest was not simply an "unintended consequence" of the unfortunate

Maggie planting a sugar maple on the river bank. A
beaver ate it, but it bounced back. (Faith Rand)

collapse of farming: today's sugar maple profusion is also an expression of
love. The tree you plant in the yard today helps determine the composition of the forest tomorrow.

   The oldest maples on our farm are dying now, but we love them,
and so we carry on the work that love requires. We dug young maples from
our hedgerows and transplanted them along stretches of the river bank
that were unshaded, though we lost most of those saplings to marauding
beaver—yet another rebounding force of nature the Bascoms didn't have
to contend with in their day. Our settler ancestors were much harder on
furbearers than on maples and almost wiped them out; but now the beaver
have returned, and woe betide any small tree that tries to grow near the
river. Still, several of the maples that were nipped back have resprouted
higher still, just like Leopold's good oak.

   But shaping the future of the forest isn't just a question of what we
plant: it is a matter of what we suffer to grow. It is mostly about what we cut,
and what we don't. When we take a saw to the hedgerows and woodlots,

we favor certain trees over others and so make a lasting impression. It isn't only sugar maple we love on this farm: in different places we have encouraged shagbark hickory, black cherry, white pine, white oak, red oak, and black birch—often contesting, as I have related, with the tastes of white-tail deer. Again, we aren't the only ones making choices. But when we make those choices, our vision moves from three dimensional to four dimensional, because now we are seeing the place *in time.* We are engaging with the woods our ancestors bequeathed to us, and we are helping to create the woods our descendants will inherit.

There is a saying, attributed to the Iroquois and now ubiquitous in Native American culture and far beyond, that we should do things for the sake of seven generations. This has become such a cliché that I am reminded of it every night by the brand name on my plastic bottle of dish soap. But who exactly are these seven generations, anyway? Doing anything in this life while worrying about its consequences seven generations from now is quite a stretch—those are not people whose lives I can easily imagine. Seven generations *sounds* wonderfully sustainable, but it's far too ambitious a span to be truly meaningful, at least to me. It assumes a kind of cultural stability that is imponderable, especially to a historian.

But some say the generations to come aren't the only ones we should bear in mind. To some, the saying means living in ways that are mindful of the three generations who came *before* us, as well as the next three to come along after—a span of time stretching from our great-grandparents to our great-grandchildren, with ourselves in the middle. *We* are the seventh generation—or the one centered among the seven, as are all the others, in their turn. Our obligations run both ways—to honor our ancestors and to prepare the world for our descendants over a more familiar and embraceable stretch of time.[9]

White environmentalists are perhaps too prone to look to Native Americans for spiritual guidance in relation to nature, but there is an injunction that is strikingly similar in European agrarian culture. It is this: "leave the land to the next to come a little better, or at least no worse, than you received it." I have heard many farmers and owners of woodlands say that—including quite a few whose politics I suspect are a long way from mine. Teddy Roosevelt said it, and George Perkins Marsh said it not much differently. The saying is older than the conservationists, however: John Calvin, in his *Commentary on Genesis* in 1554, declared that it was an obligation imposed upon the very first farmers by God, who put them in the garden to "dress it and to keep it." To a farmer, dressing and keeping land means to manure it and to cultivate it—to "improve" it. In his commentary Calvin said the passage means this: "let him who possesses a field . . . endeavor to hand it down to posterity as he received it, or even better cultivated."[10]

In this exacting agrarian worldview man is indeed granted dominion over nature, but with that dominion comes the obligation of stewardship—of care. I doubt Puritan farmers got this idea from Calvin, although their ministers often praised improvement; I think they got it from their own yeomen sires. The injunction to pass things along slightly better appears earlier than Calvin in Western heritage as the "Athenian creed," although in that case it is directed not explicitly at land but at the polis, the community. But in agrarian culture, of course, the two are closely intertwined. No matter what its origin or train of transmission, recorded in literature or unrecorded in vernacular culture, this covenant of reciprocity is difficult to keep.

We often seem to think that no one in Western culture (with the possible exception of Saint Francis of Assisi) cared much for nature until recently, with the rise of the Romantics and the conservation movement—that is the moral that the saw disclosed in the rings of Leopold's good oak, for example. And there is certainly plenty to atone for. Our record of dominion in America has been far from exemplary, and the garden is looking increasingly ravaged and unkempt. But I think the worst damage is recent, while the longer record is mixed. I think it is wrong to place the blame upon some deep alienation from nature in Western culture. I place it almost entirely on the rise of the unbridled market economy. All I have to do is look at my row of maples along the old river bank, and I can see that somebody before me from my own culture cared for this place, and cared for it deeply. Those trees are not here by oversight or entirely by chance. They are not unintended.

When I look at nature in rural New England today and contemplate the work of my Yankee forebears, on balance I am more grateful than repentant for what I see. Yes, they took the land by force from Native inhabitants who had long cared for it perfectly well in their own way, and there is work of atonement to be done for that. We need to make space for Native people to participate more fully in the stewardship of their ancient home-

Maple and cherry stairs at the center of the house. The stove bench is a live-edge slab of cherry. (Michael Lovett, courtesy of Brandeis University)

lands once again—granted. Yes, in the nineteenth century the Yankee farmers cleared more land than they should have, and they used it hard to wring profit from it—granted as well. Not everything they tried with the land turned out the way they intended; but some things did. Agrarian culture is not irredeemable. The two ways of looking at nature—Indigenous and agrarian—are different, but not incompatible, at their best. Those maples show it.

When we call the trees by name and look through the wall of green, the woods open and become three dimensional in space, and that runs in two directions: we reach out to touch nature, and it reaches in to touch us. But when we step through the door and *work* in the woods, they open to us in four dimensions, including time, if we are paying attention—and that fourth dimension runs in two directions as well, backward and forward. With the power to make change should come a sense of belonging to what has come before. We need not be irrevocably torn between progress and nostalgia, between a human earth and a wild earth. We are not called to divide the world in two and cut ties forever with our blighted settler heritage, but instead to bind respect for the past to responsibility for the future: to leave the place a little better than we found it. We are called to work our own redemption in nature, not to retreat from it in shame, because of who we are or who we once were.

To see the land in four dimensions, in time, through the intention, the exercise, and the memory of work across its surface, is also to see it with affection. Perhaps the fifth, binding dimension is love. I mean, it better be love: what else do we have left?

EIGHT

Wood, Fire, and Stone

FAITH AND I HAVE HEATED PRIMARILY with wood for al-
most fifty years, always cutting it ourselves. We've often cooked with wood,
too. As much as sheep, cows, or clover, woodstoves have been at the heart
of our relationship with nature from Ireland to Massachusetts to Kansas,
tying one winter's work to the next winter's warmth. Burning wood is a
satisfying way to make use of a local resource while enjoying good exercise, in the spirit of the old saying quoted by Henry Thoreau (and everybody else) that wood heats twice: once when you cut it and again when you
burn it.

Twice? I'd say at least *five* times, depending how finely you care to
parse that little word "cut"—there's many a step between the stump and
the stove. We have cut, split, hauled, stacked, and burned wood (or, in
Ireland, wood mixed with "turf," which is small bricks of peat, sliced from
the bog and dried) in a long series of iron stoves and cookers—at least a
dozen that I can recall. These stoves became, on average, cleaner-burning
and more efficient as the years went by. But we knew that if we ever built
a house of our own, we wanted to enjoy the most rewarding of all ways to
burn wood: a masonry heater.

Harvesting wood has two seemingly opposite purposes: you can
build with it, or you can burn it. These are analogous to the role of food:
a small part of what we eat goes to build the body, but most is burned to
run it. While our bodies are alive, structure and combustion are held in
creative tension within them, just as they are in a wooden house that is
heated with wood. And just as we take great pleasure in eating food, we
should likewise take pleasure in burning wood.

Few would contest the fundamental human need to ingest and metab-
olize food (except animal protein, which has indeed become contested),
but burning wood is another matter. Building with wood is still widely

The masonry heater in action, with Innes Donahue, my nibling, reading by the fire. (Maren Leyla Cooke)

accepted; burning it is now suspect. The primary existential challenge facing our species, climate change, amounts to a struggle to either contain or entirely transcend our ancient kinship with fire, which has gotten out of hand these past two centuries, thanks to the unearthing of fossil fuel. So how, if at all, should we now burn our primordial fuel, the one that made us human in the first place and still gives us such pleasure, wood?

» » « «

For most of human history, wood for cooking and heating has been gathered from local woodlands. In those agrarian societies where populations grew dense and most of the forest had been converted to farmland to grow food, cyclical cutting of the remaining woods to produce fuel had to be carefully integrated with other needs, such as materials for building. Wood is difficult to transport long distances. Providing wood fuel for cities was a challenge, one of the constraints that limited urban growth in pre-industrial societies. The concentration of wood smoke was another burden for city dwellers to bear, long before the advent of coal. Coal, as it became available, solved that logistical problem and allowed cities to expand enormously—without bringing any relief to most people's eyes and lungs. In fact, mining and shipping coal to heat urban homes was a key early driver of the industrial revolution, first in England and subsequently in America. That transformation in heating, in the first half of the nineteenth century, in tandem with the shift in how lumber was supplied for building, broke the ancient bond between homes and local woodlands.

The relationship of European colonists to local woods on this continent was initially shaped by the conundrum of encountering abundant forests while grasping inadequate tools: a seemingly unlimited supply of large trees that needed to be cleared to create an agrarian landscape, but only clunky axes and saws for cutting them. I previously discussed how this meeting of plentiful resources with limited technology influenced the construction of houses, but it was expressed just as strongly in the way those houses were heated. Big trees and bad tools meant burning exorbitant quantities of firewood in big pieces, in enormous fireplaces. But as generations passed, older settled communities developed a more sustainable relationship to their dwindling woodlands. That relationship revolved around the ability of hardwood trees to sprout, the perfection of the American ax, and the development of smaller, more efficient fireplaces and stoves. The result: wood was grown and burned with less waste, in smaller pieces.

From the beginning, a key feature of the New England frame house was its central chimney. This innovation in home heating, once confined to the rich, had begun to appear in the humble cottages of English husbandmen in the late medieval period. Before that, smoke from an open hearth made its way up through a hole in the roof. Adding a chimney made the house less smoky and also enlarged its usable space—the loft over one side of the open hall below could be extended across the entire structure, making a complete second story.[1]

In America, that chimney became an imposing edifice of brick, rising from a stone (or brick) foundation near the center of the house and emerging through the roof peak. It often provided a flue for a fireplace in every room. The kitchen fireplace was a cavernous walk-in affair, which could be more than eight feet wide and three feet deep. Women cooked by swinging iron pots over the fire and by roasting and baking. An oven was often built into the back wall, the smoke from its fire exiting into the fireplace to find its way up the chimney. In time the oven was moved to the chimney face next to the fireplace and provided with its own flue. Even so, cooking was arduous, uncomfortable, and dangerous.[2]

Historians have duly remarked on how inefficient these large open fireplaces must have been, as they drew a mighty draft of cold air in through every crack in the walls and spewed warmed air up the chimney. They weren't that good at projecting heat, either. True enough, but on the other hand the enormous thermal mass of the chimney stack radiated warmth to the entire house all through the night, long after the embers were banked in the ashes until daybreak. Placing a massive heated masonry core at the center of the house was good design, even though the open fireplaces it contained wasted wood. But again, at first there was plenty of wood to waste—and it was less work to burn it in long pieces than to conserve it by cutting to shorter lengths. The sheer quantity of fuel that these households consumed, for both heating and cooking, was prodigious, especially in the early days. We hear reports of as many as thirty or even forty cords a year. Even with bulky pieces, forty cords is an insane amount of firewood to put up every winter: picture a stack of four-footers piled four feet high, as long as a football field. By the eighteenth century, the average New England household probably burned more like twenty or twenty-five cords—not a trivial amount.[3]

At first, firewood was mostly generated in the course of clearing land for farming or felling trees for framing and other uses, and much of it came from tops—it was easier to cut smaller diameter pieces to length than to work up the big trunks. Until the rise of the potash industry many of the hardwood butt logs, if not hewed for house timbers or riven into boards or barrel staves, were simply left to rot or burned to fatten the ground. I have often done something similar, content with cutting only the tops of the gnarly old mother maples by the river, when they come crashing down. I can't easily make use of anything over three feet in diameter, and I don't need to. Early white settlers, with copious trees and clumsy tools, were prone to felling large trees for the choice bits and leaving the rest.

As time passed, New England farmhouses grew larger and sometimes added chimneys, but the fireplaces inside them shrank—existing ones were often bricked in to make them smaller. This improvement was partly drawn by convenience, partly driven by necessity. Smaller fireplaces projected more heat into the room. By the turn of the nineteenth century the shallow Rumford fireplace was widely adopted, except in the kitchen. Not long after that cast-iron parlor stoves became available, and the fireplace was covered over completely, leaving just a small hole for the stovepipe. Like the timber frame, the chimney had vanished into the bones of the house. By the second quarter of the century, iron cookstoves were in wide use, greatly easing the daily lives of women, not to mention the comfort of the entire family. These smaller fireplaces and iron stoves were capable of heating rooms and cooking meals with much greater efficiency—that is, more heat from burning a given amount of wood was retained inside the building, and less was lost up the chimney. Houses got warmer, even as less fuel was consumed—down to a mere dozen cords or so each year.[4]

A fortuitous meshing of demand and supply drove these changes: a growing taste for middle-class comfort, which was satisfied by new iron manufacturers who could turn out stoves at affordable prices. Wood and coal stoves were a key early consumer good of the industrial age. But for this to work, firewood had to be cut smaller, too—so, less wood but more work, unless the cutting tools also improved. In fact, another technological innovation made these more efficient burning devices possible: the single-bit American ax. Improved incrementally by thousands of local blacksmiths, the ax had been perfected by the middle of the eighteenth century. The axes that had come over from Europe in the seventeenth century had long, narrow blades; they may have been adequate for cutting small wood but were too light and glancing for chopping larger timber. American blacksmiths made the blade more compact and put a heavier, squared-off poll at the back. This gave the ax head more heft and better control—if you have never swung a good ax, you should, just to feel it bite. By the time of the Revolutionary War any country blacksmith could make one in the preferred local style. Half a century later, about 1825, these axes moved beyond the local smithy and, like stoves, were widely manufactured—first made with a welded steel edge and then entirely of steel. This simple tool laid low the great American forest. Two-man cross-cut saws did not take over felling until the later part of the nineteenth century, and then they were used mostly for larger trees. To clear the continent, all it took was the thirty-two-inch, four-pound ax. It was a modest tool with formidable power.[5]

But for turning *big* trees into firewood, the ax was still far from perfect. The problem was the chips. To subdivide a log with an ax requires a wide kerf—two wide kerfs, actually, that meet in the middle. You make them by standing on top of the downed log and chopping back between your boots, notching and then splitting out nice, fat chips. I do this once a year to impress my students, and I still have all my toes. All this chipping produces a yawning triangular kerf that starts out nearly as long as the log is wide and then narrows toward the center, and the same on the other side. Start the kerf too small, and you wind up with a "boggled notch." To buck a two-foot log into four-foot cordwood with an ax, you would have to turn about a quarter of the wood into chips, and it would take you all day. Until the advent of affordable mass-produced steel, a heavy iron saw was less wasteful, but still laborious. Accordingly, once most of the big trees had been logged off within two or three generations of a town's settlement, thrifty New England farmers began to manage their remaining woodlots primarily to grow *small* trees that could be efficiently turned into fence rails and firewood, using the ax.[6]

Better woodlot management was also encouraged by the high cost of overland transportation. By the early nineteenth century the American economy was moving from local toward national-scale production. High-value concentrated commodities, such as flour and cloth, had begun to be mass-produced and to travel long distances, undercutting local household and artisanal manufacture. As we have seen, some value-added forest products such as pine shingles and potash could also bear the cost of transport, but shipping in house timbers, fence rails, and firewood was not practical for most rural communities, which were usually a long, slow ox-cart haul from the nearest seaport or river landing. Basic, bulky wood products still had to be grown close to home. Until the railroad arrived, this practical necessity helped preserve working farm woodlots.

In frontier towns such as Temple, New Hampshire, an ample wood supply could still be garnered as a by-product of clearing land, for the first few generations. Older towns such as Weston and Concord no longer had that luxury: by the late colonial period they were already four or five generations old and packed with all the farms they could hold. Woodlands had been reduced to little more than a quarter to a third of the landscape, the bare minimum required to sustain the local economy—generally covering the most rugged and least farmable rocky hilltops and sandy barrens. This proportion would hold for over half a century, from before 1775 until about 1825. Settled households in older towns, long beyond the pioneer stage, were faced with the challenge of harvesting their wood sustainably from a fixed acreage of remaining woodlots in the back corners of their farms or their towns ("Walden Woods" is one famous example). To ensure supplies of these key renewable wood resources they had to live within local limits and conserve them.[7]

In response to this challenge, these farmers reinvented a system of coppicing similar to what their ancestors had practiced centuries earlier in the tightly circumscribed woods of old England—and one that may have been practiced by many Native American nations for millennia as well (also employing fire), though there is scant evidence of that in New England. Many American hardwood trees sprout vigorously from the stump when the main stem is cut back—this natural ability may be an adaptation to fire or a means for young trees to persist in spite of repeated nibbling by rabbits and deer, while awaiting a disturbance to make room in the canopy. Taking advantage of this useful propensity, farmers began deliberately managing their oak, hickory, and chestnut stands as "sprout woods." Woodlots were cut clean every twenty-five or thirty years, with each stump immediately sending up multiple shoots. These sprouts made rapid growth, driven skyward by the well-established roots beneath them— like the unstoppable black birch in our pine lot that we tried to suppress, but in vain. Cutting it back just encourages it.[8]

When they were perhaps fifteen feet high and a few inches thick these shoots were often thinned to three or four per stump. The harvested white oak and hickory rods were split lengthwise and sold to coopers to make barrel hoops. The remaining stems were allowed to continue growing until they were forty or fifty feet tall and ten or twelve inches in diameter, whereupon they were felled again for small timbers, fence rails, and firewood, repeating the cycle. Here and there, straighter (usually seed-grown) oaks and pines might be reserved to eventually tower above the lowly sprout land through several cuttings, in time producing larger saw-logs for boards and timbers, or stock for riving. By the early nineteenth century, there was no longer anything haphazard or wasteful about the way these Yankees were managing their woodlots.[9]

This was an efficient way to grow wood, engineered by and for the ax. It kept the fully developed root system beneath the woodlot boiling away, sending up a multitude of sprouts that quickly intercepted all the available sunlight, growing much faster than seedlings ever could: a cord per acre per year. These thrifty young stems could be felled and cut to length with a few swift strokes, without requiring an absurdly wide and wasteful kerf. For cordwood, the standard length was four feet, and even the chips were sometimes collected for kindling. The round, double-pointed firewood stick could be split lengthwise, by driving a wedge into one end and fol-lowing the rift with more wedges, or just the ax—like Abe Lincoln splitting fence rails. It might be quartered, making pieces that were small enough to handle easily and dry quickly. The split cordwood was stacked in the woods to season or delivered green, and it was cut to length by the cus-tomer at home in the woodyard, typically on a sawbuck, using a bucksaw. Four-footers were a handy length to load crosswise on a sled or cart, and twenty-four inches for the fireplace, sixteen inches for the parlor stove, and twelve inches for the kitchen range became standard firewood lengths that endure to this day.

By the middle of the nineteenth century New England houses had evolved from the rude structures of the early settlers, with their exposed timber frames and enormous open hearths, to larger, more refined houses with smaller, well-appointed rooms; and the surrounding woodlands had evolved along with them. The heavy frame was still holding up the house but had been all but banished from sight. The massive central chimney had devolved into smaller stacks that still stood in the house but that served more efficient small grates or stoves distributed in every room. Improved wood and iron tools and appliances both indoors and outdoors made for comfortable houses that still connected directly with local woods, hand-some structures that embellished the landscape and live on in our cultural memory—the New Republic, more than the colonial era, was the birthplace of the classic, white clapboarded New England village. This was America's wooden age in full flower. But that thriving connection was about to give way before a tidal wave of industrialization.[10]

The nineteenth-century revolutions in lumber extraction and home construction that I described earlier were made possible by another, more fundamental transformation, which began with how homes were heated: the advent of coal. Supplying rapidly expanding cities such as Philadelphia, New York, and Boston with wood fuel was a problem, and urban firewood became expensive. This challenge helped drive innovations such as better fireplaces and eventually the rise of wood- and then coal-fired stoves. By the second quarter of the nineteenth century coal stoves became ubiquitous in American cities, and soon coal was also favored in small towns and even in many farmhouses, as it burned hotter and held a fire longer than wood. By the end of the century, central heating with a coal furnace became a widespread reality, and the revolution was complete.[11]

Coal had been mined for centuries in deforested England but only became a revolutionary power source in the late 1700s with the perfection of the steam engine. This energy transition was delayed in America by the abundance of wood and water power, but by the early nineteenth century, coal mining got under way in northeastern Pennsylvania. New canals made the anthracite available in New York and Philadelphia, and the business of mining grew. Demand for home heating generated an abundant and inexpensive supply of coal, which in turn made possible (and profitable) new industries such as manufacturing rails, boilers, steamboats, and locomotives. These engines burned plenty of wood, but ultimately they relied primarily on coal. Once rail lines spread, dirtier but more widely distributed bituminous coal was mined up and down the Appalachians, across the Midwest, and out to Colorado. Coal mines didn't just drive locomotives, they drew them: the trains had to find coal before transporting anything else. By the turn of the century coal was being hauled everywhere, just like lumber—every one-horse town had its railroad siding with a lumber and coal dealer.[12]

The advent of coal made the farm woodlot redundant as wood for heating and cooking became optional even in many rural homes, barbed wire replaced rail fences, and local timber was no longer needed for building. With this loss of economic importance many (although certainly not all) woodlots were left to grow as they pleased, and the ancient practices that had integrated firewood and timber production were lost, along with the corresponding architectural integration of hearth and frame. Distant sources supplied both construction materials and fuel more efficiently than local ones. Between the time of the Civil War and World War I, the familial ties between the house and its surrounding woodlands that had prevailed in almost all human cultures for thousands of years all but died away. The frame made of local timber, which had faded into the walls in the previous Georgian period, vanished entirely in the Victorian era. It was replaced by stud-wall construction using uniform materials that came from anywhere, assembled into a house of any shape imaginable. And the central hearth that once burned local firewood was replaced by "central" heating that burned coal, which came straight from hell.

There is nothing intrinsically wrong with stick framing or central heating; with good design and workmanship they made for many an attractive, cozy home. The real problem lay outside the house in what was less visible (though hardly invisible, during temperature inversions): the sources and sinks of the energy and materials. These buildings were expressions of an emerging national system of large-scale resource extraction, driven by the ascendancy of the market economy with an abundant supply of fossil fuel to power it: the first stage of what Lewis Mumford memorably called "carboniferous capitalism," which is now in its late and possibly terminal stage, with fading hopes of timely remission.[13]

The coal boom equitably despoiled both cities and forests. In the burgeoning market economy of the nineteenth century, nature was rapidly commodified. Water power and wood had given rise to a boisterous industrial adolescence—with coal, industrial capitalism really hit its stride. Railroads consumed vast quantities of wood in the form of trestles, crossties, and fuel; they hauled still vaster loads of lumber to the cities. But they consumed and transported even more coal (which dominates rail freight tonnage to this day), the fuel that enabled the rise of modern cities—directly or indirectly building, powering, and provisioning them. The result was greater indoor comfort, at least for the upper and middle classes who were well housed and lived upwind, but outdoor calamity. Inner-city neighborhoods and small towns alike fell under a pall of toxic coal smoke, creating a darkness at noon—true, wood smoke is also unhealthy, but coal allowed a scale of urban concentration and a level of combustion that wood alone could never have achieved. As forests were ravaged and burned from Maine to Minnesota and then across the South, the cities they served also turned black with soot.[14]

By the twentieth century, ubiquitous central heating (now powered by oil, natural gas, and coal-generated electricity) relegated the fireplace to recreational status, and the simple and elegant Rumford design was largely forgotten, too. If you are like me, you have probably cursed (more than once) a poorly built modern fireplace that wouldn't draw properly—an issue of engineering that was solved two hundred years ago, reincarnated. More often than not, chimneys were exiled from their place of pride at the center of the house and stuck on an outside wall, out of the way—often with their backside bricks scandalously exposed to the great outdoors, sloughing heat. The fireplace became irrelevant to heating the house—in fact, with the furnace going, a fireplace becomes a net thermal loss, reduced to a wasteful amenity. Even renowned architects who celebrated the ancestral hearth as the focus of the living space often parked their fireplaces on outside walls—visit Taliesin sometime, and see how many inside chimneys you can find. Not surprisingly, come winter the bold Modern architects fled Wisconsin for Arizona.[15]

The energy crisis of the 1970s inspired a revival in heating with wood. Faith and I were part of that movement, not only burning wood ourselves but also cutting and selling it, with our pickup sporting its "Split Wood—Not Atoms" bumper sticker. But the houses we lived in were seldom designed for heating with wood. They were designed around the assumption of limitless coal, oil, and natural gas. A woodstove's ability to keep a house warm depends on insulation, configuration, and above all the placement of the chimney. We vowed that in any house we built the chimney would go back to the center, where it belongs. Ideally, it would rise from a masonry stove: the ultimate in wood-burning efficiency, and a thing of real beauty.

Masonry stoves are an old technology that comes from Northern Europe—Scandinavia, Germany, Russia. (China and other cold parts of the world have similar versions.) Like timber framing, these stoves have experienced a small renaissance since the 1970s, thanks to a devoted guild of masons. Not surprisingly, masonry heaters and wood frames go perfectly together. Designs vary, but in essence masonry stoves consist of a core made of firebrick (a ton of thermal mass) encased by a fancier facing. The core encompasses a firebox, a bake oven, and a winding maze of chambers and flues through which the flames must pass before escaping up the chimney. Surrounding that core (but separated from it by a small gap) is a facing that can be stucco, tile, brick, or stone, adding another ton or two. The complex interior architecture of the stove affords ample opportunities for exterior benches, shelves, alcoves, and cubbies. Even mated with a handsome timber frame, the masonry heater becomes the focal point of any house it occupies—especially on cold winter nights when the stone is quietly radiating warmth. The wooden frame encloses the stone hearth in the same way the woods and fields enclose the house, and all is well.[16]

A good masonry stove has three cardinal virtues, plus a pizza oven. First, due to its extremely hot fire, secondary combustion chambers, and a long flame path, it achieves close to complete oxidation of the wood fuel, maximizing efficiency and minimizing pollution. Second, by the same means, the firebrick captures almost all of the heat in the flue gases before they can escape. Third, the stone facing absorbs the intense heat of the core and then transmits it to the house at a comfortable 100–120 degrees Fahrenheit. You can sit on it, lie on it, or rub up against any part of it (except the firebox door), even while the fire inside is raging. People touch it a lot: they snuggle up to it like a kindly old grandmother—if they can get the dog off the bench. Warmth is maintained by burning one or two large fires a day and pulsing the core, rather than by constant feeding: most of the time, there is no fire to tend. It doesn't matter if you are out all day or sleeping all night—the trusty stone warms the house at a constant rate. This makes heating with wood more convenient than using a conventional iron stove, but also more ceremonial. As for the oven, on a good night it can cook a pizza in ninety seconds—almost faster than you can slide it in, turn it, and peel it back out.

Our stove was designed and built by Carsten Homstead, a local mason who has mastered both the form and the function of his heaters. We hired Carsten toward the end of the house project, so the space for the stove was already tightly circumscribed—a constraint he might not have chosen, but the sort that often inspires fine art. Carsten's stone heater faces the living room and is framed by the stairs behind and catwalk above. On one end it connects at right angles to a smaller (but still imposing) brick cooker of similar design, which defines the kitchen. The cooker is great for quicker warmth and making tea and oatmeal in the morning and for stovetop cooking in the evening. It is true that, from a cold start, water boils faster on a gas or electric range; but, as everyone knows, on the woodstove it boils more holistically.

Our heater is faced with two complementary species of rock: Ashfield stone, a local mica-schist that is blue-gray with silver and bronze streaks; and golden Connecticut granite-schist with dark red garnets—a handsome combination. On one end is a heated stone bench that runs into the brick chimney at the back of the cooker; on the other end Carsten built a wooden bench and cubbies using live-edged cherry slabs left over from the braces, tying the stove into the stairs behind it. With that bench joining wood to stone, the house was spiritually complete. If you want to sit dead center in our house, midway between the two inside bents, you sit on that cherry bench. We surrounded the stove with a hearth laid up from mica-schist shingles that we collected from shoals in our river, and we repeated that in the entry hall. An intermittent stream of local stones runs from our front door around the center of the house.

Inside the masonry stove wood is burned, completing a transformation by which sunlight captured by photosynthesis and stored as chemical energy in the form of cellulose and lignin is oxidized and released as light and radiant heat—everything going back to where it came from. The fire warms us directly through the glass door while it is burning and indirectly for hours on end through the stone—the memory of fire. It also warms us more deeply as it recalls our connection with the living world surrounding us, through the energy of our own work. But is the satisfying warmth of heating our home with wood a harmless indulgence, a wasteful extravagance, or a genuine social virtue?

Wood heat is only really satisfying if the wood is cut and burned responsibly. If the tools and techniques are deficient, disenchantment reigns: a hacked forest, a smoldering planet, and a crippled old chopper. In that spirit, let us explore responsible cutting and burning of wood. Others may have their own ways of heating with wood, which is fine by me, as long as they strive to meet the same standards—because this is a matter of public health as much as personal satisfaction. This is how we do it.

Heating with wood is hard work, so it is safe to say that the only people who stick with it for long—unless driven by necessity—are those who enjoy it. Few Americans cut wood entirely by hand (bucksaw, splitting ax, wheelbarrow) anymore, but I still know a handful of these stalwarts, most of them weathered old hippies much fitter than I am. I cut enough firewood that way when I was young to know what it takes. Modern woodcutters augment their muscles with mechanical power—chainsaws, hydraulic splitters, tractor buckets, pickup trucks—in whatever combination suits their own philosophy. As with all hand labor, the key to cutting wood is to organize the work so it flows smoothly from tree to stove; and so that the muscle-powered segments, while strenuous, do not break the body—but also so that the mechanical-powered segments don't make the muscular parts more difficult. Also, since cutting, storing, and burning wood all leave their mark on the world, the virtuous woodcutter is obliged to ensure that each step is done beautifully.

Before firewood can be burned, virtuously or not, it must be felled, limbed, bucked, split, hauled, stacked for seasoning, and carried into the house. The road to reasonable efficiency lies not only in the practiced execution of each of these steps but in the ease of the transitions from one to the next. For me, this means reducing the wood to small pieces as quickly as possible and then picking those pieces up and moving them as few times as possible. Wood is heavy: minimize handling! These days almost all of our firewood, both at the farm and in Weston, is cut along fence lines and hedgerows or in small woodlots where we can get a pickup right to it. I have already described the proper method for felling trees, using the bore cut and trigger when a controlled fall is required. I should again stress the importance of proper safety gear, including stout boots, ballistic nylon chaps, and a helmet with eye and ear protection. Practice the many-layered approach to personal safety.

Once your tree is horizontal, you are ready to limb and buck it. If you can, fell the tree over some downed logs, or anything that will keep it up off the ground—the high-tensile fence often works well for me, for smaller trees. Cut small wood from branches that are at a comfortable height, working them back to the trunk. Keep the tree intact as you work it up, because the big tree holds the branches for you, making them easier to cut. Resist the temptation to saw the tree into shorter sections, bring those home, and cut them again into firewood, unless the situation demands it. You will handle the wood an extra time and end up with a lot of irregular lengths and awkward cuts. Avoid that—use the whole tree to your advantage.

I run two saws: a light one, about 40 ccs displacement (I now have a battery-powered equivalent), for limbing and bucking small stuff; and a larger saw, over 50 ccs, for anything exceeding about six inches. Of course there are much bigger, more manly saws out there, if you think you need one. As I grow older, the weight of saw I can comfortably handle keeps getting smaller; but meanwhile, saws themselves keep getting lighter—so far, so good. At this rate, by the time I die, I will have a saw that is infinitely powerful yet weighs nothing, like a light sword—woodchopper's nirvana.

I am a stickler for cutting precise lengths; just ask Liam. I carry a slender sixteen-inch measuring stick in my trigger hand. It's easy to get used to. Most people, if they measure at all, turn their saw bar sideways; but I find that awkward, especially on small branches, and I notice that few who do it that way cut accurately—although that may be more a matter of attitude than technique. Measuring quickly with the little stick between cuts I find I am consistently good to within half an inch. When I encounter pieces of firewood that are more than an inch off, I am not happy—particularly if they are too long. Exact lengths make for even stacking and fit properly in the stove.

Most American stoves are designed to burn sixteen-inch wood—probably because that is one third of an old four-foot piece of cordwood, as I said. Many European stoves are smaller and work best with pieces that are about thirteen inches long—which is so, I suspect, because that is a third of a meter. We cut a small amount of slender oak, maple, and hickory to twelve inches for grilling. For years we burned a lot more twelve-inch wood in an antique kitchen range with a small firebox, but cutting and splitting wood down to that size takes forever. I once counted, and there are as many pieces of wood in a quarter cord of twelve-inch wood as there are in a half cord of sixteen-inch wood: it is *twice* as much work. Sixteen inches is the way to go.

Once the wood is cut to length, it must be split so it will season. If you are going to split by hand, sixteen inches is an ideal length. Twenty-four inches might seem more efficient as fewer pieces will make a cord, except it is significantly more trouble to stand a two-foot piece of wood on end and split it with a single stroke. If you have a wood furnace or boiler that burns two-footers, it is a safe bet that you also have a mechanical splitter and that your philosophy of wood burning involves a different economic calculus than mine. We are valuing our woodsplitting time in different ways—you are trying to save it, I am trying to savor it. I like splitting wood, and I like watching it burn. To split wood with a machine and to burn it in a boiler down in the basement or out in the yard, where I can't even see it, would leave me with no reason to heat with wood in the first place. Don't get me wrong: processing and burning wood that way may be satisfying for you, especially where heating larger buildings or compounds is concerned, so go right ahead. As long as that wood furnace burns clean, which the newer gasifying models do. If your wood-burning device doesn't burn clean, then you and I have nothing further to discuss.

I like to split the wood right where I bucked it. This is a major saving. If you oblige yourself to carry logs home to a mechanical splitter (or even a chopping block), you are going to be hoisting heavy unsplit rounds into your truck, then heaving them back out of your truck into a pile, and then someday (typically months later) wrestling them *again* onto your woodsplitter. You have already picked up and moved that wood three times before it even gets split. Then you will chuck the split pieces into another heap and someday stack them, when you get around to it. Whereas I split the wood where it lies into pieces that I can easily toss five or ten feet into the truck without wrecking my back or— too often, anyway—my plastic taillight cover (those things now cost as much to replace as a whole cord of wood, but that is a defect in the truck, not in my philosophy). Then we stack it right off the truck—all done.

To split the wood, I use a six-pound maul. You can use an ax, of course, but I find them too light in most cases. The maul is a shapely wedge of iron on a thirty-six-inch handle, a cross between an ax and a sledgehammer. It is not designed to cut wood, only to split it. The edge is just sharp enough to enter the end grain of a log without sticking, and it has plenty of "cheek"—it widens rapidly to force the wood fibers apart as it descends, delivering tremendous leverage by virtue of a long swing. Finding one with the correct shape can be a little difficult, these days; they are mostly too fat. Eight-pound mauls are also available, but those are for young guys with more upper-body strength than I ever possessed, let alone retain. So-called monster mauls weigh fifteen pounds—they sure do split wood, but few people can operate them for more than a few minutes. There are also lighter splitters somewhere between a maul and an ax that work decently, especially if you are of smaller stature, but I have seen plenty of women use a six-pound maul with devastating effect. Basically, you should use the heaviest tool that you can swing comfortably for a few hours and that you are strong enough to control when the head strikes— whatever works best for you.

The maul handle should be straight with the grain running parallel to the swing like a baseball bat and oval in cross-section rather than circular—

a little round handle will turn in your hands, and it will snap at the first overstrike. Fiberglass handles are great for tyros because they won't get all chewed up and break, but fiberglass doesn't feel right if you are accustomed to hickory—it's too stiff and jarring. You are not going to take a wild, over-the-shoulder, roundhouse swing. You are going to square your feet, raise your maul straight up over your head with your hands sliding apart, and then bring it straight down with your right hand sliding back to meet your left at the bottom of the handle (presuming you are right-handed). Bend your knees as you strike and, if you can, snap your wrists for extra power. You are aiming to finish your stroke in the ground at the bottom of the split log—this is important mentally as well as mechanically. If you don't believe the wood is going to split, it will probably prove you right.

Like revenge, wood splitting is best enjoyed cold. Wood splits more easily when it is frozen. It also helps that the hard ground doesn't overly cushion the force of your blow. Moreover, your body stays more comfortable if the temperature is below freezing, because this is real work. Even if there is snow your gloves stay dry, so your hands stay warm. You will soon be in shirtsleeves. Winter is best for woods work, but you will sometimes find yourself splitting wood when the heat has softened even your bones and sweat is washing sunscreen into your eyes and dripping from your nose, and it still works fine—the maul powers through. I have been known to split wood on my birthday, and I was born the day before Henry Thoreau.

Here's the main thing: winter or summer, you are going to split the wood *on the ground*, right where you cut it. Just stand it on end, split it, throw it in the truck, and it's done. With a maul, you don't need a chopping block. Wood might split a little better on a hard block than the soft earth, but there are several problems with that. First of all, firewood tends to be crooked and uneven, and it can be hard to get it to stand up on the block, especially small pieces. On the ground you can easily make it stand, and you can lean it back slightly against the next piece—the sequence becomes second nature. When you hit a log on the chopping block, it tends to go flying; if it doesn't split, you have to fetch it and set it up all over again. Also, splitting wood on that unyielding chopping block is going to ruin your wrists after a few decades; mine are still pretty good. But worst of all, chopping blocks are fixed in place. You have to bring the wood to them—at which point, you have already lost the race. By then, I would have split that piece and thrown it in the truck. Using a chopping block suggests that you think splitting wood is difficult. But splitting wood is not difficult, and you should never let the wood suspect that you think it is. It will tense up and resist you. Your job is to make the wood feel comfortable and relaxed, and then it will split willingly, usually with a single stroke.

There are three things you need to split wood successfully, besides the proper attitude. The first is power, which you get either by being young and strong or by years of practice that optimizes whatever strength you have left. The second is accuracy, by which I mean the ability to consistently hit your spot, let's say to within a quarter inch of where you meant to. Half an inch is usually close enough, though sometimes it's surprising how much difference a quarter inch can make. Because last, and most important, is knowing where to hit it. This is a bit hard to describe—it's something you learn from having done it a million times. The first split, usually right down the middle, is going to follow a line that avoids the worst knots (if the log is too big to split easily through the center or has tough grain like elm, you can whittle it down by slabbing pieces off the outside). Later splits are either going to isolate those knots on their own pieces or finish the job by going right through the biggest knot of all, cleaving it into bookmatched pieces—in which case, you better have the log turned so you are swinging up the tree, not down into the crotch. In general, wood splits more easily going up the tree than down, but this slight tendency is often overruled by other factors. In particular, if your split is going anywhere near a knot, you want to hit whichever end of the log is farthest from it. You want the widening split to have all the leverage it can muster by the time your maul reaches the twisted vicinity of that knot—if you strike the end nearest the knot, the crooked grain will stop you cold.

Mostly I don't think about any of this much: I see the line that is going to split most easily in the end grain and the bark, adjust my feet and the angle of my stroke as I raise the maul, and swing through that line as gently as possible. I don't hit the wood any harder than I need to, which is constantly recalibrated by the resistance of the last few pieces I've split. The key to this, obviously, is being able to consistently hit your spot. Once I see the right line, the whole thing just unfolds—I could do it with my eyes closed. In fact, sometimes I *do* close my eyes when I swing, just to feel that rush of power—and to make sure I can still do it.

When I go out to cut wood these days, I usually plan to put in two or three hours of work—about all I am good for, and about what it should take to cut and split a quarter-cord, which is what my little Taco can hold. I gas up and fell a few small trees that are leaning over the fence, then cut pieces off the butt ends as far as the wires, using my big saw. Then I step back into the pasture and limb out the tops, cutting small pieces from the branches and then working the trunk, using my little saw until the wood gets too thick for it. The sawing generally takes me about an hour, and by halfway through I am warmed up and feeling good, ticking along nicely even if the day is way below freezing. If it's really cold out I might switch briefly to splitting after cutting the first few pieces, to get the blood moving to my fingers and toes. Sawing is colder work than splitting.

Once the cutting is done I set the saws aside, back the truck up to the wood, and pick up my maul. I throw the smallest pieces into the bed in the round, but I split most everything over four inches thick because they season better that way. Every now and then I switch to dragging brush to the fence, throwing it out of the pasture and beyond the strip I clear annually with the brush cutter. This extra step to dispose of the brush is the one drawback to felling trees into the field. I generally wrap up the job by stepping back over the fence and splitting the butt pieces, tossing them into the truck over the side panel, so I'm not endangering that taillight. After an hour of splitting I am finished, and feeling great. I am a little tired, but working as smoothly as I ever did.

I hoist my saws and mauls back into the bed on top of the wood, and I just have this one question: why is my truck only *half* full of wood?

They don't make trucks like they used to.

Now we come to stacking the wood, and here is where you can easily lose much of what you have worked so hard to gain. Wood needs to be split and stacked so that it can season—that is, dry to less than 20 percent moisture content—and burn efficiently, without wasting energy evaporating its own sap. Wood does not season well until it is split, unless you live in a dry climate. In Kansas, they don't have to split their wood—though of course I still did. In New England, if you pass a woodpile that is stacked in the round, you can be sure that when you drive by ten years later that same pile will still be there, untouched except by squirrels and fungus and unmoved except by gravity, quietly rotting away. Nobody who actually burns wood here stacks it unsplit—it's just a useless extra step.

For years, I made wood stacks three feet high and sixteen feet long, with crisscrossed abutments at both ends. Such a stack won't fall over, and it measures exactly half a cord (sixty-four cubic feet), so you know what you've got. The stacks look good—the proportions seem right, at least to me. But they have one glaring defect: the need to cover them. Through the summer they stand drying in the open, looking crisp and providential. But come fall you have to cover them against the weather or you will be burning wet wood by winter, a betrayal of everything you hold dear. You could use rusty old sheets of corrugated roofing, but that's a bit New Hampshire. For many years I used strips of heavy mil black plastic, but frankly that looked crappy and didn't reliably keep the wood dry either. Lately I've taken to using larger, heavier-duty plastic tarps to cover several stacks once they're dry, but that is awkward and ugly. It always bugged me to build such nice woodpiles and then not know how to cover them with something equally attractive. We were planning to build a woodshed at the new house, which is probably the best solution, but then something else turned up.

What about those round piles? While researching timber frame houses and masonry heaters I bumped into a couple of these *holzmieten* and they looked kind of cool, but I wondered if they actually worked. By the time we were building the house, Liam, who had been helping with firewood since he was little, had reached that middle-school age where building a circular woodpile seemed like a fun project. Better yet, several of the attempts that we viewed ended in classic YouTube fails, which posed a suitable challenge: it couldn't be *that* difficult, for anyone who understood the art of stacking wood, could it? What, did you have to be German, or possibly Norwegian, to keep one of these things from falling over?

So we set up a base of pallets by the kitchen porch in Weston big enough for two holzmieten, side by side, and gave it a whirl. The pallets keep the wood off the ground and provide air flow up the middle. First you make a ring of split wood laid end to end, and then you build your outer wall on that circle, taking care that the pieces always slant down inward. They will keep wanting to tilt the other way because they are jammed together more on the inside, so shim early and often, using thin splits turned sideways. Once the ring is high enough, you can begin to fill the middle with vertical pieces—the idea again is to allow good air flow. We tend to put small stuff in the middle so it packs a little better, and that is the supply for the kitchen stove. Tilt those guys in toward the center, too.

First (and next to last) holzmiete collapse, back in Weston. (Faith Rand)

We decided on a slender pod only six feet in diameter, because we wanted to be able to reach the middle when taking the wood out to bring inside and burn. Four and a half feet tall would measure a full cord, so that seemed like a good design—a remarkably compact way to store wood, if it worked. Such a slim pile might have stability issues, but that only heightened the challenge. Just keep it straight and true, right? So up we went, without much difficulty, over a few weeks—bringing home a quarter cord at a time. When we reached the desired height, we mounded up the center fill and then went to work on the roof. The idea, all the web sites said, was to build a shingled cover of thin splits to shed water. That seemed simple enough, but a couple of courses up, the whole thing unraveled: it went spiraling around and down with a long rippling crash like you hear in a bowling alley on Saturday morning, and our holzmiete lay in a heap at our feet.

Rats. We got a cup of tea, contemplated this mess for a few minutes, and decided to change tactics. We shimmed more assiduously. But this time, we also put an eight-foot pole in the middle: first, because I thought these things really ought to have a center pole, aesthetically speaking—sort

Two holzmieten: they usually come in pairs. The first hat is in place, with the second under construction. The hats have lasted ten years so far. The chopping block is for making kindling. (Brian Donahue)

of like the old meadow hay stacks on the cover of my Concord book; and second, because this time I was going to make my *holzhaus* a nice hat. That shingled roof thing bothered me: how were you supposed to get the wood *out?* As far as I could tell, the function of these round piles in Northern Europe was laudable, but laborious. The idea was to build a large, stable wood house (all sorts of fanciful designs were then possible, depicting Beethoven, Elvis, King Harald, Batman, or Angela Merkel) and let the wood season for a year. Then you restack it on the porch for the winter you burn it. Much as I admire letting wood season for two summers, I'm not keen to restack it. There had to be a way to get the wood out of the stack *and* keep it covered and dry. So I thought okay, let's make a hat, and just let it float down as the pile gets smaller. It worked.

I make my holzmiete hats out of three-eighths-inch CDX plywood, duct tape, and latex paint—the cheapest, lightest materials I could think of that might last a few seasons. But like a lot of cheap prototypes they've now lasted ten years, and so far we've made eight of them. I repaint them every summer or two and retape them when they need it. The hats are two feet high and octagonal, with a small center hole for the pole. The triangular panels for two hats fit nicely on three four-by-eight sheets of plywood, though that sixteenth panel requires splicing two end half-pieces. We build six or eight wood pods a year, adding up to more than fifty to date. The second year another one collapsed during construction, but no more since then. We have refined our technique: we have a little plywood ring that fits over the center pole, with three-foot-long radial arms. It rides up during construction and can be rotated periodically as you stack, keeping the pile round and true; then it is removed. Liam and I call this device "the technology," as in "we have the technology to put a man on the moon, so why can't we end world hunger or stop global warming?" With more of *this* kind of technology, maybe we could.

I sometimes tell my students, once I have taken them out splitting a time or two, that cutting firewood is a lot like writing a research paper. I say this to get a laugh, because for them, getting out in the woods is about as far from normal coursework as they can imagine. It might be a rueful laugh, too, because for all the fun we have swinging mauls in mud time, the term paper in my forest course is famously grueling in a more conventional academic way. But actually, woodcutting and writing *are* similar: you take a complex natural world and break it down into its constituent parts— pieces of wood or nouns and verbs with discrete, unitary meanings. You then reorganize these elements into a new, simplified order—sentences and paragraphs, stacks of wood.

Of course, in making the subject legible you lose much of the wonder of the original—a wood stack only represents one small slice of the complex, living forest, as does a house, or a book, for that matter. Such are the perils of reductionism. But you hope that some of the energy, that enchantment of nature, comes through between the lines—even in linear stacks, the wood is edgy and expressive. The same way you want to throw a craggy word into a smooth sentence, or an orthogonal sentence into an orderly paragraph, to keep the reader on their toes. One nice thing about the round piles with their whimsical hats is that they retain more of that magic of the wildwood, while still being well organized. A timber frame house has some of that going on, too. But where you really get that wild energy back from wood—not just in a physical but in a psychic sense—is when you burn it.

» » « «

The last step in responsible heating with wood is the care you take with its combustion. The goal is to make as little smoke as possible. With a normal woodstove, you light the fire in the morning and then faithfully tend it, hour after hour, day after day—as people have done since time immemorial. Every hour or two you add wood and maybe adjust the air flow, all depending on how hot you want the stove to run. Perhaps you fill the stove in the evening before bed and turn the air down—but not too low, as you don't want it to start emitting toxic fumes. There is a nice rhythm to it, and you have the pleasant company of the fire all day.

But of course this means you have to *be* there all day, and you have to enjoy dealing with clunky pieces of firewood, unless you are using an automated pellet stove. To me, every piece of firewood is an object of spellbinding beauty, but that is perhaps abnormal. But even presuming you like putting wood in the stove as much as I do, you are not going to tend the fire like that in a masonry stove. Instead, you are going to build a big fire just once or twice a day and burn it down to ashes in a single roaring inferno, and let the brick and stone take it from there. This is a very different rhythm than a conventional stove, and much more flexible. It also gives you one heck of a fire to enjoy, while it lasts.

Laying a fire in a masonry stove requires ten to twenty pieces of wood. The firebox accommodates sixteen-inch pieces both ways, and it is quite tall. You build the fire with four to six crisscross layers, depending on the thickness of the pieces and the size of the fire you want, keeping the pile nice and even. I usually lay three pieces across in each layer, but it could be two or four, depending. As you build you want to use slightly smaller pieces for the middle of each layer, to keep the stack from rocking, to carry the fire down more rapidly in the center, and to help it collapse inward as it burns. These rules are more important for starting a campfire in the open than in a closed firebox, which is more forgiving because of the reflected heat from the walls, but they are always good to practice for when you really need them.

Once the main stack is ready, you build a smaller kindling fire on top. There are many ways of successfully lighting a fire, of course, but for serious wood burners, top-firing has become de rigueur. There are places where top-firing is difficult—in the smaller firebox of a normal woodstove, for example, it won't easily fit—so you build the kindling fire first and then add to it. But in a masonry heater, top-firing is ideal. One reason for putting the kindling fire on top is simply practical: if something goes wrong and the fire doesn't catch right away, it's easier to get at and feed it or try again. But the main reason for top-firing is that it is the cleanest, most efficient, most beautiful way to burn wood.

Wood is composed of cellulose and lignin, which are long, hairy organic molecules made of carbon, hydrogen, and oxygen, stiff enough to provide structure to plants. When they are heated, they cook off as highly combustible gases—and that's most of the potential energy that is locked up in wood (and also the basis for the wood chemical industry). But if there is no handy source of ignition, those hot rising gases can't fully combust as they exit the fire. They go on to become either tarry creosote in your chimney or foul smoke in your neighborhood, and their potential is wasted.

If your kindling fire is at the bottom, gamely heating the pile above it, you've got the whole thing upside down. It will burn someday, but by then a lot of good fuel will have been smoked away, and the world will be defiled. Whereas if you put the merry little kindling fire on top, like lighting a candle, the gases being elicited from the heated wood beneath it must rise through the flames, where they are consumed forthwith. The fire, which is hottest at the bottom, begins to work its way down, gathering strength as it descends. Nothing is wasted, and the whole process is a joy to behold.

A fire in the masonry stove lasts about two hours, during which time it passes through all the stages of life. For the first ten minutes the kindling fire burns alone, unprepossessingly perched atop a pile of inert material, like an oblivious child at play. In the next ten minutes the top layer of firewood (which should be made of smaller pieces) becomes engaged, first in the center and then side to side. The orange flames begin to leap up through the throat at the top of the firebox and their flickering peaks appear in the oven above, with exuberant but erratic adolescent yearning. Over the next twenty minutes the fire descends to the bottom of the pile, and now everything is burning at once. The yellow flames are long and shoot up into the oven above the firebox, where they make one full turn and then swirl off and disappear into the heater core at the right, with its secondary combustion chambers. This is the adult stage of the fire, when it burns with full force.

Oddly, in spite of the vigorous continuous upward streaming of the flames, the structure of the woodfire stands there just as you built it, intact and unmoving, slowly charring—it is only burning in spirit, not yet in body. Most of the energy in wood is in spirit. In its second hour, the fire settles and burns more calmly, orange and glowing red. It is in its fully mature, reflective stage now, its carbon structure slowly collapsing into coals. The volatile hydrocarbons have been consumed, and all that is left to burn is the charred body, the pure carbon.

There is a memorial service at the end of a fire in the masonry stove— a brief resurrection that you don't often see in other fires, which just die away to lingering embers and then to ashes, when no longer fed. Once all of the structure of the fire has crumbled, you can rake the coals into the center, shut the airflow through the door, and fully open the under-air from the ash pit to burn them out. Small blue flames appear and shimmy across the bed of bright red coals; the most intense flames appear purple at the base. Then, as the air begins to blast through from beneath, a brilliant cloud of luminous, swirling yellow gas arises, sometimes filling the entire firebox. It shines like the northern lights. Occasional bursts of sparks flash up through it, crackling like tiny fireworks. Sometimes, we think we can see hints of green in these flames—some say at the base, others say at the tips. We quarrel about whether we have really seen the green flame, and what could cause it—iron from the grate? Copper scraped from the brass shovel? Some other trace mineral in the wood—boron, or something? In any case, green flame or not, the billowing cloud of brilliant gas is a celebration of the life of the fire and of the wood, the final spirit rising before it fades away to nothing but warm stone, the lingering memory of fire.

While I am drinking my morning tea and updating my to-do list or unwinding with an evening shot of single malt, I contemplate the latest fire of the thousands I have built. There it stands, either just starting to burn or already fully encased in flame but still intact, this neat rectilinear structure whose intersecting but slightly irregular horizontal lines mimic those of the stone masonry that encloses it and the timber frame that encloses that. This is a trivial observation—after all, the same interplay of verticals and horizontals at right angles in two or three dimensions is also visible in books in their cases, picture frames on the wall, file cabinets, window panes and casings, these lines of words on the page, you name it—it's just the way we humans make things, for obvious reasons of stability and security. Still, I take great satisfaction at least once a day in building this abstract replica of our house, bringing the uneven layers up to level in a slightly different architecture each time, determined by whatever pieces of firewood are at hand—and then incinerating it. Adding that fourth dimension, if you will: going from structure to story. Every day, I symbolically sacrifice this miniature dwelling to propitiate the briefly indulgent but ultimately merciless gods of oxidation, and so far it seems to be working.

Warming ourselves with fire, cooking food with it, and telling stories around it are thought to be fundamental to human evolution, so fire is something to which most of us are powerfully drawn. I am, however, keenly aware that in recent years burning wood (especially when it goes by the wonky name of "biomass") has acquired an uncertain, not to say unsavory, reputation among environmentalists. Those 1970s Volvo bumper stickers that said "Split Wood, Not Atoms" have long since disappeared. A more politically correct sentiment for today's electric vehicle fenders might be "Burn Nothing, Not Ever." Sleek, immaculate electrons, conceived without combustion, rule the utopian dreams of climate warriors.

The objection to burning wood turns on three concerns: its impact on air quality, on climate, and on the forest. I take them all seriously. As to the first, burning wood can be dirty (especially regarding particulates) compared with natural gas or even oil and coal. Wood needs to be burned in devices that meet stringent air quality standards. If properly designed and operated, masonry heaters have low particulate emissions, because they foster very hot, complete combustion—it is the heat that lingers, not the toxic dregs of the fuel. The Masonry Heater Association has worked with the U.S. Environmental Protection Agency to develop testing procedures to set emission standards, but in the meantime masonry stoves are exempt from certification—which is a good thing, because it would be painful to replace ours now. Once he built our stove, Carsten tested it rigorously to determine the most efficient air flow settings.[17]

Given clean combustion, burning wood for heat seems harmless enough in places where there is plenty of wood and likewise plenty of atmosphere in which to disperse the smoke relative to the number of lungs that have to breathe it. The denser the settlement, especially where winter inversions can trap smoke, the cleaner the combustion devices must be and the fewer of them are tolerable. This all stands to reason: wood is an appropriate fuel mainly for rural areas.

The impact of wood burning on climate is a bit more complicated.

Wood emits carbon dioxide when it is burned, just like coal, oil, or natural gas—in fact, usually a little *more* carbon dioxide to accomplish the same heating task, given achievable efficiencies of combustion and conversion. Growing forests, on the other hand, sequester carbon and store it in the form of living biomass, coarse woody debris that decomposes only slowly, and soil carbon that accumulates over time. The recovering forests of the Northeast are mostly middle-aged, just approaching maturity. Studies show that they continue to grow and to store more carbon than they respire. Presumably they cannot grow at the same rate forever but will slow until they reach an equilibrium where they are sequestering no more carbon through photosynthesis than they release through death and decay, but we do not know when that plateau will be reached—only that in most places we aren't there yet.[18]

So there is something to be said for simply allowing forests to grow and keep sucking down at least some of the excess carbon dioxide that is being produced by burning fossil fuel—and some environmentalists are vigorously making that case. If that growing wood is harvested instead, the carbon impact will hinge on several things: what change that makes in the rate of growth and storage in the forest, how the removed wood is used, and what that use replaces. If you are burning wood to replace fuel oil and burning it cleanly, as we have been for forty years, that can look pretty decent. If you are burning wood when you might have installed a solar electric heat pump, as we could do now, that begins to look a bit more problematic.[19]

Let's set the vexed issue of comparing wood fuel with other energy sources aside for a moment and look more closely at what is happening in the forest when wood is cut. In the case of our masonry heater the origins of the fuel are benign. For the first winters we burned maple and cherry from the mill slab and tops of the trees I had felled for the stairs and braces, so that had a certain charm. It was a homemade version of burning logging and sawmill residue—parts of trees that had already been cut for another purpose and so were going to decompose and release their carbon anyway. Since then, we have mostly burned trees that fell on the pasture fence or looked like they had that in mind; thus, we generate fuel as a by-product of routine farm maintenance, and the forest proper is only grazed around the edges. If a big sugar maple limb falls on my fence and I cut it up to dispose of it, it is hard to see a meaningful difference in carbon dioxide release between burning it the next winter or allowing it to molder at the edge of the woods over the next decade—except that in the second case I would *also* have to burn an equivalent amount of propane in its place. To find fault with that you would have to insist that we let the forest take back our entire farm and move to a solar-powered city (if such existed), where we can eat food grown from algae in tanks, flavored to taste like grass-fed beef if we crave it—which is the world I sometimes think the fiercest opponents of burning wood and eating meat are really envisioning, if you press them hard enough. A world where fond memories of home fires are something to pull up on your cell phone at Christmas.

Be that as it may, deriving your firewood directly from farm upkeep is admittedly rare, and statistically insignificant. If society as a whole is to burn wood as part of its energy portfolio, some can be recovered from waste wood or trees that are being cut anyway, but most must be generated by harvesting from the woodlands that cover much of the landscape—and there the trouble begins. If this biomass is produced by periodically razing forests after only a few decades of vigorous growth, that is carbon neutral only in the narrow sense that the wood, once burned, simply returns to the atmosphere the carbon dioxide that it sequestered while growing. What is squandered, as many have pointed out, is the capacity of those trees to continue growing *and storing* that carbon for many decades, if not centuries, to come. Fossil fuel may be replaced by burning wood, but carbon storage is thrown away, and for some years after harvest the rate of growth of the forest may be slowed, as well.

There may be other environmental reasons to prefer biomass to fossil fuels. Cutting and transporting wood, however ecologically disruptive, is seldom as destructive as stripping coal, drilling oil, fracking natural gas, or mining tar sands, not to mention refining, shipping, and inevitably spilling those toxic subterranean hydrocarbons that have no rightful place up here in the biosphere. As a forester I know once remarked, if a truck hauling biomass goes off the road, all you have to clean up is a pile of wood chips. Nevertheless, having a large part of the forested landscape alternating between early succession and recent cutover, generating biomass and then just burning it up again, is not an attractive proposition, doesn't achieve anything for the climate, and isn't what I am talking about. There is little to be gained, and plenty to be lost, growing forests simply to produce combustible biomass.[20]

What is going on in our woods, whether in the Weston town forest or here at the farm, is different. We practice what the New England Forestry Foundation calls exemplary forestry, or what others call ecological forestry: long rotations aimed primarily at maintaining the other environmental benefits of the forest while producing *timber,* with periodic improvement cuttings along the way. During the first century of growth of a well-managed woodlot, we harvest five to ten cords per acre of low-grade wood every fifteen or twenty years, ideally starting about year forty. Each improvement cut, called a "commercial thinning" in the forestry trade, removes perhaps a quarter or a third of the standing trees—mainly the most suppressed or crooked ones. After a few years you would scarcely know our saws had been there, because there is as much standing volume as if we had never cut a thing—the woods look about the same as they would have, with slightly fewer but larger, more upright stems.[21]

This is the key point: *a young growing forest will do that thinning on its own anyway.* It starts with many more trees than will live to maturity and squeezes most of them out along the way, to die and gradually decay so that most of their carbon is released through respiration of the creatures decomposing them, only slightly more slowly and less completely than through harvest and combustion. When people take over the thinning, much of that carbon is burned to warm us instead, but the growth of the woods overall is scarcely interrupted—it is merely redirected, or even accelerated. The thinning serves to concentrate that growth into trees of the highest timber quality, which expand their crowns and quickly take up the photosynthetic slack. This may even achieve a *faster* overall rate of growth than if the stand were left alone, because we have removed the struggling members of the community that were soon going to die and reallocated their sunlight to the most vigorous more expeditiously.

That is the way we have been doing it for forty years in the Weston town forest. This is not just some theory to me: I have watched it achieve its aim. In our hilltop woodlot here at the farm, which had not been managed before we bought the place, we made up for lost time with a more sweeping low-grade harvest. Comparing such a managed stand to one that has been left alone, after a century we might find a slight difference in how much carbon has been oxidized and how much is left standing, but that difference is so trivial it is not worth getting all worked up about. In essence, such management simply captures mortality and carbon dioxide release that would have happened anyway and puts it to use, mainly for heat.

By the later improvement cuts, as the stand matures, part of what is removed can be used for timber as well as firewood, as was the case in our low-grade harvest here at the farm. Once the stand has passed one hundred years of age, the rate of growth typically slows, because the remaining trees have reached full height and now only add girth. This varies from one forest type to the next; research continues, because many of our forests are just reaching that age. Eventually, over the next few decades, the mature, high-quality trees can be cut for timber (usually in several stages), releasing young trees that have been springing up on the forest floor all along, awaiting just such a disturbance, natural or cultural. At this point a substantial part of the sequestered carbon goes into buildings, where it can be safely locked up for many more decades if not centuries, barring some catastrophe. Meanwhile, back in the woods, younger trees are rapidly growing, absorbing more carbon from the air.[22]

When larger trees are harvested for timber and much of the stand is regenerated, the carbon computation becomes more complex. The amount of carbon stored in the forest is dramatically reduced for many years, so now the argument turns mainly on what becomes of that harvested material. The object is to store as much of the removed carbon for as long as possible, in buildings like our house. I will return to that question shortly, but my main point here is that harvesting fuelwood should never be an end in itself. It should be ancillary to ecological forest management that is aimed primarily at maximizing the production of mature timber, while maintaining other ecosystem values.

That is the most important connection between our masonry heater and the timber frame that encloses it. The two go together—wood heat and wooden house—and reflect a coherent philosophy of ongoing forest stewardship that is similar to the one that existed in our region before the industrial revolution but more appropriate for our time. Burning biomass as the main end of forest management makes no sense. Honestly, biomass has little to contribute to meeting our greatest challenge, which is to reduce and then eliminate fossil fuels: it can never amount to more than a small fraction of our total energy supply. Especially electricity: biomass currently generates only 1 or 2 percent of the nation's power; even with strenuous efforts that could only be increased by a tiny bit. Burning wood to make electric power is not a serious solution, except locally where there is a lot of waste material to dispose of anyway, at sites such as a large sawmill or pulp plant. The serious solutions lie in energy conservation and in expanding solar, wind, and geothermal power to take over the major jobs of running industrial society: generating electricity and driving transportation. Wood has comparatively little to offer in that arena.[23]

We do not need more fire in this world; we need far, far less. But fossil fire is now most of our fire by several orders of magnitude, and that is what must be extinguished. Wood fire we stole from the gods when we were young, and it made us human. That is worth cherishing, because that is who we are—we are creatures of fire. Subterranean fire we stole from the demons of hell, and, for that, hell must be paid. That is who we have more recently become, and who we must stop being. Once fossil fire has been safely locked back beneath the bedrock, wood fire can burn on in the ancient place where we have long cherished it: on the hearth, warming our buildings and cooking our food, at least in country places. Not many of us live in country places anymore, but the rest can visit from time to time and enjoy a nice wood fire—that is good for the soul, as well as the rural economy. Cutting wood fuel should be mainly a means to improve timber and secure other ecological benefits, giving forest managers an outlet for low-grade material that will at least pay its way out of the woods. If we can keep firewood in its proper place, heating rural buildings, we needn't lose sleep either fantasizing about a major role for biomass in replacing fossil fuels or fretting over the relatively trivial amount of carbon dioxide it releases.

Heating with wood is a lifestyle choice; it makes good sense for country people who like to do for ourselves and count the hours we spend cutting wood as contributing to our wellness. For us, heating with wood isn't really about savings: it is sheer gain, start to finish. It is analogous, actually, to hunting deer and eating venison: not a significant source of protein for modern industrial society, but central to maintaining rural landscapes and culture.

Well-managed woodlands are capable of producing two overlapping products: firewood (and some timber) while they are growing up and being periodically thinned, and timber (and some firewood) when they are harvested and regenerated to grow anew. Much of the living carbon that is captured and combusted early in this process would have died and decomposed anyway, releasing approximately the same amount of carbon dioxide—not hundreds of years from now, but routinely, in the course of the growth of the forest. The timber that is harvested in the end does not store all of the carbon that would otherwise have been left standing in the woods (some of that typically gets burned as well), but it can lock a significant part of it up in handsome buildings.

To the extent that either combustion of firewood or construction with timber reduces the use of fossil fuel today, that is all to the good, as long as it is harvested well and burned cleanly. Once solar and wind power have taken over the bulk of our energy base, burning that small amount of wood won't matter anymore. The masonry heater standing in the timber-framed house reflects a healthy, dual relationship with the surrounding woodlands, calling on them for both energy and structure, in a direct, satisfying way. To do away with such relationships entirely would be to cease being human, to become an entirely new species—zoo creatures that the machines keep alive for their own amusement. To perfect such ancient relationships—and hold the robotic predators circling the campfire at bay—is one more way of keeping hope alive.

NINE

Wood Is Green

SO, HOW MUCH OF A TYPICAL HOUSE could be grown locally?

Thus far, I have advocated building and heating with wood that comes directly from the surrounding forest, especially if you enjoy doing some of the work yourself. I've claimed that this wood can be cut sustainably, still leaving the forest healthy and beautiful. But I haven't tried to pretend that *everything* in our house came from our own woods or that *everyone* is in a position to build in such a direct, simple way. That obviously isn't possible or even desirable. What we need is a broad range of workable ways of combining sustainable forestry and green construction, ranging from local artisanal woodcraft to larger-scale mass timber.

Our house exemplifies this synergy, but it is only one point along the spectrum. The direct connection between our house and our woodlot only worked for us thanks to industrial technology. First, there was all the machinery we used, to harvest and process the wood: chainsaws, tractors, skidders, trucks, sawmills, kilns, and planers. True, that was once accomplished mostly by ax and by ox, with maybe a little waterpower thrown in, and horses can still do the skidding very nicely; but I am not pining for the return of two-man crosscut saws. Even for a local wood economy, powerful machines are handy to turn big trees into boards and beams. I *am* looking forward to the electrification of all that oil-burning horsepower. I will enjoy the return of relative peace and quiet, not to mention a cooler planet.[1]

Second, many key components of our house were *not* sourced locally. We have a conventional basement, a conventional roof, and conventional interior walls: we chose to use local wood mostly where we could see it. Being selectively artisanal saved money, especially in the roof, where the intricately angled joinery of heavy timbers would have been exorbitant,

Liam, Brian, and Maggie, going on hemlock logs. (Faith
Rand)

yet invisible—not a match made in Yankee heaven. If you want to lean back
in your grandma's rocker to savor your soaring rafters and purlins, your
living room will need a cathedral ceiling. You will pay dearly for that high-
falutin roof and for heating all the empty space between you and it. We
opted for conventional roof framing and attic lofts, which provide extra
usable floor space along with glimpses of the ridge beam and loft ladders
from below, giving a more subtle sense of upward movement.

Our interior wall framing disappeared behind sheetrock, so it made
sense for the carpenters to use standard two-by-fours. We could have generated rough pine or hemlock studs from our woodlot and had them kilned
and planed as we did for the flooring, but we couldn't see much point in
that. Or in putting genuine timber-framed sills and joists underfoot. If you

go down cellar and look up, you will see nominal two-by-ten joists on sixteen-inch centers running over beams of laminated veneer lumber that are supported by steel lally columns, just like anybody's basement. You will see chipboard. Others might make different choices, and that's great—if you find satisfaction knowing there is local wood even deep within your walls where nobody can see it, all the more power to you. Using local wood wherever *you* want it is the point, not following the one correct path.

Otherwise, our frame is mostly unchanged from the seventeenth-century model brought over from England; but just as in those days, the key innovation is not the old bones but the new skin: the sheathing. Back then it was pine boards, clapboards, and shingles in place of wattle, daub, and thatch; today, the skin includes extra layers of fat, for added warmth. In colonial times, the exterior walls were filled with brick nog and plaster (coincidentally the name of a bracing Yankee cocktail made from red rum, apple jack, milk, maple sugar, and nutmeg plunged with a hot poker, if I remember correctly—as in, "I'll have another Brick Nog and Plaster, please"), leaving only the inside faces of the frame timbers exposed. Today, we have "structural insulated panels": two layers of oriented-strand board with eight inches of foam insulation sandwiched between them. SIPs don't sound as appealing as brick nog (except when abbreviated) but do have the redeeming quality of standing entirely outside the frame. Nothing else is needed inside that shell except drywall, slipped in behind the posts, and trim. This leaves the frame members fully exposed on three faces, to stunning visual effect.[2]

A house feels extra snug when it can project that kind of bone structure. Together, the timber frame and SIPs make a solid marriage between traditional craftsmanship and modern technology, employing each to best advantage. For exterior siding we went with traditional white pine clapboards, but not from our own woodlot, even though we had plenty of pine. We bought them from Ward Clapboard Mill in Vermont, which employs an ingenious nineteenth-century mill to produce radially sawn, beveled siding. These vertical-grain clapboards are stable and weather-resistant—they evoke the riven pine and cedar siding of the seventeenth century. We stained them pumpkin and let them weather brown. Like the frame that sits inside the modern sheathing, our exterior siding is old school. The traditional elements of the house catch the eye, but they are more than ornamental. The industrial elements tend to be hidden.[3]

But again, not everyone can build such a house, coming straight (at least in part) from their own woods. This raises a fair question: was our timber frame house just an atavistic indulgence—another privileged piece of do-it-yourself cabin porn? Can it serve as a useful model for how a post-industrial urban society manages its forests and provides decent, attractive housing for everyone? I think it can: the *principles* we applied can extend throughout the countryside and reach back into the city. By extension they speak to the entire nation, for ours is a well-wooded land.

To answer this question, we need to consider both demand and supply: what is the need for wood (and its advantage in comparison with other materials); and what is the best way to fulfill that need without undermining the other benefits that forests provide? With ten billion people likely to walk the planet within the lifetime of most of those alive today, it is pointless to think about what is best for the forest in isolation from human needs. To do so would be to embrace a future in which people live entirely separate from the natural world, dependent on artificial systems that bypass wild ecosystems altogether—a breakthrough into half-earth hell, if you ask me. I can't stress this enough: it is fine to oppose brutal industrial logging, and it is fine to designate more wild and indigenous places; but somehow, we still have to meet the legitimate material needs of billions of human beings mostly living in cities.

The basic need for wood is shelter, but the broader imperative is to rebuild urban, suburban, and rural communities in greener ways that both reduce their environmental impact and make them better places to live for everybody. What can wood contribute to that fundamental transformation that it is not providing already? How can our forests be protected even as we necessarily wield chainsaws within them?

Even though building a house with timber harvested from one's own woods is not feasible for everyone, most Americans do live reasonably close—within a one- or two-hour drive—to sufficient timber to build a home. Our country contains well over seven hundred million acres of forest that is capable of growing timber—about two acres for every person. That is easily enough to supply the lumber and paper we consume: the United States still harvests the great bulk of its own wood products and is only a small net importer (mostly from Canada), even though a large part of our forest is seldom cut. The American forest is found primarily in the

Northeast and Upper Midwest, the South, the higher elevations of the
Rocky Mountains and Sierra Nevada, and the Pacific Northwest—a distribution that matches quite well with that of our population (as can be
seen in the maps of forest ownership in Chapter 6). With the exception of
the cities of the arid Southwest, most Americans live in or near a forested
region.[4]

My argument, in a nutshell, is this: it would be better for Americans
to draw their wood products not exclusively but primarily from the forests
of their own places: as close to home as possible. To put it in economic
terms, there is comparative advantage in an increased measure of regional
self-reliance in timber (even granted some loss in absolute advantage in
narrow economic terms), because of the large social and environmental
co-benefits. The same can be said for food, by the way. What we might lose
in efficiency we would more than make up for in sustainability, resilience,
and satisfaction.

New England is broadly representative of the nation as a whole, in
terms of timber supply. The region is both heavily populated and heavily
forested. Like the country, New England has two acres of forest for every
inhabitant—about thirty million acres of trees for fifteen million people.
We live smack in the middle of a magnificent forest. It runs continuously
from suburban backyards through farms and rural getaways to the nearly
deserted North Woods, linking private and public ownerships from Cape
Cod to the Canadian border and beyond. These woods cover 60 percent
of the landscape in southern New England and almost 90 percent in the
north—about 80 percent of the region as a whole. This makes New England the most densely forested region in the country, but it is also one of
the most densely settled, so our forest is close to home. Each regional forest
is different—for example, the Northeast is more dominated by hardwoods
than the conifers of the South and West—but in general, what holds true
for Massachusetts also holds for Georgia, Minnesota, Colorado, Washington, or any other state with plenty of trees within a few hundred miles
of where people live, if not right out the back door. I will use New England
as a model for other forested regions, with the understanding that your
exact wood usage may vary.[5]

The demand for timber might usefully be divided into two categories: a local, mostly rural market; and a regional, mostly urban and suburban market. Today, that distinction doesn't exist: construction everywhere

utilizes lumber from pretty much the same national supply chain, with regional production feeding into it. But putting a more intentional local and regional system in place could transform our relationship with the forest. The first of these two kinds of demand is the subject of this book: a revival of timber framing and related artisanal construction could draw mostly upon local woodlands, which would maximize the benefits of resurrecting face-to-face economies in rural areas. Meanwhile, the green rebuilding of urban America could draw primarily on revived regional timber industries, based on the same ecological forestry but using larger-scale processing and more innovative building methods. To succeed, they need to share identical principles: protect and carefully steward the forests, extend affordable housing to the whole community, and build with local and regional wood.

Rural housing today is a quandary—a boom for the few and a bust for the many. The United States typically adds a little more than a million units of new housing every year, fluctuating between half that and twice that number, depending on the state of the economy. About one-fifth of Americans live in "non-metropolitan" areas, but only about one-tenth of new housing is built in these rural places and small towns—most is still going up in the sprawling suburbs of the South and West. This contributes to an affordable housing crisis in the countryside. At the same time, something like one hundred thousand new homes *are* built in rural places every year, which is a considerable market. Many of these houses are built by newcomers from the cities and the suburbs who arrive with strong environmental convictions—or so they would have you believe. While many rural counties across the nation have been losing population for generations, others are now being resettled by urban migrants—a trend that appears to be accelerating, thanks to the Covid pandemic. There is no telling how long this latest wave of upscale reverse migration will last or what it will mean for rural America. But virtually all of these new homebuilders could utilize local wood by employing some version of the direct "forest-to-house" method that I have been describing, which could be a major boost to the communities where they settle.[6]

Rural population recovery is good, in principle: it is difficult to have a thriving town (in the New England sense of a township: a village plus surrounding countryside, under the same local polity) with fewer than a thousand inhabitants. Yet even in western Massachusetts, let alone northern

Maine, many towns are in this perilous condition. The same is true across much of rural America, so one way or another urban migrants are sorely needed. The question is what sort of communities the newcomers will help rebuild, and whether they will make it possible for local people to remain and thrive alongside them. Will they reinvigorate the rural economy and keep the land available for farming and forestry, or will they simply treat it as a private getaway? Will they ship in most of their lumber from parts unknown (perhaps degrading faraway lands), while creating little more than low-paying service jobs at home? Will they leave room for, and help create, more affordable housing? In short, will they support rural places where those who were born here want to live and are able to stay?

The first impact of rural resettlement will be determined by what these migrants build and where they build it. The money they spend on their new digs will not be matched by what they spend on dinner for many years to come, so how they build will have consequences. Yet few seem to think about it like that. People tend to build whatever they desire in terms of style, size, and features, within the limits of what they can afford, without giving much thought to the origins of their materials. Many will eagerly seek out a local farm to patronize, without noticing the miles of forest they must drive through to reach it—or at least without recognizing all those trees as something houses could be built from, just as bodies are made of food.

Yet New England's recovered forest is so pervasive and so packed with superb timber, reaching far back into the suburbs, that *all* of the new construction and renovation in rural and even many exurban towns could directly incorporate a substantial amount of local wood, without dinging that forest much at all. Anyone who wants to build as we did could engage a timber framer and visit the trees that will be cut to build their house, should they wish to take a walk and see them. Through good forest management, rural areas can easily cover most of their other wood needs, as well.

How much cutting are we talking about? How much wood an American really "needs" is difficult to specify, because it depends on factors such as the average size of a house, how long it lasts, how much paper we consume, and how much we recycle. We could certainly reduce our average consumption. Making some conservative assumptions, my colleagues and I have calculated that between an acre and an acre and a half of forest could supply an amount equal to the wood consumption of each American, forever. In other words, something like four acres of forest stand behind each household. A bit less than half of that goes for lumber and the rest for paper and other "low-grade" uses such as fuel. In New England, we have that much forest close at hand, and then some.[7]

Let me put that another way: over a hundred-year period, two acres of well-managed forest can grow enough wood to build an average house—to frame, floor, finish, and furnish it. And repair and remodel it from time to time, as well. Two more acres will supply that household with all the paper it needs, not to mention the pencils to write on it. Plus a steady supply of fuel, if you live in the country, which you can kindle with your crumpled-up notes, as I do. This is a bit notional, of course: a given acre is unlikely to have the exact mix of woods you might want to build your house, and I am not suggesting you make your own pencils. But a *town* that has at least twice as many wooded acres as it has homes could pretty much keep itself housed forever, provided that it builds those homes to last at least a century. Slow houses. Even many exurban towns on the expanding fringes of suburbia, which typically contain a thousand or two homes, have that much forest—and much of it is now one hundred years old and therefore ripe for judicious timber harvesting. Most truly rural towns have far more at their disposal.

The average *rural* New England town contains from five to ten thousand acres of wonderfully diverse forest, typically covering three quarters of the landscape, if not more. That is enough timber to handily maintain and expand the local housing stock and also supply urban markets. Most rural towns contain about a thousand people, if that, occupying a few hundred dwellings. You can readily see that if those houses are built to last at least a century, just a handful of new ones every year is all it would take to maintain the stock. Add a second handful and you could expand that housing to a healthier level—providing homes for enough people to once again support local schools and other services. That double fistful of home construction projects, together with outbuildings and renovations, would suffice to keep a local network of wood craftspeople busy with highly skilled, well-paid work, forever.

Trust me, these people exist. They are eager for work. There are plenty of young people who would love to apprentice with them and learn their skills, if it meant steady employment doing something they love and

perhaps an opportunity to branch out on their own. Building just five or
ten timber frame houses *from local woodlands* every year would drop a few
million dollars into each rural town's economy and keep it there. That
increased local demand would multiply the shops of custom sawyers, millworkers, and framers and thus bring them closer to the work, reducing the
inordinate timber schlepping that we had to do—Dave Bowman's shop is
six towns away from ours. A couple of framers building with local timber
in every town would do wonders for these strapped places and could help
build a stronger constituency for conserving forests, too. This is a far cry
from city people who show up only to campaign to "protect" the forest by
stopping all logging.

Building locally holds great potential to improve the rural economy,
but it will require an equally great change of heart. Chainsaws are a different way to engage with forests than binoculars—not incompatible (I often
carry both in my truck), but a bit jarring to the uninitiated. Everybody
talks about eating local food, yet we live completely surrounded by local
wood, and hardly anybody talks about that. It probably does not occur to
many residents of the leafy outer suburbs that they could keep themselves
snugly housed forever by harvesting only 1 percent of their forest every
year, or that this might be a good idea. Instead, cutting trees has become
anathema: the forest is increasingly seen as precious sequestered carbon
that should be left alone to grow unmolested: "proforestation" (which is
nothing but a new name for preservation), or never cutting anything.

But how can we justify imposing a moratorium on timber harvesting
when we live in houses made of wood? That ethical framework is riddled
with termites of the genus *Nimby,* unbraced except by fantasy, and it cannot withstand the slightest breeze of reality. Today, we in Massachusetts are
harvesting only about one quarter of the annual growth of our forests and
congratulating ourselves on all the carbon we are storing. Yet at the same
time we are consuming *four times* that annual growth. In other words, in
my heavily wooded state we consume sixteen times the wood we are willing to cut in our own back yards—a mere 6 or 7 percent of what we use.
New England as a whole, which is even more heavily forested and has
an established wood industry up north that cuts hard, still supplies only
about three quarters of the wood products it consumes and just a little
more than half of its lumber. The issue is not whether trees will be cut to
produce two-by-fours and toilet paper, because they will be: the issue is
where and how those trees are cut.[8]

Too often, environmentally minded homebuilders acquire a lovely piece of wooded land and clear a site in the middle of the property, way up the hill where the views are grand. They build with lumber that comes from they know not where, harvested and milled by they know not whom. There they live remotely by Amazon and Zoom, zealous defenders of the forest in which they bathe, but whose trees they usually cannot name. They would never think of cutting trees on their own property (except for those necessary to clear the generous house site, half-mile-long driveway, and sweeping viewscape), and they often decry cutting any trees they can see beyond the swath that allows them to see. They consume wood products from distant lands, in order to preserve the illusion of wild nature close to home.

In this way the rural landscape is steadily fragmented and rendered less ecologically coherent and workable—by the passions of tree huggers. There is a better way, but it requires thinking like a village. It would be more honest, and more neighborly, for newcomers to place their houses closer to existing homes near the road so that the forest behind them remains intact, to build with wood from forests they can see, and to work as engaged citizens to ensure that more woodlands are conserved while development is concentrated in fewer places. That would ensure not only a permanent supply of timber but also other ecosystem benefits such as water quality, biodiversity, and, yes, carbon storage.[9]

Much of this new rural construction could be framed with local timbers. If you feel the need to clear an acre or two for your house, fine; but that's most of what you need to build it, right there. With timber framing many oddball and crooked trees, including hardwoods, that would be worthless for conventional stick framing become useful—in fact, in the right hands, the crookeder the better. If your builder doesn't know how to build a house like that, find one who does.

If you are going to build with local wood, you might as well enjoy it. It will cost about the same as conventional framing—maybe a little more, depending on what choices you make. Timber framing has a reputation for being extravagantly expensive, but it needn't be. A lot of the fancy frames you see in glossy magazines obviously cost a fortune, but *you* don't have to build like that. A timber frame is ravishing enough without ostentation. The only extravagance in our frame was the cherry braces, but those came from low-grade trees. Unless you are seduced by soaring hammer beams (which I'm sure your framer will be delighted to provide), the structure is

Faith retiring another slice of the pizza debt. (Kielan Donahue)

not going to affect the cost of your house that much, relatively speaking—instead, it's how many bathrooms, back kitchens, and breakfast nooks you think you need and above all how *big* you end up making the place. Our biggest indulgence was the masonry heater, but we're paying that off with the weekly savings on pizza. We do have a few payments left to go, admittedly. Someday, perhaps our grandchildren will retire the pizza debt, which will be like burning the mortgage, only amortized with prosciutto and Kalamata olives. After that, the next few centuries of wood-fired pizza will be free and clear.[10]

  If you can afford to build a house, you can afford to use local wood in whatever style you choose. By drawing your house directly from the surrounding forest you will support not only the usual contractors in the building trades—carpenters, plumbers, electricians, painters—but also the less familiar upstream woodworkers: foresters, loggers, sawyers, millworkers, timber framers, and cabinetmakers. Not to mention the stonecutters and masons, if you include a little local stone. We used Ashfield stone rough for the masonry stove but also cut and polished for kitchen countertops and bathroom tiles—a wonderful addition to the house. The impact of your choices will resonate, since you will want to show the place off. You will be insufferable, but the house will be great. By showcasing the beauty of local wood, you can expand the clientele for timber framing and the constituency for good forest stewardship, far and wide.

So far, so good: if those with ample means would build their new country places more conscientiously, connecting to local forests as avidly as they connect to local farms, that would do something to rebuild rural economies. But that alone cannot build just, sustainable communities. Affluent homebuilders drive up the price of land and often scrape away existing low-cost dwellings to replace them with something pricier, locally sourced or not. This gentrification has long been under way in many rural towns. It is better than towns being perpetually rundown—unless you are one of the people displaced by the new dispensation. To be truly sustainable, local economic revival must have mechanisms to rehabilitate existing affordable housing and create more. Protecting forest and farmland makes the remaining building sites more expensive, so land protectors must work equally hard to be housing providers. Otherwise, there will be no decent homes for the people who cut the trees and build the homes.

Providing adequate housing means first repairing and renovating existing housing and ensuring that it remains affordable, whether as rentals (sorely needed in most rural areas) or as a bridge to homeownership. Homes can remain affordable through some form of shared equity, such as that provided by a community land trust, which balances the community's need to keep housing costs from rising too fast with the homeowner's desire to build wealth in the appreciation of the property. Community land trusts can also develop new housing, as long as they are supplied with adequate means to acquire the *land.* Housing trusts can work hand in hand with conservation land trusts and regional planning agencies to coordinate protection of farmland and forests by dedicating appropriate sites for housing, sometimes on the same property. The key for both affordable housing and land protection is to shift more of our land base into some degree of local community ownership and control. Much more of this kind of collaboration between community housing and conservation is needed. The market, unassisted, has shown itself indifferent to satisfying basic human needs and instead delivers upscale sprawl in grating harness with homelessness.[11]

In rural areas, housing projects represent an opportunity to use local wood. Since the object of affordable housing is to maintain thriving communities, it only makes sense to stimulate the local economy all the way back to the woods. Using local materials and building to a high standard will make the resulting housing all the more affordable in the long run. If public funds are used to support the construction of housing, we should get the broadest benefit from it. In rural areas, such houses can be economically heated with efficient woodstoves, as well. Increased demand for rural homes that are built from local wood will create a reliable supply of the needed materials, close at hand, which is a virtuous cycle we want to encourage. Affluent newcomers who build timber frame houses can help rebuild that supply chain—the loggers, sawmills, and millworkers who provide local wood—which can then be more readily utilized by larger developers, for whom timely availability of materials is often as critical as price. In the countryside, the local wood economy can supply a range of attractive housing for everybody, if responsibly supported.[12]

The "conservation subdivision" of our own farm exemplified these principles on a small scale. We created a new home next to an existing one, protected the rest of the land, and built our house mainly from local timber. But that was not all: Tom and Joan renovated the rundown nineteenth-century farmhouse, opening the downstairs into a more modern configuration with a new kitchen, while blowing in foam insulation, putting in tighter windows, and trimming it all with red oak from our woodlot. But before Tom embarked on that project, he renovated the ell at the other end of the house and turned it into a cozy rental. Between us, we created three housing units where before there had been only one. We utilized local wood, while developing only two out of 170 acres of a still-working farm and woodlot. Why couldn't something similar happen on every rural property in the nation that comes up for sale?

Timber frame housing can give a welcome boost to the rural economy, as long as the right principles are applied. But there is a much larger demand side beyond the rural and local, which is unlikely to exceed 20 percent of the housing market. Can the same principles be applied to a regional forest and construction industry to help rebuild our cities?

Rebuilding urban areas with regional wood could elevate a valuable but limited niche market into a transformational movement. Rural revival must not neglect or abandon the city, as it so often has in the past—particularly during the period of postwar suburban sprawl, when white flight and disinvestment left behind urban decay—a double disgrace. We do need repopulation of rural areas, but more than that we need green and just redevelopment of our cities, especially those that have been hollowed out by the loss of industry and the middle class. Obviously, to make this possible we first need a decent living wage and full health benefits for working people. Given that, the best way to protect the countryside from sprawl is to make cities attractive, healthy places for people to live and build them to last. Can timber play a role in this monumental social imperative that is more beneficial than using other materials, such as steel and reinforced concrete? If so, rural revival could go hand in hand with urban renaissance.

Once again, the place to start is with adaptive reuse—minding the dictum that the "greenest building is the one that is already built." Great swaths of many older American cities are burdened (or potentially blessed) with thousands of old houses and commercial buildings that desperately need to be renovated—revitalizing neighborhoods with residences, shops, offices, and gathering spaces—if only adequate resources were sent their way. The nation is full of successful examples; the challenge is to ensure that all the property isn't snapped up by speculators and that public funding (often funneled through tax credits) doesn't get hijacked for private profit and gentrification. Too often, the poorest neighborhoods—frequently communities of color—are bypassed or pushed out, repeating the legacy of redlining and misguided "urban renewal." Public funds that flow to these neighborhoods should be directed by community groups that can make the best decisions about redevelopment: which old buildings to restore and which to demolish, what new buildings to build, where to incorporate community gardens and green spaces, who has access to the housing that is created.[13]

Given community control there is ample room for new urban development, and here timber has an exciting new role to play. Wood can help rebuild cities and towns, using technologies that are a modern version of timber framing, with a similar look and feel. Mass timber construction, which is suitable for office and institutional buildings as well as multi-unit housing, utilizes "engineered wood products" (EWP). The first important EWP to appear a century ago was plywood, followed by laminated veneer lumber (LVL), which is made of strips of plywood sandwiched together to form a beam—much stronger than solid wood of the same size. Those are now standard in conventional framing; like us, you probably have plywood on your walls and roof and a couple of LVL beams in your basement. The next generation of EWPs includes cross laminated timber (CLT) structural panels and glulam beams, which are analogous to plywood and LVLs, only composed of two-by-fours instead of veneer. These compound wooden materials, which are structurally comparable to steel and concrete but lighter and easier to install, could soon transform a significant part of the construction industry.

Mass timber construction opens up new possibilities in the realm of affordable housing. A good example in our region is the 340+ Dixwell project in New Haven, Connecticut. Dixwell is a historically Black neighborhood, plagued by decades of job loss and disinvestment. This four-story retail and housing development, sited on land owned by a local non-profit, is creating sixty-nine new units of housing, fifty-five of them affordable. The CLT and glulam structural design adds about a 5 percent construction cost premium, but it creates a more durable, healthy, and attractive structure with exposed wooden walls, ceilings, and stairwells. As mass timber becomes more widely adopted, and especially when used to reach greater heights, we can expect those costs to drop. But the concept is the key: high-quality housing for *everybody,* made of familiar and comfortable wood that people can see.[14]

Now we are talking about moving wood back into cities, growing like trees—not so much the downtown cores, but the residential and commercial rings that have rolled out from them over the past two centuries, where growth has been mostly horizontal. Many of these places cry out for denser, better-designed, mixed-use redevelopment. They can be connected to mass transit and surrounded by resurrected green spaces: rediscovered riversides and harbor fronts, daylighted streams, community gardens, parks, bicycle paths, and trails. Creating both denser development and green space is not paradoxical, but synergistic: first by reclaiming space from the automobile, and second by going up—but only as high as a majestic white pine. Such smart growth is hardly a new idea: state climate and housing plans have long embraced it, and many such projects are on the drawing board or under way. What is new is the idea that these new structures can be built primarily with *wood.* That can make it twice as smart, by connecting to the region's forests and thus helping rebuild rural economies at the same time.

Mass timber is perfect for redevelopment, especially in the mid-range. This makes for a carbon footprint trifecta: adding density to existing cities

and suburbs around transit hubs, storing carbon in buildings, and supporting a revived forest economy that also holds more carbon on the landscape
through better forestry. Mass timber buildings can safely rise to at least
twenty stories, but their greatest promise lies between six and twelve stories: too tall for conventional low-rise stick framing, but too short to justify
the higher fixed costs of much heavier high-rise structures made of concrete and steel. CLT wood panels are lighter and come prefabricated, making them relatively fast, economical, safe, and quiet to assemble. They can
store carbon for decades or centuries, while the forest they came from
continues to grow and scrub more carbon dioxide from the atmosphere.
They are an inhabitable carbon sink.[15]

Even better, CLT panels replace steel and concrete, the mining and
manufacture of which leave behind long, toxic environmental trails, pol-
luting the air and rooting up the earth. If there is anything we desperately
need to curtail on this poor pitted planet, it is more mining—including the
seemingly innocuous sand that goes into concrete. Wood alone cannot
provide the infrastructure of a modern industrial society, but it can bear
significantly more of the load. The carbon advantages that accrue to timber by "life cycle analysis" vary according to the projected lifetime of the
building, how much of it is ultimately recycled, and the different manufacturing processes assumed—but they are substantial. Concrete and steel are
not going to disappear, and the environmental impact of their manufacture
must also be improved. But if done well, building with timber has over-
whelming environmental advantages. Plus, timber buildings are more livable, which adds to the lifetime of both the building and its occupants. If
we want buildings to store carbon for generations, they must be built so
that generations of people are inspired and empowered to care for them.[16]

Mass timber is also ideal for mid-sized commercial and institutional
buildings, which may represent an even larger market than multi-unit
housing. Not far down the road from our house stands the prize-winning
John Olver Design Building, which houses the University of Massachusetts building and construction technology program, along with its architecture and regional planning departments. This handsome five-story
structure, which opened in 2017, is a modern timber frame. Outside, the
Design Building is an ordinary-looking glass and aluminum-clad modern
campus edifice. Inside, it is a revelation. With its exposed wooden frame
it feels uncannily like our house, grown up to the size of a cathedral. The

frame is made of glulam posts, beams, and diagonal braces, many of them left exposed. The walls and stairways are composed of CLT panels, a five-layer sandwich of crisscrossed two-by-fours. The atrium is crowned with the modern equivalent of a medieval timber truss: a soaring steel and wood "zipper truss" that supports a roof garden. The floors combine CLT panels with a concrete slab on top, for added stiffness and ease of maintenance. There is no need for a dropped ceiling beneath those floor panels: sitting in a classroom or lab you look up and see massive wooden beams supporting a ceiling of crossing planks, which is the underside of the CLT panels holding the floor above. The structure *is* the decoration—the sub-flooring *is* the ceiling. When I visit, I feel right at home.[17]

Steel beams were used for a few longer spans, but even those were clad in wood for fire resistance. Wait—how can wood be more fireproof than steel? Well, it isn't generally the structure of a building that ignites and burns—it's all the stuff inside. A key safety concern is how long the structure holds its integrity before it collapses. A steel beam reaches a maximum temperature and then droops like a noodle, whereas wood of sufficient thickness chars on the outside and maintains its strength much longer. So, counterintuitive as it seems, wood cladding can insulate and fireproof steel. Now I know what I have been trying to conjure into being by burning all those sacrificial wood structures in my masonry stove, of a cold winter's night: a brave new world of mass timber construction.

Throughout the Design Building, wood, metal, glass, and concrete are used together in creative and attractive ways. But wood predominates, generating a warmth and comfort that is missing in most modern office and classroom buildings, as those who spend most of their working lives inside them can attest. People are generally biophilic: we prefer to live surrounded by wood, which mass timber construction accomplishes. There are efforts under way to certify CLT panels made from New England softwoods such as spruce, white pine, and hemlock, with the goal to begin manufacturing them in the region. In Europe, CLT panels are often composed of hardwoods, as well, which would suit our prevailing forests in the Northeast even better. That is the critical next step in mass timber construction: connecting it to regional manufacturing and sustainable forestry, thereby completing the circle and bringing it home.[18]

Wood can join the need for affordable housing and revitalized urban communities with the need for sustainable forestry and revitalized rural economies. But the crucial underlying connection is political. It may not be obvious, on the surface, that urban and rural people share these interests. Indeed, one could argue that those working to rebuild urban neighborhoods should use the least expensive materials they can get, whereas those working to revive regional lumber production shouldn't worry too much if their products are going mostly for gentrification. But the market hegemony that has long kept both communities from gaining control of their own destinies is one and the same, and the solutions are strikingly similar: more community ownership of land, and more stakeholder control of decision-making that is in the common interest. So, this connection isn't just about the flow of lumber: it is about building regional political coalitions that are strong enough to overcome vested interests, breaking the power of those who profit from business as usual.

Similarly, mass timber buildings *could* take the ecological principles that are embodied in our timber frame house, translate them to modern construction, and tie them back to regional forests in the same healthy way. But those principles are hardly a given: they must be imposed by political force. The greenhouse gas and other environmental savings of wood construction could be substantial, but only if the forestry supplying that timber is sound. The largest carbon benefits come from improved forest management. Whether we are talking about building a traditional timber frame, putting up a mid-rise mass timber apartment building, or burning low-grade wood for heat, the benefits of using wood are hardly automatic. They do not accrue simply by substituting wood for concrete, steel, oil, or coal. They come only when the spirit of sustainability by which the building is constructed is successfully carried back to the forest, with ecological values placed foremost at both ends of the chain. Cities should be made green, and their residents should be happy that trees are cut to house them—but only if they are also pleased with the manner in which those trees are cut. Like our farmhouse, urban mass timber buildings should reflect pride in the ecological health of the forest from whence they came.[19]

Realizing the full environmental benefits of building with wood hinges entirely on the forestry that provides the timber. That supply side of the equation returns us to rural New England, or any other forested region. The carbon value of "worst first" silviculture is substantial, but let's not focus too narrowly on carbon. We need to account for all of the forest's ecological and social benefits: water quality, wildlife habitat, recreational use, beauty. That is the central premise of this book: beautiful buildings that stand within beautiful landscapes should be inward and outward reflections of the same thing. So, while we are harvesting wood products to build our homes, here are three principles that will safeguard the health and beauty of our forests: conserving land, designating wildlands, and improving ecological management.

First, let us permanently protect all the forest we can and strictly limit its conversion to other uses. This principle has already been invoked on the demand side of the equation, because it requires the concentration of housing—here, I will elaborate on it. Second, let's devote a meaningful portion of that conserved forest to expansive wild areas that are only passively managed. Third, and most important to this discussion, let us manage the productive portion of the forest on long rotations that maximize timber (rather than pulp or chips), maximize carbon stored in living trees, and maximize the other ecological benefits that the forests provide. That is, instead of ecological values surviving (or perishing) as unintended consequences of financial decisions, timber harvesting should be constrained by ecological values. Ecology should drive forestry.

For ecological forestry to be practiced, the forest must first be kept safe—not only from conversion to hardscape, but from ruthless wood extraction. I am among the authors of the *Wildlands and Woodlands* vision for the future of New England (first published in 2010), which calls for *at least* 70 percent of the region to remain in forest, permanently protected from development. As New England is presently 80 percent forested, this is close to a "no net loss" policy that still allows for a small amount of clustered rural "smart growth" and energy development. It could also accommodate some expansion of farmland (as proposed in *A New England Food Vision*), all of which should also be protected. Protecting at least three quarters of the landscape in forests and farms obviously won't happen overnight, but we believe it can be accomplished within the next fifty years or so. About 25 percent of New England has already been protected over the past century, with a quickening pace in recent decades, so this isn't such a wild and crazy dream.[20]

Why so much formal land protection? After all, most of the remaining forest isn't about to disappear. Given the present rate of sprawl it isn't as if the entire region will be overrun by tract housing and shopping malls (or even solar panels) anytime soon, although there are places where that is a real danger. The greater threat to rural New England is landownership that becomes increasingly fragmented, leaving the forest perforated by widely dispersed vacation homes. This "parcelization" interrupts the ecological fabric of the forest and makes it more difficult to manage in a coherent way. It also tends to remove scarce farmland from food production, a parallel problem. The most basic layer of land protection aims to at least prevent this scattered low-density development. In recent decades, this has been accomplished primarily by acquiring conservation easements on private land, such as our farm. Much more needs to be done along these lines.[21]

That level of protection is far better than nothing, but it is not nearly enough. In northern New England, enormous tracts of such "protected" land remain in the hands of absentee corporate owners whose financial interest lies in short-term wood extraction rather than the long-term health of the forest or of rural communities. Having cashed in the development rights by selling an easement to some obliging non-profit, they continue to cash in the trees by cutting them as fast as they can grow. The resulting ecological degradation is not a theoretical possibility: it is the well-documented outcome of decades of routine behavior by financialized forest owners who control twelve million acres of our region. They are doing just what their shareholders expect them to do, which is hew to the bottom line—exactly what private industry has been doing to American forests for two hundred years, as we have seen. Acquiring over two million acres of conservation easements on such lands has thus far accomplished next to nothing.[22]

I can see no justification for private ownership of tracts of thousands (let alone millions) of acres of forest in a world running headlong into a climate crisis. Private ownership ought to be limited to the farm woodland scale—or at least, public and philanthropic funds should not be squandered to purchase easements that primarily benefit private owners of more than, let us say, a thousand acres. Large tracts of forest would better be held in a mixture that includes wildlands owned by state governments, community woodlands owned by municipalities and non-profit land trusts, and tribal land rematriated to Native communities. Over the years, a handful of commendable large private owners have taken good care of their forest, but most have not. What hope is there that these principled outliers will long survive in an economy increasingly ruled by private equity? The days of large-scale private forest ownership, upon which the sun should never have risen in the first place, should now be left behind. If public money can be invested to "protect" large swaths of corporate forest by purchasing easements, why not go one step further and acquire the land in fee as community forests, to be managed in the public interest by local people who really care for them? This approach would cost substantially more in the short run but yield real, rather than illusory, public benefits in the long run.

Once the forest is protected, how should it be managed? Should it be allowed to go wild, or should it be sustainably harvested? Why not some of both? In *Wildlands and Woodlands* we suggest that at least 10 percent of the landscape should be designated as unmanaged wild reserves. In our region that would amount to four million acres, which could include wild tracts in northern New England of a million acres or more, as wilderness advocates have long advocated. But it would also include wildlands of intermediate size—thousands of acres—even in more densely settled southern New England, along with numerous smaller local wildlands on the scale of a few hundred acres. Henry Thoreau envisioned such a wild reserve surrounding Walden Pond, for example, in some of his last writing. His call to preserve Walden Woods has long since been answered, and it should be echoed in every town.[23]

Wildlands allow for the development of old-growth structure, and large reserves provide ample room for natural landscape-scale disturbances to drive forest dynamics. Similar ecological conditions were widespread in the past when Native people were stewards of the land, and such conditions should be well represented in the future to support a full range of biodiversity. Where harvesting occurs, even the best-managed productive woodlands can never be dominated by large ancient trees, standing dead snags, and voluminous coarse woody debris on the forest floor—precisely because long-rotation management for timber means eventually cutting and removing most of those big old trees. Therefore, for the sake of full biological diversity we need to devote some portion of the landscape to wildlands where no wood at all is harvested.[24]

Affording overcivilized modern citizens access to wild, unmanaged natural places for respite and inspiration is a cultural benefit as well. This book is deeply concerned with reforging a working relationship with harvested woodlands, but that active connection needs to be balanced with the humility that we experience in places where nature is allowed to take its own course. Yoking wildlands alongside productive woodlands in an expansive vision makes not only ecological but political sense. It is a plea for harmony not just in nature but in the conservation community, with everybody pulling together toward an ambitious common goal, rather than wrangling over each little slice of a shrinking pie. Some might argue for more wildlands in that mix, but even by the most generous accounting, only 3 percent of New England is formally designated as wilderness today. We might aspire to having more than 10 percent of the region set aside for wildlands someday, but making that first tithe would be a good start.[25]

To walk in wildlands with a clear conscience, we should put our house in order by producing the wood we use more sustainably. The need for timber remains great, and *most* of the ecological benefits of wild forests, including biodiversity, can be provided just as well by diverse, well-managed woodlands—and over a much wider area. To care for productive woodlands responsibly, we need ecological forestry. Of course the existing forest products industry—including regimented fast-wood plantations, which are rapidly expanding globally—likes to claim that it is sustainable. But to be legitimate, that term must adhere to one simple idea: ecological values must be placed first and wood production second. Harvested forest needs to take on this larger environmental role because there is no practical alternative. We do not presently have half an earth to spare for "more-than-human" nature. Because there is little or no prospect of setting aside enough wild forest to safeguard all the ecological services we depend upon, we must manage productive forest so that it also delivers those benefits: carbon storage, water quality, biodiversity. The responsibility of striking this difficult balance over the shared earth cannot be shirked. It falls to everyone who consumes forest products, especially those who live in regions that have forests.[26]

To put ecological values first, forest managers need to pay attention to natural processes. These vary among forest types, which are composed of different mixes of species corresponding to a wide range of soils, climates, and disturbance regimes. Disturbances, such as windstorms or fires, are the primary drivers of natural forest dynamics. Ecological foresters aim to roughly mimic two aspects of those dynamics: how young forests grow and how older forests are regenerated. This is inescapably a "rough" process in two senses of that word: it cannot precisely replicate

natural dynamics but it can come close; and it involves toppling and removing trees, which is rough stuff. In nature trees might indeed be toppled, but they would not be removed—at least not by dragging them away.
Such impacts cannot be avoided in productively managed forests, but they
can be softened. Let us examine one cycle of this process from start to
finish (which is also a fresh start).[27]

Whenever a disturbance creates an opening large enough that the
canopy cannot close and a burst of light reaches the ground, forests start
to regrow. At first, many more seedlings spring up than will ultimately
survive—in fact, in most cases they are constantly appearing before the
disturbance even occurs; foresters call this advance regeneration. The
mother trees may help nourish these seedlings through networks of roots
and mycorrhizae, but in the end only a few will make it into the canopy. I
have already described how the inevitable mortality of a large portion of
this exuberant young growth can be captured by periodic thinning and
turned into products such as firewood, while nudging the remaining trees
toward higher-value timber and accelerating their growth. Earlier I argued
that removing and burning such young trees is essentially carbon neutral,
because most of them would have soon died and decayed anyway. Meanwhile, the overall growth of the stand has been concentrated in the most
valuable remaining trees. But what comes next, once those favored trees are
larger and becoming mature?

At about one hundred years of age, hardwoods such as red oak and
sugar maple have generally reached their full height, though taller white
pines may emerge above the canopy and continue to ascend. By that time
early successional species such as black birch and red maple have mostly
disappeared, or they are trapped beneath the canopy and will likely be
squeezed out over the next few decades. From that point on, the remaining dominant trees slowly add not so much height as girth, ring by patient
ring. Now any disturbance, whether natural or man-made, will create an
opening large enough to release that continuously replenished layer of
seedlings and saplings on the forest floor, initiating the next cycle of growth.
The most consequential silvicultural decisions concern the scope and timing of harvesting most of those large trees: how long to wait, and how hard
to cut?[28]

Mature trees that have reached the canopy are capable of living for
centuries, and much is often made of this romantic fact. We tend to feel

reverence for beings so much older and larger than ourselves, which is only natural—like any hobbit, I bow to the ents of Fangorn Forest. But that potential does not mean that *all* such mother trees will live that long, because being a towering tree is a perilous occupation, even in the absence of orcs equipped with chainsaws. Among northern hardwoods, single trees may die from a variety of causes, often taking several neighboring trees down with them when they fall; or groups are shredded and snapped in localized windstorms. Such disturbances tend to create small gaps that again favor shade-tolerant species such as sugar maple, beech, and hemlock. Southward and toward the coast, larger disturbances such as hurricanes and fires sometimes let in more light, favoring medium shade-tolerant trees such as oaks and pines. These sporadic dynamics take place over a topography of varied soils and slopes, creating a complex mosaic that shifts with time. That mosaic is dominated by older trees at most times and places, but it also contains many patches of younger trees, which harbor their own suite of forest creatures.

Following European colonization, this already jumbled pattern has been thoroughly scrambled by sweeping pendulum swings of unprecedented, crosscutting disturbances: agricultural clearing, agricultural abandonment; fire promotion, fire suppression; herbivore extirpation, herbivore explosion; heavy cutting, cutting cessation; invasive insects and diseases; and now, rapid climate change. Many of these anthropogenic impacts are ongoing, and some are accelerating; but even were people to suddenly disappear, the consequences of what has happened in the past four hundred years would continue to play out for centuries to come. It is not possible to restore the forest that once was, even if ecologists could agree on the exact nature of that forest—which, believe me, they never will. But perhaps we can care for the forest that has emerged from this unsettled past in ways that keep all the remaining species in play and that at least resemble the structure and dynamics that once prevailed, while we also use most of that forest productively. That is a more useful and achievable goal than striving for, and endlessly wrangling over, some chimera of complete ecological restoration.[29]

Ecological forest management aims to maintain or enhance existing species diversity and mimic natural disturbance patterns, while harvesting wood products. This is a restrained approach: good foresters are humbly uncertain about what they are doing, so they tend to take it easy out there.

They know that there are more variables to how the forest they are "managing" will actually develop than they can comprehend, let alone control—and they won't even live to see most of it. In our region, dominated by long-lived deciduous trees, restraint means extending the age to which trees are allowed to grow so that mature forests always dominate the landscape and, when it's time, cutting trees in ways that maintain diversity at every scale. This creates a landscape mosaic in which the vast majority of plant and animal species will be able to move about and thrive, under shifting conditions that are similar to what they have experienced for thousands of years. A forest that is producing timber cannot be expected to reproduce old-growth structure—but it can move a long way in that direction. Besides, with the "Wildlands and Woodlands" approach we will have plenty of unmanaged wild reserves to play that old-growth role, so we will not need to replicate it exactly in the forests we productively manage.

Woodlands should be managed so that at any given time a large part of the forest is mature, while the rest is made up of scattered patches in earlier successional stages. This does not generally require precise planning, which human beings don't do well over such long time scales anyway. It can be accomplished collectively across a town or an entire region more or less at random, simply by extending the age to which existing trees are allowed to grow while maintaining steady output overall—in other words, never cutting too much at once. Under this philosophy, northern hardwoods are typically managed by periodic single tree selection or small group harvests, which create small gaps. This eventually produces "uneven-aged" stands that closely resemble the ancient condition of this forest type, although the mature trees will never get quite as old. Oaks and pines can be favored through group selection that creates larger gaps, or by shelterwood and seed tree harvesting, letting in enough light to help regenerate these valuable species—along with an early surge of red maple and black birch that is eventually overtaken, as we have seen on our place. In other regions such as parts of the South and West, ecological forestry might call for the inclusion of prescribed burning to maintain more open stands of scattered timber trees and to help prevent more catastrophic fires.

In our hardwood region a good average rotation to produce the highest quality timber and get the most value from the mature trees might be at least 120 years, varying from site to site. This allows the trees several decades to grow the outside "clear" lumber that forms once the canopy has closed and lower branches have been shed. Under a harvesting regime of well over a century, whether in a town forest of a few thousand acres or across millions of acres of New England woodlands, less than 1 percent of the forest would be subjected to a regenerating harvest and set back to zero in any given year. The majority of the landscape would be covered with mature and middle-aged stands, with early successional patches scattered here and there, along with old-growth reserves that are never cut. My colleagues and I have calculated that about twenty million acres of New England forest managed in this way—50 percent of the region, or a bit more than 60 percent of its forest—could provide all the wood products we need. That is a diverse forest that every tree hugger and birdwatcher in New England can learn to love—and in fact the Audubon societies of Vermont and Massachusetts are working with foresters like Lincoln Fish to help create it.[30]

And every logger and homebuilder should love it, too. Consider the revived forest economy that such management could support. The resurgence of white pine across southern and central New England, so keenly desired by twentieth-century foresters and now finally coming into its own, can provide structural material for both rural timber frames and urban mass-timber apartment buildings, for many decades to come—forever, if managed properly. The same is true for hemlock across central New England (for as long as it survives the adelgid) and spruce across the north. The best of the pine and spruce will also yield clear boards for casework and trim, provided the rotations are long enough to grow knot-free wood. As for hardwoods, red oak in the south and sugar maple in the north, along with black and yellow birch and the myriad other species that grow alongside them, will offer a nice selection for flooring, trim, cabinets, and furniture—and can play an important role in timber framing as well. These are the high-grade timber products for which we should be managing. They correspond to a forest dominated by large, mature trees that are harvested at a slow, steady rate. That is the dual beauty of slow wood.

Practicing ecological forestry will also generate plenty of low-grade wood—there is no getting around that. There will always be tops and crooked trees to thin. Such low-grade wood can be utilized as fuel and pulp, as part of a sustainable forest economy. But these short-lived uses, which quickly return carbon dioxide to the atmosphere, should be minimized. Producing low-grade material efficiently should not be the goal of

forest management, as it has long been in industrial regions dominated by
pulp. We do not need a slew of biomass plants across the region, and we
do not need to fully resuscitate the paper industry. Our society can prosper using far less paper—as indeed we have been for decades now, since
the rise of the internet. We do not need short-rotation cutting for pulp,
biomass, or anything else. Management that externalizes social and environmental costs is the hallmark of fast wood. To internalize social and
environmental benefits, we need slow wood.[31]

Many durable and appealing products can be made from low-grade
wood—from curved cherry braces to live-edge bars to spalted maple bowls.
Or even peeled-pole balusters like those on our stairs, which are *below-
grade* wood—saplings that mostly weren't going anywhere anyway. Such
artisanal niche markets may never amount to a large volume, but they stand
for the wide array of diverse goods that might flow from a healthy regional
forest economy and forest culture—a second American Wooden Age, more
conscientious and sustainable than the first. New engineered wood products are appearing that might utilize much more of the low-grade feed-
stock, such as wood fiber insulation. This material locks up carbon and
lowers home energy consumption at the same time. In contrast to biomass
or paper, it could provide a high-volume use of wood chips that is non-
consumptive. Wood fiber insulation can be applied not only as blown-in
fill but as rigid boards that also serve as exterior sheathing. If we were
building our timber frame house today, we might be sheathing it with
wood-fiber boards instead of SIPs (or perhaps with a wood-fiber version
of SIPs), upgrading from a high-tech product made largely of petroleum
to a high-performance product made of waste wood. Now, too, weather-
resistant thermally modified woods can replace pressure-treated lumber
in siding and decking, and these products can be made from low-grade
species such as red maple. As we have seen in our house, low-grade hardwoods can play a stand-out role in traditional timber frames, and they can
be incorporated into mass timber panels and beams as well. With the
proper commitment, we can find environmentally friendly wood products
that make use of every stick that comes from ecologically minded forestry,
shrinking our carbon footprint until the atmosphere can no longer detect
our presence among the trees. That is the future to which every lover of
forest should be laboring to give birth.[32]

» » « «

Building a traditional timber frame house from local woodlots is scalable, by endless repetition. All it requires is that thousands of like-minded homebuilders make similar choices, patronizing local woodworkers. It can be repeated at the scale of the community across rural America and again at the scale of entire regions to rebuild cities. Building single-family houses with local wood is straightforward—it may be less efficient than relying on global lumber markets, but it builds a more robust and resilient local economy. Connecting urban housing to sustainable use of the region's forests involves a more complex (though strikingly similar) set of timber construction technologies and supply chains, but it can draw upon exactly the same silviculture. This is all very doable.

Getting it to happen is another matter. It will require radical changes in who owns the forest and how we incentivize its management, in place of raw market forces. When it comes to ownership, I have long argued that forest land needs to move steadily from private ownership toward several kinds of reclaimed commons. These can range from conservation easements covering smaller private woodlots (such as our farm) to community forests owned by land trusts and municipalities (such as the Weston town forest) and to much larger tribal lands and state-owned wildlands, in places where the forest is held in vast tracts. In terms of management, the restrained ecological forestry I have described is not as profitable as cutting early and often, because time is money. But for patient owners willing to think of the future, slow wood yields a steady return over the long haul, along with satisfaction day by day. This should make it sufficiently rewarding to family and non-profit forest owners and to the stewards of community-owned forests. It will never be attractive to private equity, but to repeat: people for whom a sustainable return is not fast enough should be relieved of the burden of owning forest, or for that matter anything else whose intrinsic worth transcends its productive capacity.

Slow wood stewardship yields much more important returns to society as a whole, in the form of water quality, carbon storage, and biodiversity. Therefore, society should make a slow but steady stream of payments to owners who protect their land and adhere to the high standard of practices that provide these ecosystem benefits. Some of this support should flow to rural municipalities as well, which tend to lose tax revenue when land is protected—although that loss can be made up if protection is balanced by the clustered construction of new homes and other needed development. In addition, both private and public buyers of wood products should be encouraged to patronize local and regional sources of timber where ecological forest management has been certified. This may be a matter of choice for private consumers; it should become a matter of policy for public agencies. In short, as a society we need to find ways to reward owners who care for their woods as if their grandchildren depended on it. State and federal climate plans can help provide incentives and funding, as long as they don't focus too narrowly on carbon but rather on all the ecological benefits of well-managed forests. The forest is not going to save us from climate change, but it can do its part.[33]

This returns us to the role that can be played by affluent people who move to the country—people like Faith and me. The Covid pandemic has set off a new wave of urban refugees. Who knows how far this surge will reach or how long it will last? More waves will surely follow, just as they have in the past, and climate change will drive them. These new owners may pose obstacles, if they plant their fine house on the hill, stand on their presumed environmental principles, and use their wealth and influence to resolutely oppose all logging that takes place within their view. Instead, they should use the same power to help show the way. In building their house, they can provide a welcome market for local wood that is hewn by local woodsmen. That is a good start. It is similar to the demand for local food: over the past few decades regenerative farmers have successfully created a strong niche market among the well-to-do; now that must be systematically expanded to become available to everyone, as it always should have been. Getting local food to more people will require deliberate policy aimed at greater equity of access, *not* lower cost of production. The same is true of local wood.

It is not enough that wealthy homebuilders patronize local wood, but at least it is a step in the right direction. The key is taking that next step. Just as important as becoming enlightened consumers, these people can take action to conserve land as engaged citizens. Instead of crowning the hill, their home could be set closer to the road and to their neighbors, leaving the woods on the hill permanently protected and available for sustainable management, with a trail climbing to the top, where everyone can walk to survey a lovely landscape of wooded hills also not crowned by showy houses. Beyond conserving their own property (instead of consuming it) conscientious owners can also contribute to protecting surrounding woodlands, collaborating with land trusts to acquire land for community forests and working farms. These are social investments in the village that new property owners should feel obliged to make. We need to think about the privilege of landownership in a new way.

I feel comfortable dispensing such sweeping edicts because we have followed them ourselves, in a small way. Our land is protected, and we chose to site our house close to our neighbors—who were also, conveniently, our farm partners and friends. I know others who have quietly done more and who do not appear to have suffered—just the opposite. For most of the past half century Faith and I lived in a wealthy suburban town whose citizens have been willing to tax themselves to buy and protect one quarter of the landscape as common forest and farmland, even as it was being relentlessly developed. Time and time again since the 1950s, Weston conservationists have gone to town meeting, and time and again we have come away with the funds to conserve more land, usually by landslide votes. Similar things can happen in rural towns such as the one where we now live, but their citizens often do not have such ample means to conserve land as do those who live in affluent towns like Weston. Yet our goals should not be modest, but audacious: to conserve not just one quarter, but *three* quarters of the landscape. We consequently need to attract outside funding to these efforts—we cannot leave it to impoverished rural communities themselves. Community forests are being created in rural New England towns where land is protected both for recreation and for the kind of productive economic engagement I have been describing, so that the whole town benefits. As a society, we must devote adequate resources to carry on this work at a much larger scale, because it benefits all of us.[34]

Even the most positive actions taken by affluent landowners who move to rural towns are not enough—they still risk creating enclaves of privilege. Ultimately, local land protection needs to be supported by ample state and federal funding so that it can succeed in all communities, and it must be directed by community stakeholders to aim at broader social goals, including affordable housing. Securing that funding will require a long, patient struggle, just as it always has. But in the meantime, in this time of social and environmental crisis, those with ample means have not only an opportunity but an obligation to contribute, and contribute amply. They need to invest not just in their own property but in the permanent protection and stewardship of the surrounding landscape and community. Buying a piece of the country should come with a social covenant to work for the betterment of the countryside as a whole.

Our farm from the west: the new house is on the right, with the woodlot on the hill behind it. This remains a working landscape. A century ago the hill would have been clear halfway up; a century and a half ago, it was perhaps clear to the top. (Brian Donahue)

The way we build our houses matters. It matters obviously in reducing the carbon dioxide that buildings emit by heating and cooling. It also matters in a way that should be equally apparent but has long been ignored: reducing the ecological footprint of the embodied materials from which houses are made. Yes, the walls should be better insulated, but what are those walls made of? The greenest material is wood, which connects us directly to the world's forests, for better or worse. For the sake of both satisfaction and responsibility, it should connect us to our own forests, where we can also go walking to gaze upon our handiwork. In New England, we need houses, and we have trees. We live in a forest: why should anyone else be growing our timber? Much of the world is on fire, and our forests can help quell the flames and cool the planet—but not by benign neglect, which demands nothing from us. We are blessed with an opportunity and confronted with a duty: to join the construction of our houses to the conservation of our home forests.

TEN

Slow Food, Slow Fire, Slow Wood

LIKE MOST PEOPLE, I LOVE WOOD FIRES. Unlike most people, I live by wood fires. We heat with wood, and we often cook with it, sometimes directly over the coals. This was normal for most of human history—but not anymore. On planet Earth, there is not much difference between lighting a fire and being alive. Like fire, our bodies draw air to oxidize carbon compounds; we emit carbon dioxide. We are creatures who burn slowly from within, until we are gone.

Fire can destroy as easily as it creates, and never more so than now. Fire is our friend until it burns down the house, or the planet. This is not a happy time for people who love fire. According to my fellow environmental historian Stephen Pyne, when humans jilted Primeval Fire (organic carbon) for the seductive wiles of Promethean Fire (fossil carbon), we conceived and brought forth upon this planet a new era: the "Pyrocene." That may be a better name for our time than the nearly synonymous "Anthropocene," because mastery of fire is the prime mover of the modern world. Fire has elevated our species, though it is not clear who is mastering whom. We have met burning man, and he is us.[1]

The paradox of fire as both creator and destroyer defined life on earth long before *Homo sapiens* rubbed two sticks together and stared into the flames, but it has only recently become an existential problem for most living matter—well, maybe once before, but that was long, long ago, before there were people around to fret about it. How much fire is too much fire? Even in this time of crisis, I can't accept that the only correct answer is "any fire." Solar electricity may seem innocent of combustion, but I'm not sure we want to completely disown earthly fire. Will we still be human if we do? Surely not all fire is evil. Besides which, fire is not going away.

In this book I have written about using wood to build our homes and

The house in winter. (Michael Lovett, courtesy of Brandeis University)

to warm our skins. But our deepest relationship with wood is doubtless to cook our food, to warm us from within. Fire for warmth allowed a handful of our ancestors to venture from Africa into temperate and polar latitudes in spite of the looming ice of the last glaciation; but several glacial cycles before that, at the dawn of our species, it may be that fire for cooking made us human in the first place. It rendered our food (both animal and vegetable) softer and more digestible, giving us a surplus of metabolic energy. It shrank our guts and jaws and made room for our swelling brains to exploit that surge of energy, so they say. It gave us a comfortable place to sit under the stars and tell the stories that came spilling from those overstuffed, overstimulated heads, tales to console ourselves for the gift of conscious mortality. Those stories and the knowledge they encode are the basis of culture. They are given poetic shape and musical sound by our repurposed tongues, in a futile (though often amusing) attempt to make sense of our existence. But from a planetary perspective, the meaning of human existence is plain to see.

Even though our ultimate purpose remains obscure, the central *mean-*

ing of our existence, our place on earth, has thus far been to make fire. Fire is what sets us apart, as a species. This is our edge: all animals oxidize their food; we can burn *everything*. Up to now, our business has been mainly to set the planet ablaze. The evidence is incontrovertible, but the verdict is still out. Are we the crown of creation, or is making fire a crime against nature? Once a misdemeanor, now bumped up to a felony? Possibly a capital offense? A jury of our peers, drawn from the pool of living creatures, is filing back in, looking grim. The hanging judge is rising from the bench, waiting to pronounce sentence.

This is stuff you think about while cooking dinner; at least, I do. Especially when you are alone on a Friday night, as I often am when I come out a day early to get some farm work done and the house warmed up for the family, loading heat into the stone. Presumably, the original way to cook something was to grill it, as boiling requires more gear. It has been suggested that perhaps our forebears first came upon cooked meat and tubers while scavenging in the ashes following wildfires, before we were capable of bringing the embers home. Be that as it may, ever since I learned how, I have been grilling over wood coals at least once a week, year-round. I don't grill anything fancy, just beef steaks, pork chops and ribs, lamb kebabs, chicken, striped bass, shrimp and scallops, stuff like that. Every now and then I smoke a duck. Nights I don't grill, we make more complex meals, some with meat, some without. After pork chops, we are ready for pesto. Beef and pork from our farm are my usual fare, cooked over wood cut along the fence line.

Among local woods, sugar maple, oak, and hickory make the best coals. Sugar maple likes to volunteer by falling on the fence. You wouldn't want to spurn such generosity, though sugar maple burns the coolest. That just means leaving the steak on an extra minute, especially when the air temperature is well below freezing like this. I cut my grilling wood twelve inches long and split it about two inches thick. I have two stacks side-by-side on the back porch, one of which rises and seasons while the other one shrinks and burns. They look like a caricature of real woodpiles. Hey, that must be the kids' pile, you think—how cute. But no, it's just dad amusing himself with yet another way to stack wood and burn it.

I light the kindling fire of birch bark and twigs that sits atop my crisscross stack of maple splits in the Weber kettle. Top-firing is perfect for grilling, partly because it minimizes smoke, but mostly because it optimizes coals. Once the top layer has caught, I go inside and put the fingerling potatoes and olive oil in the oven to roast. The cubed butternut squash and coarse-chopped garlic will join them after about twenty minutes. The potatoes and garlic come from the garden, the squash from the farm—we are still in the squash and pumpkin business, in a small way, growing a few tons to deliver to farmstands and CSAs back in the suburbs. It's a good way to get some cash return while reseeding a few acres of pasture every year. Also, as I stated earlier, I hate driving back to Weston with an empty truck—I feel more virtuous with eight hundred pounds of squash riding behind me. We eat a good bit of squash ourselves, and by December the butternut is just hitting its peak of nutty sweetness. We can keep it to next July or August—butternut (which is gooseneck crossed with blue hubbard) has amazing antioxidant properties, though it gradually loses its flavor. We also feed about half of what we grow to the pigs—some say they can taste the pumpkins in the pork, but I can't.

Back outside, the fire takes hold as the afterglow of sunset fades in the west—a smooth transition from celestial to domestic illumination. That's a switch we learned to flip a long time ago. The flames are still mostly on top but working their way down. It is a calm evening so the fire sinks slow and steady, the orange flames rising straight up. Every now and then I re-center pieces that burn in half and tumble down the side. Properly tended, the fire descends evenly to the bottom, so soon the whole pile is burning as one, the flames showing more yellow as their temperature rises. This ensures a uniform bed of coals about forty-five minutes after I light it. Everything else—the roasted potatoes and squash, the steamed broccoli, what have you—has to be timed to that moment. Such is the discipline of grilling with wood—at least, the way I do it.

Grilling this way the cooking window is brief: not many coals are produced, and they don't last long. The steak goes on just before the flames disappear, when the heat is most intense, to get that good sear. It will finish with a few more minutes on each side as the coals fade. The heat is being conveniently reduced. As the steak cooks, I drop small pieces of hickory bark on the coals, whose smoke has a spicy cinnamon smell that is evocative of something vaguely familiar yet indescribable, both earthy and ethereal. I'm not sure you can taste hickory smoke in the steak crust, but if you smell it while you are cooking, you will remember it while you are eating and *think* you can taste it, which is just as good or possibly even better. If I'm grilling pork or chicken, I use apple or black cherry chips for smoke and cook it longer and slower, and even I can taste that.

What I like about grilling with wood, beyond the superb texture and flavors, won't surprise you. It joins slow food with slow wood—flesh from animals we have raised with wood from trees we have cut. I have described New England farming as an eternal contest between forest and field—on the grill, they are reunited, at least for one night. The breeds we raise— Devon cattle, Tamworth and Old Spot pigs—are tasty, and they lead care- free lives on pasture, finding shade by the woods. I like to remember the work of tending the animals and cutting the wood, which is what I have been doing this cold winter afternoon, after all—so in a sense, I can taste that, too. In summer, I sometimes grill steak with the cattle grazing peace- fully not ten yards away in the warm glow of sunset, blissfully unaware of our true relationship. We try not to eat too much beef—one Porterhouse steak is plenty for Faith and me to share, once a week at most. Since I am alone tonight, I'm grilling a nice little rib-eye. If we're at a pub and I want something to go with a craft brew, I'll order a spicy black bean burger or fish and chips. I eat all the beef I need at home. We believe Americans need to eat less meat, but better meat, and we try to adhere to that prin- ciple ourselves.

I stand by the fire with the last of my India pale ale, or my first glass of Côtes du Rhône, and watch the silver twilight fading in the southwest. Venus is riding high this evening and will soon be blazing, just below the slender crescent moon. At that wide angle from the sun, our sister planet must be just about a hundred million miles away—you know, as the crow flies. Another bright planet, Jupiter no doubt, is above the moon and chas- ing Venus down toward the horizon—it looks like it will catch up in an- other day or two, with the moon swung further east, out of the way. That will be another nice conjunction, if the weekend stays clear.

If I were my father, this steak and that planetary spectacle would rate at least a Gigondas, if not a Gassac; but I am alone and not inclined to push the boat out that far. That would not have stopped Dad, mind you. He was on the team that sent the Pioneers to Venus forty years ago to examine its surface and atmosphere (and the Voyagers the other way, past Jupiter to the outer planets). This was accomplished without the use- less baggage of sending actual human beings into space, of course. Years before that, I remember him telling us at dinner about the hypothesized "runaway greenhouse effect" that their Pioneer measurements would later confirm—the first time I ever heard that ominous phrase. Long ago, the Venusian ocean boiled away, he said, the water vapor triggering warming that was then locked in by carbon dioxide—something worth avoiding here on Earth. It turns out we don't have enough coal to pull that off (Venus accomplished it without coal, by being closer to the sun), but we can still cook almost everything currently alive, if we put our big brains to it. Standing by my modest fire reminds me of such epic sagas and the high stakes involved. What ancient culture could look up from their cook fire and tell such a story about the planets—or have to face the consequences?

A hard question. Fire is good company on this cold, clear evening, even so. Fire and those disheveled stars, and my wandering ancestors— Irish, Scottish, and Yankee herders and farmers, inventors and entrepreneurs, teachers, scholars, plumbers, and railroad conductors; English colonial settlers intermarried generations later with Celtic exiles from English colonial settlement. I turn my steak and look out over the farm in the dusk, past the feeders behind the barn where the circled cattle tuck into the hay bale I have brought them, to the dark maples by the river and the invisible oaks on the slope beyond, up to the jagged black fringe of pine tops on the hill half a mile away, etched against the fading winter sky. From somewhere on that slope a sardonic barred owl asks who cooks for me. That one, I can answer: they all cook for me. It is December, the earliest sunset of the year that falls about ten days before the solstice, just as the latest sunrise occurs in early January—an offset symmetry I love. It reflects the imperfect fit between the modern need for uniform twenty-four-hour days and the hidebound Earth's slightly elliptical orbit. Ask an astronomer to explain it to you in a noisy pub after you've had a few, for rare amusement. Ah, you see, that's just the equation of time, the scientist will shout over the din, sketching incomprehensible sinusoidal curves on a cocktail napkin.

I think about what this world needs to remain as beautiful as it is to me at this moment. That is, beautiful for *everyone*, not just the smug few who jet around to consume it as they please or launch themselves not quite far enough into space, while those living closer to the ground suffer the consequences; and me somewhere in between—more comfortable than most, surely, but still fuming that the whole thing is so screwed up, when we know how to fix it. None of the earthly pleasures I enjoy can escape this simmering anger that has dogged me since I was not quite fifteen years old: Earth Day, 1970, followed just two weeks later by Kent State—a whiplash between hope and rage from which I have never fully recovered. It can't be fixed until we cast off the bloodsucking parasites who produce nothing of value but hold the world in thrall, so we can steer the industrial economy in a democratic direction that allows everyone to live decently. I have an agrarian mentality and fervently believe that people who get rich by hiring machines to tunnel through mountains so that their computers can conduct futures trades nanoseconds faster than other computers are fundamentally corrupt and should be cast into the abyss—preferably in a device of their own contrivance—and sealed therein for a thousand years, so they can trouble us no more. Sure, Faith and I have modest retirement investments, and we are lucky to have them, but that bears about as much relation to the real problem of economic inequality as my cook fire does to global warming. Everybody could and should have a decent shared stake in genuine economic growth. Our relative privilege does confer an obligation upon us to stay in the fight and not just sit back and enjoy our steak and wine.

Given a more sensible redeployment of super-abundant wealth and power, the major solutions to living sustainably on this planet do not involve wood fires, any more than the major problems do. A livable future does not require all of us to go back to small-scale farming and cutting our own wood—an outcome I might have advocated (or at least relished) when I was twenty years old, back in the 1970s when we thought the world was running out of oil. I now understand that wholesale decentralization to an agrarian condition is neither practical nor desirable—it would be a calamity. But a livable future does not require us to move to Mars, either. The major solutions lie in the reform of modern industrial technology to sustain, justly and decently, a largely urban society, here on earth. They lie in finally realizing a version of Lewis Mumford's "neotechnic" revolution: clean solar electric power, green reconstruction of cities (including more engineered wood products), and electronic communications that reduce the tonnage of stuff we think we need to quarry and dispose of. But also *unrealizing* the kinds of neotechnic miscarriages that tormented the prescient Mumford, such as nuclear weapons, microplastics pervading the oceans and the air we breathe, disappearing insects and songbirds, and of course global warming.[2]

I have no quarrel with the primary necessity of cleaner (not just less) modern technology—I am my Modernist parents' son. People have looked up at the moon and stars and told entertaining stories for a million years. Not many of them have also sent spacecraft to the evening star to take a closer look. With science, we have powerful new stories to tell and secrets to share. Somehow, though, we need to bring the old stories into conjunction with the new science, because the wild old tales are worth heeding. They convey complex warnings of the wages of arrogance and greed, and they can perhaps help us temper and redeem our industrial power. We know what lights the stars, but few of us can even *see* the stars anymore, especially as brightly as I can this evening. Was that such a good deal? Where was it written that technology surpassing travel by ox cart and illumination by candle had to render the stars invisible, lost somewhere high above our smog, contrails, streetlights, and satellites? Are we destined to obscure them completely behind the haze we will have to deliberately inject into the stratosphere, in a last-ditch effort to dim the glow of the star that gives us life? Can't we have both scientific clarity and clear skies? If not, what is the point of that clarity, of knowing all about that which we can no longer see? That is a one-way plunge down the dark hole of virtual reality, the abyss that awaits us. The light that puts out our eyes is darkness to us, said Thoreau—and here we are putting that proposition to the test.

My steak is sufficiently done—medium rare, if that. I place it on a cutting board, put the lid over the lingering coals, say goodnight to Venus, and head inside. Simple pleasures. While the steak is resting and the broccoli is steaming, I light a fire in the masonry stove to keep me company until bedtime, and a candle on the table—one match, two fires. A man should dine by candlelight, this darkest evening of the year. This particular table is not made from local wood. It is Danish Modern, made of teak (no doubt from Southeast Asia), which my parents bought sometime in the late 1950s, or thereabouts. I sat down to dine at this table for twenty years growing up in Pittsburgh, then for thirty years visiting the folks in Ann Arbor, then for another decade having Christmas with my mother and brothers, back in Pittsburgh again after dad died, when all our kids were still young. Now it has come home to roost—childhood stuff does have a way of tracking you down. And more than family furniture has found its way back to me: my share of the equity that accumulated in those houses over half a century is what built this wonderful house that encloses me now. It couldn't pay for the whole thing outright, but it provided enough to buy the land, avoid a chafing construction loan from the bank, and pay my brothers back by getting a mortgage after we had a certificate of occupancy. This table is a talisman of all those earlier houses in this one.

A Danish Modern table tells a different tale than the local wood in our house. This one has acquired layers of meaning that don't depend on personal acquaintance with the trees that grew it or the work that went into making it. Perhaps it stands for the major part of the overall solution to climate change, the Modernist side that my parents admired: not just handcrafted things, but those nicely designed in the spirit of handcrafting, economically mass-produced, and made to last for generations. There is certainly a great need for that, done right. It's not all one or the other, all global or local, all industry or craft, all modern or traditional. I don't want to go back to making *everything* by hand. But I don't want to see all the working bonds with local farms and woodlands broken, either—or trivialized into forest bathing, seeking an unblemished spiritual connection with the trees that fails to account for the table or the house. Bathing in nature is fine, but it can't wash away the stain of industrial extraction, which is more than skin-deep. We also need to learn how to use nature responsibly and lovingly—to muck about and then really scrub in nature, if you will. Those cows feeding contentedly outside aren't just meat, but they're not pets, either.

The trees talk to one another, and we should listen, you say? Well, maybe they do, but what if some of what they are whispering to each other isn't so nice? Trees can be pretty mean. For example, all the oak trees over a wide area quietly agree which year to make acorns, so that they can provide *more* than enough food for the animals who disperse their young in the process of gathering nuts. This is called "masting"—it is one method rooted species use to reach forest openings, like the oaks planted under the pines on our hill. Extended over millennia, it amounts to a way to move thousands of miles up and down the continent—a necessary skill, given those eccentricities in the earth's orbit that drive cycles of glacial expansion and contraction. The trees aren't just talking to each other: they're throwing a block party so they can go *walking*.

But this generosity has a dark side: the mast trees must also make sure there aren't enough animals around to eat *all* their acorns, year after year. So every few years, they get together and decide to produce *no* acorns, and consequently most of those squirrels die. How is that abrupt switch from kindness to cruelty any different from the way we treat our cattle? If you believe that trees and their mycorrhizal networks are collectively conscious, are they not also morally culpable? The whole cycle is a neat example of reciprocity in nature, until you contemplate that last little trick. Of course, a few rodents survive to carry on, and their numbers explode again the year *after* the next masting—but tell that to the rest.

I think I can hear the oaks, when I walk among them. They are whispering to one another, "Look, we figured out how to annihilate millions of squirrels every few years by cutting off their food supply—isn't there some way we can kill these morons, too?" If there is a pervasive saprophytic intelligence underlying the forest, that is what it should be thinking. Something involving mutant fungus, perhaps? I love the trees, but I am under no illusion that they love me. The trees can help assure all our fellow humans a pleasant stay here on earth and a decent standard of living, both by being forests and by being wood; but it won't be out of the goodness of their hearts. They have other fish to fry. It has to be out of the goodness of *our* hearts, and also the sharpness of our saws. Until we pick up a saw and eye the local mother trees to judge the direction of their lean, we're just kidding ourselves, while giant machines we don't have to watch grind on through other forests thousands of miles away, turning them into biomass and chipboard in our name.

After dinner I settle in front of the masonry stove, with what is left of my second glass of spicy Grenache and Mourvèdre, or perhaps a smoky single malt—neither of which puts you in mind of a real forest, but more of garrigue scrub or heather bog. Both the Mediterranean maquis and the Highland moors were proper forests once, until ancient pastoralists (including those Celtic ancestors of mine) took to relentlessly grazing and burning them. Over thousands of years, that turned them into ruined forests now much beloved by inhabitants and tourists alike. You can surely taste the buzz and soot of those two pyrophylic cultural landscapes in the wine or whisky, take your pick. Both go well with a brisk evening fire, as does the music of Jock Tamson's Bairns that I have put on to keep me company. Now here's a lovely slip jig, composed for gathering sheep on South Uist—are my balusters skipping right along? They seem to be taking it all in stride. The house is warm now, especially here where the glass doors of the stove allow the rapid escape of visible radiation from the long, spiraling flames. I am too beat from working with the saw to write anything, so I let my mind wander with the fire, as it releases the spirit of the wood. Not surprisingly, I reflect more deeply on the consanguinity between forests and fire, and the future of this flammable world.

Until there was forest on earth, there could be no fire. Half a billion years ago, when life was still locked in the sea and had released only a small amount of oxygen, there was nothing to burn and no way to burn it. Once plants crawled onto the land there was plenty of fuel, but it took millions of additional years of photosynthesis to raise the level of oxygen to where there was enough to sustain combustion. It took life to make fire! What a surprise *that* must have been. Over the eons that followed the level of oxygen in the atmosphere has fluctuated, but during fiery eras such as our own, many plants had to adapt to being periodically incinerated. In time, they learned how to re-sprout from their roots, or grew thick bark, or gained the ability to disperse their seeds quickly to new places that had recently been scorched and scourged—adopting various strategies according to the frequency and intensity of the fire regime wherever they lived and their own peculiar habits of growth and regeneration.

Meanwhile, a treacherous new paramour insinuated itself into this smoldering romance between atmosphere and vegetation. During those long epochs hundreds of millions of years ago, after plants covered the continents and oxygen levels rose, fire did not consume all the standing organic matter; nor did slow decay break down all the hydrocarbons after they fell—because there was also water on our planet, after all. Layer upon layer of detritus accumulated in vast, shallow wetlands in the form of peat, which was overlain by mud and slowly compressed into seams of coal. A similar sedimentary embrace at the bottom of the ocean took plankton and algae and patiently squeezed them into petroleum and natural gas. You remember all this from junior high school, of course, but now consider: how bizarre and totally random a twist of geological fate was that? There are certain basic parameters that presumably must be met to foster complex life on a planet, but fossil fuel accumulation isn't one of them. Caching a vast storehouse of dense carbon underground was just a gratuitous afterthought. It was an accident of creation, which then became a destructive accident waiting to happen.

Or maybe it wasn't an accident? I am not a believer in Christian (or any other) theology, being a secular ecological humanist, but the recent resurrection of fossil fuel surely follows that biblical script: an all-knowing yet oddly mercurial Creator devises a fiery subterranean trap for his favorite clever species to stumble into. His object is to discover whether said clever species will use the gift of knowledge, supercharged with this tempting supply of surplus energy, to dress the garden and keep it, or to desecrate it—which honestly didn't take much omniscience to forecast correctly. He even beta-tested this fiendish device 250 million years ago, engaging a handful of well-placed volcanoes (aptly named the "Siberian Traps") to ignite a small part of that fossil carbon, and it worked brilliantly: 70 or 80 percent of life on the planet was extinguished in just a few thousand years. The Great Dying, geologists call it. All that was needed to complete this devilish experiment was to wait patiently for some smart little creature to come along, find *all* the coal and oil, and burn it in just a few centuries— faster and more completely than even volcanoes could manage. And now, at last, here we are, shovels in hand, digging away.

Creating such an adept species took another intervention by fire. In more recent times (the last ten million years or so), as the climate turned cooler and drier in the Pliocene run-up to the latest round of glaciations we call the Pleistocene, grasslands evolved in many parts of the world, and they regularly burned. This set the stage for our own problematic kind. Human beings appeared in such open places, where natural fire was prevalent. We discovered that fire could work to our advantage, and we learned how to start it ourselves—although not always how to stop it. Not satisfied with home cooking, we also began burning entire landscapes, gleefully spreading fire far and wide. I helped with several prairie burns when we lived in Kansas, and it sure was fun—it's no mystery to me why people do it. Wherever human beings have ventured on this planet, a new layer of charcoal soon appears in the paleoecological record, like clockwork. Fire helps maintain open ecosystems that are more congenial for our species than closed forests: grasslands, savannas, and patchy wooded parklands where plenty of sunlight reaches the forest floor, producing more berries and game within easy reach. Human fire has reshaped terrestrial ecosystems in ways that have come to seem natural, in the sense that over time other species have adapted to it. Such fires may be destructive for individual organisms in the moment that they occur, but they become a regenerative force for those species (including our own) that have learned to inhabit the places where fires have become commonplace.

We are creatures of fire. We employed it first to cook our food, then to warm our dwellings. We employed it to shape our landscapes, including the structure and composition of many forests as well as grasslands. Eventually, during the present interglacial period, we learned to use it to smelt ore and fashion metal tools (and weapons), and to fire ceramics, bricks, and glass—the artisanal roots of industry. All that use of primeval fire technology was a cause for celebration (setting aside the associated advances in slaughter). Together with the advent of agriculture, primeval fire had an impact on many planetary ecosystems and possibly even on global climate—but all within reasonable bounds.

Unbinding Promethean fire is another matter. Being creatures of fire, sooner or later some human culture was bound to unearth those hidden stores of boundless energy and invent technologies to accelerate their use, orders of magnitude beyond the organic carbon available in trees. In less than no time, we find ourselves imposing changes in climate and vegetation so rapid that they threaten to cause ecospheric trauma equal to a handful of the worst disasters in the history of the planet. The Sixth Extinction: the Great Dying 2.0. This time, *our* doing. Ironically, one consequence of this recent surge of fossil fire appears to be a corresponding intensification of landscape fire, in places like Australia, the Mediterranean, Siberia, Canada, and the American West, rendering the horror we have unleashed more visible to us. Just to confirm that we will indeed persist in this criminal behavior even after its dire consequences have been fully revealed.

I sit staring into the convivial flames in my stove and ponder what we can do to avert, or at least blunt, this spreading catastrophe—something I have been doing now for half a century, without success. But what, exactly, is *causing* this disaster? Was it just written in stone once the coal was formed, or is it something more specific to our own time? As a historian, I warn my students to be wary of sweeping, uni-causal historical explanations—which tend to be adduced in support of simplistic, ideologically driven solutions for complicated problems. At the same time, be wary of multiplying causes to the point that your scholarly complications explain nothing. Get a sense of the relative strength of your causes and how they interact, I tell them.

For example, I asserted just now that after our species got fire "some human culture was bound" to stumble upon fossil fuels and start using them at an explosive rate. I think there is truth in that: once you start mining enough coal to invent the steam engine to pump water out of your mine, it becomes hard to get off that train. Could have happened to anybody. But this simple explanation, rooted in technology, suggests an inescapable destiny intrinsic to the nature of humans, fire, and coal. Although I have been putting a negative spin on it (I am an environmentalist, after all), at base this story reflects a positivist view of inevitable scientific progress. In turn, that way of framing the problem suggests purely technological solutions: it becomes just a matter of seeking continued scientific advances to address this new set of challenges. Soon we will have limitless solar power, nuclear fusion, nanomaterials, artificial "plant-based" foods, ways to mine the asteroids, and our problem will be solved. Among the uses of wood I have championed, mass timber construction fits this fundamentally Modernist, technocratic paradigm—as does, I suppose, 3D printing of houses with some new material derived from ground-up trees. Americans tend to be comfortable framing a problem like climate change this way, because that solution doesn't require any major change in our behavior or power structure—just more of the same kind of "disruptions" that we count as progress. And no question, one way or another we will need to deploy better technologies to get out of this mess, if we can.

But the industrial revolution and unleashing of fossil carbon didn't happen just any old day. The trap was sprung in a specific historical context: the rise of a capitalist market economy and its powerful drive for growth and profit, leading to the rapid and largely unconstrained extraction of natural resources such as lumber, cotton, and coal. That context included the global spread of colonial empires, the expropriation of Indigenous land, the rise of systematic, racially based slavery, and the rank exploitation of wage labor. This capitalist drive helps explain the stupendous generation of material wealth that came along with unlocking fossil fuel, as well as its spectacularly inequitable distribution and indifference to social and environmental consequences. The accompanying concentration of political power also helps explain the long, slow, difficult struggle to impose restraints on that engine of growth in the name of simple justice and the common good, even in a democratic society. It took a century from the rise of industrial cities before any meaningful controls on air pollution were enacted, for example; this time lag resulted in the premature deaths of millions of people.

Perhaps burning fossil fuels became inevitable from the moment human beings domesticated fire, but the profligate manner in which those fuels have been exploited—and the criminally slow response to the collateral dangers they pose—is firmly rooted in capitalism. Climate change is a particularly knotty problem partly because cheap fossil carbon is so deeply ingrained in our industrial economy that it cannot be easily replaced, but mostly because it has come to a head during a period of resurgent neoliberal corporate hegemony that has effectively hamstrung a timely response. I believe that is true, because I have spent my lifetime watching it happen and struggling against it; but I also believe we need to be careful not to fool ourselves into thinking that a catchy little phrase like "neoliberal corporate hegemony" can explain *everything* that is going on or what we ought to do about it. At this point, to survive and prosper we need to make use of the technological prowess that capitalist excess has unlocked.

I think of these explanations, one based in technology and the other in political economy, as not competing but synergistic. They work together, although as you can tell I consider the second the more urgent of the two. Blaming capitalism for the persistence of entrenched dirty technologies can't replace the need for new, cleaner technologies—and we do have scientific progress to thank for making those solutions available to us. But by themselves, technological solutions to climate change, besides being slow to accomplish because they continue to be resisted by powerful vested interests, will be inadequate, or worse. They won't address rampant inequality on the one hand or rein in the mindless growth of energy and material consumption intrinsic to a market economy on the other. If we leave the development of a solar economy to the market and the technocrats, we will end up with the upper quintile driving their overweight electric vehicles to far-flung exurbs infested with McMansions that are bigger than ever, leaving the inner cities and older suburbs still rundown and distressed. The world's forests will continue to be degraded by creeping mines, sprawling solar and wind farms, low-density high-end development invading the most scenic spots, short-rotation plantation forestry, and the spread of yet more industrial agriculture producing animal feed and jet fuel. Fossil carbon combustion will continue for much longer than necessary to meet this ever increasing demand for energy and to squeeze out all the profit left underground, even as renewables slowly gain market share—like earlier energy transitions that built upon and incorporated preceding fuels rather than replacing them. Instead of being phased out, petroleum will be diverted to making more indestructible plastics. We will go on being a petroculture, even after the petrol tank is empty. Mumford called this a "cultural pseudomorph"—the promise of neotechnic liberation locked up in a paleotechnic social and political prison, built by carboniferous capitalism.

We need better technologies, no doubt. But to bring them to bear fast enough and to create a more just, livable world from them, we have to compel the emerging solar economy to also deliver universal health care, affordable housing, and healthy food for everybody. That is a matter of organizing and exerting political power to counteract the natural inclination of the market (and those who profit from it) to mostly ignore the needs of people who don't have money and to make sure most people don't have much. For example, Faith and I recently put solar panels on the roof of our lovely timber frame house—enough to power the farm and sell some back to the grid. Tom and Joan did the same (on the roof of the new cattle loafing shed we built with pine from the hill), and they bought an electric car to soak up the surplus. That is all to the good—I don't feel guilty about it. But *we* had the financial resources to cover the up-front costs, enjoy the tax benefits, and reap the rapid return on investment through negative electric bills. Clearly, as a society we need more broadly based incentive programs to help *anyone* who has a roof to enjoy the same benefits, and to put solar canopies over parking lots, before subsidizing large developers to chop down forests to plop their solar arrays on the cheapest available land. And we should equitably apportion the cost of upgrading the grid to accommodate all that decentralized green production. Similarly, we ought to encourage clustered growth that connects to improved mass transportation and to build lots of affordable housing, putting those roofs over more people's heads—the market has proven it won't deliver that on its own. I have argued that technological innovations such as mass timber construction should be tightly linked to sustainable forestry that also serves ecological values, instead of simply incorporating the cheapest lumber available—but again, that will require the political strength to drive a "just transition," empowering communities to direct how new technologies are deployed, rather than just incentivizing private developers to run roughshod over them one more time.

Such a just transition is what I spend most of my time working on, these days. At bottom it is simply a more progressive version of Modernism than what the technocrats are foisting upon us, in the sense that the arc of the moral universe bends toward justice, but only if we keep pushing it. Nonetheless, such improved Modernism is not what *this* book has been primarily about. Here, I have argued that part of our problem lies with Modernism itself, and therefore another important part of the solution must be anti-Modern: a deliberate effort to revive older technologies such as timber framing and masonry stoves. I have argued that these pre-industrial "eotechnics," as Mumford called them, still have their place. They once created beautiful and comfortable homes, relying by necessity on sustainable management of local woodlands, and they could do so again. I have claimed that conservation and stewardship of nature is not an entirely modern invention. With the modern transformation to an industrial, urban, fossil-fuel-driven economy, a lot of useful traditional knowledge—not just Indigenous knowledge, but Western agrarian knowledge as well—was shoved aside and largely forgotten, along with the satisfaction of performing skilled work that connects directly to natural materials lying close at hand to make beautiful, functional objects, such as houses.

A vigorous anti-Modern reaction sprang up in the wake of industrialization, with the Arts and Crafts movement beginning in the middle of the nineteenth century, which persists in many forms to this day. Ours is surely an Arts and Crafts house, and we are proud of that—Faith's grandfather (her father's father) taught sloyd, which links woodworking and handicrafts to education of the whole child. Some of the furniture he made and some that Faith's father made is here in this house, as her family stuff has chased us down as well. Without Faith here this evening, I can't remember whether her father or her grandfather made this little bench my feet are up on now, for example. Sensible people have been working to revive woodcraft for a long time, for all the reasons I have been discussing. This impulse to return to hand work gains more and more emotional traction, the more complex and alienating the modern world becomes. The effort to revive deeply rooted culinary traditions is also at the heart of the slow food movement—which is why I am calling its local forest counterpart "slow wood."[3]

Environmentalism contains a strong anti-Modern current, in its desire to protect and restore remnants of a less disturbed natural world, to re-forge healthy connections to unspoiled nature, and to live more simply without consuming so much disposable junk that winds up in our air and water—the Romantic Thoreauvian strain. This urge to turn back sits uneasily alongside the Progressive drive to deploy cleaner technology and promote social justice that I have been endorsing, which seems to push in the opposite direction—unless the balance between them is carefully calibrated. There are clearly dangers in romanticizing the pre-modern world, which was rife with privations and oppressions of its own. The rise of capitalism and the industrial revolution offered important means to escape those stifling conditions, but so far has failed to fully deliver and has needlessly spoiled many good things along the way. One might easily object that turning back the clock and making everything by hand is no solution—it would plunge most of humanity into poverty and starvation. Bespoke handmade goods such as timber frame houses are so expensive that only the wealthy can afford them, one might claim, and many apologists for industrial capitalism (who often enjoy such handmade goods themselves) are happy to do so.

But that argument is a straw man, and a cheap plastic straw man at that. Industrial and handcrafted work can be complementary, not antagonistic—and at a level far beyond a tiny boutique handcraft trade for the wealthy. The more efficient we become at manufacturing useful industrial goods with minimal human labor—computers, solar panels, electric vehicles, and the like—the more room we create to spend our time making and enjoying organic goods by hand, using traditional methods. If there is room in a post-industrial world for "gaming" and "influencing" as legitimate economic activities, there is surely also room for widespread organic farming and timber-framed houses. If the bulk of the people working in all sectors of the manufacturing and service economy were decently paid, so that the benefits of industrial efficiency were more widely shared rather than accruing disproportionately to those who own capital, most people would be able to afford a reasonable share of slow food and slow wood, as well, if they so desire. This is where a just Modernism and an artisanal revival can join hands.

There were deeply layered and satisfying connections among our ancient ways of farming, cooking, woodcraft, and building. In the modern world, which cannot possibly thrive without industrial technology, we must find more than a token place for these husbandry and craft traditions, too. We need a healthy portion of the population engaged with caring for the world by performing enjoyable artisanal work, providing a fair share of the resulting products for everyone. In these realms we don't need to be more efficient, but less: we need to employ *more* labor, and have more fun. We need handsome houses made of wood, real food that is lovingly grown and cooked, and wood fires by which to tell our stories and play our music, to watch the stars and see how they run. We should have work that tires our muscles, to remind us how to create such things that are vital to our souls. Making everything by hand would be cruelly laborious, but making it all entirely by machine renders it painfully close to meaningless. When our food, our houses, and our home fires no longer connect to *anything* in the living world that our own bodies have grappled with, most of the meaning drains out of *everything*. Meaning is in part muscle memory—it can't be accrued solely on the bean-counting side of the brain. The creative lobe connects to the whole arm, not just the tip of the finger. The point of technological progress ought to be to make it possible for more of us, not fewer, to enjoy productive engagement with the natural world and with each other.

I watch the fire settle into the mature, deep red, pure carbon-consuming stage of its burn now. There is nothing new to this marriage of clean, just Modernism with the best of traditional artisanal work that I am proposing. It has been propounded for over a century, in various forms, by the likes of Peter Kropotkin, Lewis Mumford, René Dubos, and Murray Bookchin—all intellectual mentors of mine. It embraces modern science and technology, but rejects unconstrained industrial capitalism. It embraces cultural history and a satisfying arts and craft heritage but rejects retreating to primitivism. It is neither anthropocentric nor biocentric— it is a marriage of contrasting tendencies that has been called "ecological humanism," which sounds about right to me. I don't see any insuperable technical difficulty in bringing it to pass, even for ten billion people— though it would work better for far fewer, in time. I do see a harrowing political difficulty, in the face of fierce resistance from the technocratic elite who will not hesitate to defend their interests, inflicting mass misery to mobilize populist fury and burning down the planet if they must. That, not the technology itself, is now the nub of our problem.[4]

Unfortunately, ecological humanism cannot now conceivably come to fruition fast enough to wholly succeed. That window has closed. We will just have to do the best we can. When we first came to this little valley in 2007, I hoped that by moving inland I could return to the colder winters I had enjoyed in Concord and Weston, back in the 1970s—at least for a while. But we have passed that point already. This New England forest that I love will change, perhaps dramatically. I am reconciled to some loss. I remind myself that the forest would change even were the climate to remain stable, as all the other disturbances we have wrought in the landscape over the past few centuries continue to play out. Life is change, I suppose—even as my traditional instincts long for greater stability. Our beautiful timber frame house is an expression of the forest that was here at the particular moment we built it, not an emblem of its permanent state. Forests are resilient and contain many nimble species, and we are near the northern edge of many of those that grow here now. I am confident that if we can keep the rate of climate change within tolerable bounds, beautiful trees will continue to grow, and more beautiful houses can be built from them. There is still time for that. We shall see—or somebody will.

These changes might be painful for our generation to contemplate, but they will seem only natural to those who grow up after us. Hemlock will probably decline and withdraw to a narrow band somewhere to the north—let's hope it can find a zone of safety that is too cold for the adelgid but not for the hemlock, or that the impact of the adelgid subsides over time, perhaps with some help from us. Sugar maple will no doubt become less pervasive here, too—but maybe not overnight, because maples live a long time. Boiling maple syrup will become marginal south of Canada, because the early spring sap run already passes by too quickly, most years. Black birch seems poised for an upsurge, wherever the canopy is breached by disturbances. Oaks may be regenerating poorly at the moment, but they should remain dominant long enough to give themselves many more chances to propagate their kind. Unlike maples, oaks in our region should benefit from warming—if disturbances provide them with enough light, and if deer don't consume all their seedlings. I would not count oaks out too soon. White pine, similarly, will continue to deliver its seeds to openings that give it enough light to thrive. It may never enjoy another bonanza quite like the wholesale abandonment of pasture from the mid-nineteenth to the mid-twentieth centuries, but that explosion has given pine momentum that should last for generations. Hickory may rebound as the climate warms, and, who knows, a hybrid variety of disease-resistant chestnut may rejoin the forest, with a little help from those who are remaking it to withstand the blight. I am starting to see tulip poplar popping up here and there, and it grows fast and tall. Black cherry should do well, at least for a while, and, of course, that unstoppable generalist red maple is likely to thrive, come hell or high water. Perhaps, in a disturbed world where we can use all the help we can get, we in the Northeast will stop labeling black locust as an invasive pariah and welcome it as a long-lost native son that just took a long time getting back up here after the last glaciation, probably because it lost the megafauna to transport it—but now it has us.[5]

But all this will take time—perhaps centuries—to transpire, as most mature trees of our region can handle the degree of warming we are likely to inflict upon them: it is their offspring that will be most affected. Ironically, the more widespread logging that I have advocated in this book might make for a faster change in forest composition—as would an increase in natural disturbances such as windstorms, for example. Some of these species may not thrive for other unforeseen reasons, such as new outbreaks of pests and pathogens. But any combination of those that remain or move in will give us functioning forest ecosystems, full of lovely trees, shrubs, wildflowers, fungi, insects, birds, mammals, and all the rest. Which of these possibilities would you call natural, or native to this place? Which is the forest that belongs here by ecological design? They would all be fine with me, and if introduced species like Norway maple join in, so be it. There is no way we can stop them now, anyway, so we might as well accept such well-established "invasives" as a fact of life. All trees are pretty much invasive, and all ecosystems are ephemeral. Let's not lose too much sleep over invasive plants, which do little widespread harm unless you believe particular ecosystems were meant to be homeostatic and eternal. If pest species—such as hemlock woolly adelgid—threaten species we love, let's fight them in targeted ways where we might do some good, not as a class of ecological evil. What we really need to worry about is a calamitous rate of change that strands a large portion of our current species, unable to reach new places where they might regenerate and thrive, while other species that might do well here are unable to reach us in time. That still seems unlikely in temperate New England, but it is a grim possibility in many other parts of the world that are more tropical, more boreal, or more arid. And along with such a rate of warming will also come terrible human dislocation and suffering, especially in places where people lack the wealth and power to cope.[6]

To avert this disaster, we must stop burning fossil carbon as soon as possible—there is no substitute for that. I know there is nothing new in

Staring into the flames. (Maren Leyla Cooke)

that statement, but since I have been among those making it for forty years, I might as well keep repeating it. The forest can perhaps help us repair the damage, but only if we stop making things worse. Just letting the trees grow to absorb carbon dioxide is not helpful, however, because we also need houses—that is a genuine human need that can only be slightly moderated. Burning wood for energy has only a small useful role to play, as I have explained—you can't make much of a case for it beyond a few stoves for country people, like us. *Building* with wood can play a much more important role in this desperately needed transformation, and there is nothing like living in touch with wood—that, in one form or another, is good for everybody. The best thing wood has to offer isn't burning it to replace fossil fuel, but building with it to replace materials that require fossil fuel.

But it has to be slow wood. By that I mean that the timber must be produced *not* in the most efficient way possible, which reduces forests to plantations, but as a by-product of cautious management that allows us to enjoy all the ecological benefits of complex, diverse, mature forests at the same time. One of those benefits might indeed be storing more carbon on the landscape over the next few crucial decades, even as we store more of it in buildings, too. That requires ecological silviculture. But honestly, how we manage our forest should not be driven primarily by calculating its capacity to store carbon. The most important benefits of a healthy forest are beyond calculation, and beyond carbon. Only an enduring marriage of honorable use and humble reverence will give us a fighting chance of successfully conserving the forests of our region, or of the world.

The wooden frame that supports the flames has collapsed to red embers, and my glass of red wine is down to the dregs, too. I rake the last of the coals into the center and open the blast through the ash door underneath to burn them out. The luminous yellow afterlife of pure carbon combustion fills the firebox for a few more minutes. Is that the green flame I see, there at the base of the dying fire? Maybe not—it is hard to tell. If it were just a shade greener, I could be sure. I do believe that primeval fire can be green and that it need not be banished forever. I wash the dishes and head up to bed. The stone can warm the house through the night without any further tending from me.

Acknowledgments

THIS BOOK REQUIRES TWO overlapping sets of acknowledgments: one for help in building and another for help in writing.

For making the farm happen, Faith, Liam, and Maggie; and our friends, neighbors, and partners, Tom and Joan. For help along the way, our parents, siblings, and other family members.

For protecting the land, Dick French, Leigh Youngblood, and Tony Matthews; and for leading us to it, John O'Keefe.

For forestry, Susan Campbell and Lincoln Fish. For slow logging, Ed Klaus.

For sawing and milling lumber, David Lashway, Michael Idoine, Rhys Hatch, Tony Mason, and Emily Boss and the Massachusetts Woodlands Cooperative.

For architecture and troubleshooting, Tom Chalmers.

For excavation and foundation, Doug Edson and David Bernard.

For framing, David Bowman, Neil Godden, and apprentices Will and Will.

For helping raise the frame, Paul McDonald, John O'Keefe, Jamie Pottern, Brian Hall, and other friends and family.

For carpentry, Toby Briggs, Chris Krezmien, and crew.

For sheetrocking and painting, Terry Staiger—inner and outer spaceman.

For wiring, David and Marsha Laprade. For plumbing, Jason Wallace. For heating, Mike Hubbard.

For the masonry heater, Carsten Homstead. For mica-schist counters and floor tiles, Johanna Andersen-Pratt at Ashfield Stone. For birch cabinets, Bryan Dolan.

On the writing side, for help with the maps, Brian Hall at the Harvard Forest, Matthew Peters at the U.S. Forest Service Northern Research Station, and Emma Sass at the U.S. Forest Service Family Forest Research Center.

For comments on the manuscript, Mark Fiege, Nancy Langston, Wendell Berry, and one anonymous reader.

For research support, a Charles Bullard Fellowship at the Harvard Forest, and a fellowship from the American Council of Learned Societies.

For production support, the Wildlands, Woodlands, Farmlands, and Communities initiative of the Highstead Foundation.

For editorial support, Elizabeth Sylvia, Elizabeth Casey, and, as always, Jean Thomson Black at Yale University Press.

Notes

Chapter 1. We Buy the Farm

1. William R. Moomaw et al., "Intact Forests in the United States: Proforestation Mitigates Climate Change and Serves the Greatest Good," *Frontiers in Forests and Global Change* 2 (2019), https://doi.org/10.3389/ffgc.2019.00027.
2. Our adventures in Weston are described in Brian Donahue, *Reclaiming the Commons: Community Farms and Forests in a New England Town* (New Haven: Yale University Press, 1999). Reforestation in New England is summarized in David Foster et al., *Wildlands and Woodlands, Farmlands and Communities: Broadening the Vision for New England* (Petersham, Mass.: Harvard Forest, 2017), 7, figure 3.
3. Erle C. Ellis, "To Conserve Nature in the Anthropocene, Half Earth Is Not Nearly Enough," *One Earth* 1 (2019). This article contains numerous references to the extensive literature surrounding E. O. Wilson, *Half Earth: Our Planet's Fight for Life* (New York: Liveright, 2016).
4. Brian Donahue, *The Great Meadow: Farmers and the Land in Colonial Concord* (New Haven: Yale University Press, 2004). I am descended from Samuel Hartwell and Ruth Wheeler.
5. See "Sustainable Working Landscapes Program" pages on the Harvard Forest web site, https://harvardforest.fas.harvard.edu/sustainable-working-landscapes -program.
6. "Agricultural Preservation Restriction (APR) Program" page on the Massachusetts Department of Agricultural Resources web site, www.mass.gov/agricultural -preservation-restriction-apr-program; Mount Grace Land Conservation Trust web site, www.mountgrace.org.

Chapter 2. Fencing Out the Forest

1. W. Barksdale Maynard, *Walden Pond: A History* (New York: Oxford University Press, 2004), 214–17.
2. "Environmental Quality Incentives Program" page on the USDA Natural Resources Conservation Service web site, www.nrcs.usda.gov/programs-initiatives /eqip-environmental-quality-incentives.

Chapter 3. The Woods

1. "Season 11: The Concord Barn" page on *This Old House* web site, www.thisold house.com/concord-barn.
2. "Season 30: The Weston House" page on *This Old House* web site, www.thisold house.com/weston-house.

3. "Massachusetts Forest Stewardship Program" page on the Massachusetts Department of Conservation and Recreation web site, www.mass.gov/service-details/forest-stewardship-program. Susan is a graduate of the Yale School of Forestry and Environmental Studies, as it was called at the time.

4. David Foster et al., *Wildlands in New England: Past, Present, and Future* (Petersham, Mass.: Harvard Forest, 2023).

5. Charles D. Canham, *Forests Adrift: Currents Shaping the Future of Northeastern Trees* (New Haven: Yale University Press, 2020), 59–60. This book captures the dynamic view of forest ecology and history that also informs my thinking. See also Jared Rosenbaum, *Wild Plant Culture: A Guide to Restoring Edible and Medicinal Plant Communities* (Gabriola Island, B.C.: New Society Publishers, 2022).

6. The motivations and harvesting behavior of small private forest owners are examined in Andrew O. Finley and David B. Kittredge, Jr., "Thoreau, Muir, and Jane Doe: Different Types of Forest Owners Need Different Kinds of Forest Management," *Northern Journal of Applied Forestry* 23 (2006): 32–33.

7. "Managing Forests for Birds" page on Massachusetts Audubon Society web site, www.massaudubon.org/our-conservation-work/wildlife-research-conservation/bird-conservation-monitoring/forest-birds; "Foresters for the Birds: Assessing Your Woods for Bird Habitat" page on the Massachusetts Department of Conservation and Recreation web site, www.mass.gov/guides/foresters-for-the-birds-assessing-your-woods-for-bird-habitat#-foresters-for-the-birds-overview.

8. A good overview of the geological origins of New England's stony soils and stone walls can be found in Robert M. Thorson, *Stone by Stone: The Magnificent History in New England's Stone Walls* (New York: Walker and Company, 2002).

Chapter 4. Hemlock Frame

1. Kenneth C. Parkes, "In Memoriam: Walter Edmund Clyde Todd," *The Auk: A Quarterly Journal of Ornithology* 87 (1970); W. E. Clyde Todd, *Birds of the Buffalo Creek Region, Armstrong and Butler Counties, Pennsylvania* (Pittsburgh: Audubon Society of Western Pennsylvania, 1972); "Todd Nature Reserve" page on Audubon Society of Western Pennsylvania web site, www.aswp.org/pages/todd-history.

2. For a marvelous overview of the deep history and prospects of Eastern hemlock, see David R. Foster, ed., *Hemlock: A Forest Giant on the Edge* (New Haven: Yale University Press, 2014).

3. The approach we used is similar to that described in Albert E. Mayfield III et al., *Integrating Chemical and Biological Control of the Hemlock Woolly Adelgid: A Resource Manager's Guide* (USDA Forest Service Forest Health Assessment and Applied Sciences Team, 2020), www.srs.fs.usda.gov/pubs/misc/misc_2020_mayfield_001.pdf, which contains an extensive bibliography on hemlock woolly adelgid. See also the "Hemlock Restoration Initiative," https://savehemlocksnc.org.

4. For books on timber frame construction see Jack A. Sobon, *Hand Hewn: The Traditions, Tools, and Enduring Beauty of Timber Framing* (North Adams, Mass.: Storey Publishing, 2019); Jack Sobon and Roger Schroeder, *Timber Frame Construction: All About Post and Beam Building* (North Adams, Mass.: Storey Publishing, 1984); Tedd Benson (with James Gruber), *Building the Timber Frame House: The Revival of a Forgotten Craft* (New York: Simon & Schuster, 1980).

5. In *1491: New Revelations of the Americas Before Columbus* (New York: Alfred A. Knopf, 2005), 320–23, Charles C. Mann presents an image of a transformed pre-European Eastern forest, much of it open and park-like or cultivated, that subsequently reverted to an "artificial wilderness" with the collapse of Native population, but this depiction is overdrawn and outruns the evidence. In contrast, Shepard Krech III, *The Ecological Indian: Myth and History* (New York: W.W. Norton, 1999), argues that Native impact on the land (while hardly invisible) was more limited, primarily because of low population density. This is closer to my view, although I find Krech's reluctance to credit Native people as "conservationists" puzzling. A useful overview of the literature, together with a spatial model of the extent of Native land-use impacts, is provided by Samuel E. Munoz et al., "Defining the Spatial Patterns of Historical Land Use Associated with the Indigenous Societies of Eastern North America," *Journal of Biogeography* 41 (2014).

6. There was great variation across the region in Native settlement patterns and seasonal movement, depending on the degree of agricultural reliance. For a contrast between the more sedentary Iroquois and more mobile New England Algonquians, see Elizabeth Chilton, "Farming and Social Complexity in the Northeast," in *North American Archaeology,* ed. Timothy R. Pauketat and Diana DiPaolo Loren (Malden, Mass.: Blackwell, 2005). An older overview, still good, is Gordon G. Whitney, *From Coastal Wilderness to Fruited Plain: A History of Environmental Change in Temperate North America from 1500 to the Present* (New York: Cambridge University Press, 1994), 98–107.

7. Roger Williams, *A Key into the Language of America* ([London, 1643] Bedford, Mass.: Applewood Books, 1997), 59–60. English wood scarcity is discussed in Donahue, *Great Meadow,* 71–72 and the accompanying endnotes.

8. Donahue, *Great Meadow,* 60–62; Oliver Rackham, *The History of the Countryside* (London: J.M. Dent, 1986); Robert Tarule, *The Artisan of Ipswich: Craftsmanship and Community in Colonial New England* (Baltimore: Johns Hopkins University Press, 2004), 18–28.

9. Abbott Lowell Cummings, *The Framed Houses of Massachusetts Bay, 1625-1725* (Cambridge: Harvard University Press, 1979). In *Barn Club: A Tale of Forgotten Elm Trees, Traditional Craft, and Community Spirit* (White River Junction, Vt.: Chelsea Green, 2021), Robert Somerville tells a nice story of the rediscovery of framing with English elm.

10. Cummings, *Framed Houses of Massachusetts Bay,* 4–17.

11. See the essays in Brooke Hindle, ed., *America's Wooden Age: Aspects of Its Early Technology* (Tarrytown, N.Y.: Sleepy Hollow Press, 1975); and Charles F. Carroll, *The Timber Economy of Puritan New England* (Providence: Brown University Press, 1974).

12. Cummings, *Framed Houses of Massachusetts Bay,* 40–93. For a discussion of the response of white pine, hemlock, and other species to disturbances in the pre-European forest, see Jamie M. Waterman et al., "Historic Forest Composition and Structure Across an Old-Growth Landscape in New Hampshire, USA," *Journal of the Torrey Botanical Society* 147 (2020).

13. Cummings, *Framed Houses of Massachusetts Bay,* 126–47.

14. On the expansion of colonial towns see Donahue, *Great Meadow.*

15. Two excellent accounts of early nineteenth-century New England farming and

architectural development are offered by J. Ritchie Garrison, *Landscape and Material Life in Franklin County, Massachusetts, 1770–1860* (Knoxville: University of Tennessee Press, 1991), and Thomas C. Hubka, *Big House, Little House, Back House, Barn: The Connected Farm Buildings of New England* (Hanover: University Press of New England, 1984).

16. The idealization of the colonial village and its houses during the Romantic movement of the nineteenth century and the Colonial Revival movement of the early twentieth century conveniently overlooked the many people who were marginalized and exploited in that process (Native Americans, Black slaves, women) and told a whitewashed story. See, for example, Joseph A. Conforti, "Regional Identity and New England Landscapes," and other essays in *A Landscape History of New England,* ed. Blake Harrison and Richard W. Judd (Cambridge, Mass.: MIT Press, 2011). But it is possible to come to grips with that reality and still respect some of the architectural and agrarian virtues of settler culture.

17. Cummings, *Framed Houses of Massachusetts Bay,* 158–209.

18. See the essays in Brooke Hindle, ed., *Material Culture of the Wooden Age* (Tarrytown, N.Y.: Sleepy Hollow Press, 1981).

19. Donahue, *Great Meadow,* 214–18; Massachusetts Society for Promoting Agriculture, *Papers on Agriculture, 1803,* 50–52.

20. R. M. Godman and Kenneth Lancaster, "Eastern Hemlock," USDA Forest Service, www.srs.fs.usda.gov/pubs/misc/ag_654/volume_1/tsuga/canadensis.htm.

21. Sobon and Schroeder, *Timber Frame Construction,* 53–55.

22. Ethyl E. Bieler Gould, "The Craggin Family," *Genealogy of Joseph Teel [and] Mary Stetson Alexander: Their Ancestors and Descendants,* www.oocities.org/gingercleo /JohnandSarah2.html; Lesley June Cragin Godley, *The Cragin Story, 1634–1964,* www.familysearch.org/library/books/records/item/620030-the-cragin-story-1634 -1964-descendants-who-bore-family-name-of-john-cragin-of-scotland-and-massachu setts; Henry Ames Blood, *History of Temple, New Hampshire* (Boston: George C. Rand and Avery, 1860); Historical Society of Temple, New Hampshire, *A History of Temple, New Hampshire, 1768–1876* (Dublin, N.H., 1976).

23. "Joseph Everett Chandler Diaries," Collections of Historic New England, Boston, Mass. My thanks to Tim Orwig for sending me transcriptions from Chandler's diaries.

Chapter 5. Cherry Braces

1. An excellent overview of the interaction between household and market economies on colonial farms, and how it changed over time, is given in Richard Lyman Bushman, *The American Farmer in the Eighteenth Century: A Social and Cultural History* (New Haven: Yale University Press, 2018), 1–22.

2. On potash, see Whitney, *From Coastal Wilderness,* 147–49; William I. Roberts III, "American Potash Manufacture Before the American Revolution," *Proceedings of the American Philosophical Society* 116 (1972); Ralmon Jon Black, *Colonial Asheries* (Williamsburg, Mass.: Williamsburg Historical Society, 2008); Robert P. Multhauf, "Potash," in *Material Culture of the Wooden Age,* ed. Hindle. On rafting, see Thomas R. Cox, "Transition in the Woods: Log Drives, Raftsmen, and the Emer-

gence of Modern Lumbering in Pennsylvania," *Pennsylvania Magazine of History and Biography* 104 (1980).

3. Whitney, *From Coastal Wilderness,* 178–82; Michael Williams, *Americans and Their Forests: A Historical Geography* (New York: Cambridge University Press, 1989), 146–60.

4. The classic text is Carl W. Condit, *American Building Art: The Nineteenth Century* (New York: Oxford University Press, 1960), 10–22; see also William Cronon, *Nature's Metropolis: Chicago and the Great West* (New York: W.W. Norton, 1992), 148–206.

5. Rebecca Hunter and Dale P. Wolicki, *Sears, Roebuck Book of Barns: A Reprint of the 1919 Catalog* (Elgin, Ill.: R.L. Hunter Press, 2005).

6. Donahue, *Great Meadow,* 221–34; Brian Donahue, "'Dammed at Both Ends and Cursed in the Middle': The 'Flowage' of the Concord River Meadows, 1798–1862," *Environmental Review* 13 (1989); David R. Foster, *Thoreau's Country: Journey Through a Transformed Landscape* (Cambridge: Harvard University Press, 1999).

7. See Donahue, *Great Meadow,* 178, on colonial tanning. On the tanning industry see Hugh O. Canham, "Hemlock and Hide: The Tanbark Industry in Old New York," *Northern Woodlands* (Summer 2011), https://northernwoodlands.org/articles/article/hemlock-and-hide-the-tanbark-industry-in-old-new-york.

8. Whitney, *From Coastal Wilderness,* 186–88; Kelly Berliner, "Archaeology of Industry: F. Shaw & Brothers Tannery of Maine," 2018, page on web site of the Archaeology Conservancy, www.archaeologicalconservancy.org/industry-in-the-east/; Hildegarde Kuse and Loretta Kuse, "Object History: Bark Spud" (2019), page on web site of Wisconsin 101, https://wi101.wisc.edu/object-history-bark-spud/.

9. Hugh O. Canham, "The Wood Chemical Industry in the Northeast," *Northern Woodlands* (Winter 2009), https://northernwoodlands.org/articles/article/the-wood-chemical-industry-in-the-northeast; Whitney, *From Coastal Wilderness,* 188–93; Walter C. Casler et al., *Logging Railroad Era of Lumbering in Pennsylvania: A History of the Lumber, Chemical Wood, and Tanning Companies Which Used Railroads in Lumbering* (Williamsport, Pa.: Lycoming Printing Company, 1970–78).

10. Whitney, *From Coastal Wilderness,* 198–202; Marc D. Abrams and Gregory J. Nowacki, "Global Change Impacts of Forest and Fire Dynamics Using Paleoecology and Tree Census Data for Eastern North America," *Annals of Forest Science* 76 (2019).

11. Bill Keeton, "Eastern Old-Growth Forests in an Era of Change," *Northern Woodlands* (Spring 2020), https://northernwoodlands.org/articles/article/eastern-old-growth-forests-in-an-era-of-change. Classic examples of the nineteenth-century call for better forest stewardship include George B. Emerson, *Report on Trees and Shrubs of Massachusetts* (Boston: Little, Brown, 1846); and George Perkins Marsh, *Man and Nature: Or, Physical Geography as Modified by Human Action* (New York: Charles Scribner, 1864).

12. Alejandro A. Royo et al., "The Forest of Unintended Consequences: Anthropogenic Actions Trigger the Rise and Fall of Black Cherry," *Bioscience* 20 (2021); Gordon G. Whitney, "The History and Status of the Hemlock-Hardwood Forests of the Allegheny Plateau," *Journal of Ecology* 78 (1990).

13. A good example of Game of Logging training is Northeast Woodland Training, www.woodlandtraining.com.

Chapter 6. Birch Floor

1. The percentage of birch is taken from the USDA Forest Service Forest Inventory Analysis, Timber Product Output Studies, Core 4 table "Volume of Roundwood by Industrial Product, Detailed Species Group, 2018." This table includes products such as fuelwood and pulp as well as sawlogs, and it still has all birch species (most of which is doubtless white birch) at less than 2 percent of all hardwoods harvested in the East; www.fia.fs.usda.gov/program-features/tpo/.

2. Williams, *Americans and Their Forests*, 466–88; Whitney, *From Coastal Wilderness*, 245–49; Michael Williams, *Deforesting the Earth: From Prehistory to Global Crisis* (Chicago: University of Chicago Press, 2003), 412–13, 420–93; Mark A. Drummond and Thomas R. Loveland, "Land-use Pressure and a Transition to Forest-cover Loss in the Eastern United States," *Bioscience* 60 (2010); Bill McKibben, "An Explosion of Green," *Atlantic Monthly* 275 (1995); Ellen Stroud, *Nature Next Door: Cities and Trees in the American Northeast* (Seattle: University of Washington Press, 2013).

3. Brian Donahue, "Another Look from Sanderson's Farm: A Perspective on Environmental History and Conservation," *Environmental History* 12 (2007).

4. Deborah Fitzgerald, *Every Farm a Factory: The Industrial Ideal in American Agriculture* (New Haven: Yale University Press, 2003); Wendell Berry, *The Unsettling of America: Culture and Agriculture* (Berkeley: Sierra Club Books, 1977); Thomas D. Clark, *Greening of the South: The Recovery of Land and Forest* (Lexington: University Press of Kentucky, 1984); Mark Bittman, *Animal, Vegetable, Junk: A History of Food, from Sustainable to Suicidal* (Boston: Houghton Mifflin Harcourt, 2021), 91–128.

5. Williams, *Americans and Their Forests*, 238–352.

6. James L. Howard and Shaobo Liang, "U.S. Timber Production, Trade, Consumption, and Price Statistics, 1965–2017," USDA Forest Service, Forest Products Laboratory, 2019, www.fs.usda.gov/research/treesearch/58506; Sonja N. Oswalt et al., "Forest Resources of the United States, 2017," USDA Forest Service (2019), www.fs.usda.gov/research/publications/gtr/gtr_wo97.pdf; Sonja N. Oswalt and W. Brad Smith, eds., "U.S. Forest Resource Facts and Historical Trends," USDA Forest Service (2014), www.fia.fs.fed.us/library/brochures/docs/2012/ForestFacts_1952 -2012_English.pdf.

7. A good description of these developments is found in Roland Ennos, *The Age of Wood: Our Most Useful Material and the Construction of Civilization* (New York: Scribner, 2020). For a discussion of the rise of plywood and its impacts, see Janet Ore, "Workers' Bodies and Plywood Production: The Pathological Power of a Hybrid Material," *Aggregate* 10 (2022), https://doi.org/10.53965/CPGG8794.

8. A good overview is found in James G. Lewis, *The Forest Service and the Greatest Good: A Centennial History* (Durham, N.C.: Forest History Society, 2006). See also Richard W. Judd, *Common Lands, Common People: The Origins of Conservation in Northern New England* (Cambridge: Harvard University Press, 1997), 99–111.

9. For government planner attitudes see Sara M. Gregg, *Managing the Mountains: Land Use Planning, The New Deal, and the Creation of a Federal Landscape in*

Appalachia (New Haven: Yale University Press, 2010). For trends in regional harvesting see Oswalt et al., "Forest Resources of the United States," 44–45. For harvesting trends on national forests see Anne A. Riddle, "Timber Harvesting of Federal Lands," Congressional Research Service (2021), 7, figure 2, https://crsreports.congress.gov/.

10. Brett J. Butler et al., "Family Forest Ownerships of the United States, 2018: Results from the USDA Forest Service, National Woodlands Survey," USDA Forest Service (2021), 42–43, table 4; Howard and Liang, "U.S. Timber Production," 3–4.

11. Royo et al., "Forest of Unintended Consequences"; Whitney, *From Coastal Wilderness,* 197.

12. The tale of rebounding deer is well told by Jim Sterba, *Nature Wars: The Incredible Story of How Wildlife Comebacks Turned Backyards into Battlegrounds* (New York: Broadway Books, 2012), 86–117. See also Royo et al., "Forest of Unintended Consequences," 5–7.

13. Royo et al., "Forest of Unintended Consequences," 8–11. The response of different tree species, on different soils, to a range of air pollutants is highly complex and not fully understood—see Canham, *Forests Adrift,* 110–19. Other studies classify cherry as a "nitrogen winner"; see George Van Houtven et al., "Nitrogen Deposition and Climate Change Effects on Tree Species Composition and Ecosystem Services for a Forest Cohort," *Ecological Monographs* 89 (2019).

14. The classic telling of this story is Hugh M. Raup, "The View from John Sanderson's Farm: A Perspective for the Use of Land," *Forest History* 10 (1966). I took issue with aspects of Raup's account in Donahue, "Another Look from Sanderson's Farm."

15. Donahue, "Another Look from Sanderson's Farm"; David R. Foster and John F. O'Keefe, *New England Forests Through Time: Insights from the Harvard Forest Dioramas* (Petersham, Mass.: Harvard Forest, 2000).

16. William B. Leak et al., "Ecology and Management of Northern Red Oak in New England," University of New Hampshire Cooperative Extension (2017), https://extension.unh.edu/sites/default/files/migrated_unmanaged_files/Resource006927_Rep9991.pdf; William B. Leak et al., "White Pine Silviculture for Timber and Wildlife Habitat in New England," University of New Hampshire Cooperative Extension (2020), https://extension.unh.edu/sites/default/files/migrated_unmanaged_files/Resource008113_Rep11841.pdf.

17. Foster and O'Keefe, *New England Forests Through Time;* Raup, "View from Sanderson's Farm"; Donahue, "Another Look from Sanderson's Farm."

18. Marc D. Abrams, among many others, favors fire: "Fire and the Development of Oak Forests: In Eastern North America, Oak Distribution Reflects a Variety of Ecological Paths and Disturbance Conditions," *BioScience* 42 (1992). A good summary of the oak and fire situation in Northeastern forests is presented in Canham, *Forests Adrift,* 64–74. For passenger pigeons see Joseph W. Ellsworth and Brenda C. McComb, "Potential Effects of Passenger Pigeon Flocks on the Structure and Composition of Presettlement Forests of Eastern North America," *Conservation Biology* 17 (2003); Ben J. Novak, "The Passenger Pigeon: The Ecosystem Engineer of Eastern North American Forests," page on *Revive & Restore* web site, https://revive restore.org/the-passenger-pigeon-the-ecosystem-engineer-of-eastern-north-american

-forests/. There is a large literature on deer population and its impact—see, for example, T. R. McCabe and R. E. McCabe, "Recounting Whitetails Past," in *The Science of Overabundance: Deer Ecology and Population Management,* ed. William J. McShea, Brian H. Underwood, and John H. Rappole (Washington, D.C.: Smithsonian Institution, 1997); or Brice B. Hanberry and Edward K. Faison, "Re-framing Deer Herbivory as a Natural Disturbance Regime with Ecological and Socioeconomic Outcomes in the Eastern United States," *Science of the Total Environment* 868 (2023).

Chapter 7. Maple Stairs

1. Euell Gibbons, *Stalking the Wild Asparagus* (New York: David McKay, 1962), 117–25.
2. Donahue, *Reclaiming the Commons,* 164–80.
3. On the invention and reinvention of the classic New England village and landscape see Joseph S. Wood, "New England's Legacy Landscape," and Joseph A. Conforti, "Regional Identity and New England Landscapes," both in *A Landscape History of New England,* ed. Blake Harrison and Richard W. Judd (Cambridge, Mass.: MIT Press, 2011). I discuss the history of sugar maple in Weston and southern New England in greater depth in *Reclaiming the Commons,* 167–71.
4. Fancy syrup has been recently renamed "Grade A Light Amber." No wait—still more recently it has been re-renamed "Grade A Golden Color, Delicate Taste."
5. Aldo Leopold, *A Sand County Almanac: And Sketches Here and There* (New York: Oxford University Press, 1949). The United States became a majority urban society about 1920.
6. For a thoughtful defense of Leopold's attitudes toward social justice see Curt D. Meine, "In a Time of Social and Environmental Crisis, Aldo Leopold's Call for a 'Land Ethic' Is Still Relevant," *The Conversation,* January 5, 2021, https://the conversation.com/in-a-time-of-social-and-environmental-crisis-aldo-leopolds-call -for-a-land-ethic-is-still-relevant-147968.
7. Jonathan R. Thompson et al., "Four Centuries of Change in Northeastern United States Forests," *PLOS One* 8, no. 9 (2013): 1–15. Some of the maple surge, especially in the southern part of the region shown on the map (replacing oak), is red maple.
8. Emily Silver, "Sweet Success: Sugar Maple Expansion in a Cultural New England Landscape" (senior honors thesis, Brandeis University, 2008).
9. David E. Wilkins, "How to Honor the Seven Generations," ICT web site, June 18, 2015, https://ictnews.org/archive/how-to-honor-the-seven-generations.
10. John Calvin, *Commentaries on the First Book of Moses Called Genesis,* Vol. 1, Part 5 (Edinburgh: Calvin Translation Society, 1847), 125. For further discussion of Calvinist views on improvement and stewardship, see Mark R. Stoll, *Inherit the Holy Mountain: Religion and the Rise of American Environmentalism* (New York: Oxford University Press, 2015), especially 61–69.

Chapter 8. Wood, Fire, and Stone

1. Cummings, *Framed Houses of Massachusetts Bay,* 4–6.
2. Cummings, *Framed Houses of Massachusetts Bay,* 118–23; Priscilla J. Brewer, *From*

Fireplace to Cookstove: Technology and the Domestic Ideal in America (Syracuse: Syracuse University Press, 2000); William Cronon, *Changes in the Land: Indians, Colonists, and the Ecology of New England* (New York: Hill and Wang, 1983), 120.

3. Firewood usage is discussed in Donahue, *Great Meadow,* 214–20. See also the discussion in Tarule, *Artisan of Ipswich,* 34–36. Tarule thinks seventeenth-century houses may have consumed less wood because they were smaller, but I think they may have consumed more because of bigger fireplaces burning bigger pieces. See also Max George Schumacher, *The Northern Farmer and His Markets During the Late Colonial Period* (New York: Arno Press, 1975).

4. On the adoption of stoves, see Garrison, *Landscape and Material Life,* 178; Hubka, *Big House, Little House, Back House, Barn,* 125–26; Brewer, *From Fireplace to Cookstove,* 63–117. Nineteenth-century firewood consumption is taken from Emerson, *Report on Trees and Shrubs,* 15. The kitchen fireplace at the Golden Ball Tavern in Weston, now a museum, has been excavated to show how it grew smaller over time; www.goldenballtavern.org/gallery.

5. Henry J. Kaufmann, *American Axes: A Survey of Their Development and Their Makers* (Brattleboro, Vt.: Stephen Greene, 1972).

6. The phrase "boggled notch" comes from Horace Kephart, *Camping and Wood-craft: A Handbook for Vacation Campers and Travelers in the Wilderness* (New York: Macmillan, 1917), Vol. 2, "Woodcraft," 187–214.

7. Donahue, *Great Meadow,* 214–20.

8. Emerson, *Report on Trees and Shrubs,* 24–27, discusses management of woods for fuel and timber from surveys of nineteenth-century Massachusetts farmers. William Bryant Logan explores coppicing globally in *Sprout Lands: Tending the Endless Gift of Trees* (New York: W.W. Norton, 2019).

9. Massachusetts Society for Agriculture, *Papers on Agriculture, 1803,* 50–52, discusses thinning sprouts for hogshead poles (that is, hoops); *Revised Statutes of the Commonwealth of Massachusetts, 1835* (Boston: Dutton and Wentworth, 1836), Chapter 28, Section 102, gives specifications for the width, length, and bundling of white oak and walnut (hickory) hogshead hoops, for example. Thoreau gives a vivid account of the felling of one of several century-old white pines towering over a fifteen-year-old sprout wood on December 30, 1851, in *The Journal of Henry D. Thoreau* (Boston: Houghton Mifflin, 1906), Vol. 3, 162–64.

10. See Joseph S. Wood, *The New England Village* (Baltimore: Johns Hopkins University Press, 1997).

11. Christopher Jones, "The Carbon-Consuming Home: Residential Markets and Energy Transitions," *Enterprise and Society* 12 (2011).

12. Jones, "Carbon-Consuming Home"; Thomas G. Andrews, *Killing for Coal: America's Deadliest Labor War* (Cambridge: Harvard University Press, 2008); Robert B. Gordon and Patrick M. Malone, *The Texture of Industry: An Archeological View of the Industrialization of America* (New York: Oxford University Press, 1994), 57–116.

13. This and other Mumford references are to Lewis Mumford, *Technics and Civilization* (New York: Harcourt, Brace, 1934).

14. Gordon and Malone, *Texture of Industry.* A good overview of air pollution and responses to it is provided in Joel A. Tarr, *The Search for the Ultimate Sink: Urban Pollution in Historical Perspective* (Akron: University of Akron Press, 1996).

15. I found one out of seven or eight, and that was only because Wright added a bedroom later that enclosed it.

16. A good overview is Ken Matesz, *Masonry Heaters: Designing, Building, and Living with a Piece of the Sun* (White River Junction, Vt.: Chelsea Green, 2010). Alex Chernov, "Stovemaster," http://stovemaster.com/html_en/home.html, explains the "double bell" design of our stove.

17. "Choosing Wood-Burning Appliances," page on U.S. Environmental Protection Agency web site, www.epa.gov/burnwise/choosing-wood-burning-appliances; "Choosing and Installing Wood- and Pellet-Burning Appliances," page on U.S. Department of Energy web site, www.energy.gov/energysaver/wood-and-pellet -heating; Masonry Heater Association of America web site, www.mha-net.org.

18. See Paul Catanzaro and Anthony D'Amato, *Forest Carbon: An Essential Natural Solution for Climate Change* (Amherst: University of Massachusetts, 2019) and its supporting literature, https://masswoods.org/caring-your-land/forest-carbon; Katherine Eisen and Audrey Barker Plotkin, "Forty Years of Forest Measurements Support Steadily Increasing Aboveground Biomass in a Maturing, *Quercus*-Dominant Northeastern Forest," *Journal of the Torrey Botanical Society* 142 (2015).

19. Moomaw et al., "Proforestation."

20. The case against clear-cut and plantation forestry devoted primarily to biomass production, particularly in the American Southeast, is made by organizations such as the Southern Environmental Law Center, www.southernenvironment.org/topic /biomass-energy-threatens-southern-forests-and-communities/. For an overview of the controversy see Christopher Ketcham, "Logging Is Destroying Southern Forests—and Dividing U.S. Environmentalists," *Grist* (June 29, 2022), https://grist .org/energy/logging-biomass-nature-conservancy/.

21. R. Alec Giffen and Robert Perschel, "Exemplary Forestry for the 21st Century: Managing the Acadian Forest for Bird's Feet and Boardfeet at a Landscape Scale," New England Forestry Foundation (2012), https://newenglandforestry.org/wp -content/uploads/2021/06/EF-Acadian-Forest-051421-final.pdf; Brian J. Palik et al., *Ecological Silviculture: Foundations and Applications* (Long Grove, Ill.: Waveland Press, 2020).

22. Catanzaro and D'Amato, *Forest Carbon*.

23. Fred Mayes, "Increases in Electricity Generation from Biomass Stop After a Decade of Growth," U.S. Energy Information Administration web site, April 19, 2019, www.eia.gov/todayinenergy/detail.php?id=39052.

Chapter 9. Wood Is Green

1. Garland Mill in northern New Hampshire is still water-powered and provides another nice example of artisanal/industrial synergy; https://garlandmill.com/the -mill/.

2. Okay, I made that up about the Brick Nog and Plaster colonial cocktail. On SIPs, see the Foard Panel web site, https://foardpanel.com/timber-framers. Don't forget to put furring on the outside of the frame before you attach the SIPs, so you can slip the drywall in later.

3. Ward Clapboard Mill, https://wardclapboard.com.

4. Oswalt et al., "Forest Resources of the United States"; Howard and Liang, "U.S. Timber Production."

5. For more details on the New England forest see "Wildlands and Woodlands," https://wildlandsandwoodlands.org.

6. U.S. Census Bureau, New Residential Construction, Historical Time Series, Housing Units Completed, www.census.gov/construction/nrc/data/series.html; "Housing Need in Rural America," National Rural Housing Coalition web site, https://ruralhousingcoalition.org/overcoming-barriers-to-affordable-rural-housing/; Kenneth Johnson, "Recent Data Suggest Rural America Is Growing Again After a Decade of Population Loss," University of New Hampshire, Carsey School of Public Policy, December 6, 2022, https://carsey.unh.edu/publication/snapshot/recent -data-suggest-rural-america-is-growing-again.

7. Caitlin Littlefield et al., *Beyond the "Illusion of Preservation": Taking Regional Responsibility by Protecting Forests, Reducing Consumption, and Increasing Sustainable Wood Production in New England* (Amherst: University of Massachusetts, 2024).

8. Littlefield et al., *Illusion of Preservation.*

9. Foster et al., *Wildlands and Woodlands,* 11; Jamie B. Pottern and Laura N. Barley, "Farms Under Threat: A New England Perspective," American Farmland Trust (2020), https://farmlandinfo.org/publications/farms-under-threat-a-new-england -perspective/; Spencer R. Meyer et al., "New England's Climate Imperative: Our Forests as a Natural Climate Solution," Highstead (2022), https://highstead.net /library/forests-as-a-natural-climate-solution/.

10. Sobon, *Hand Hewn,* has numerous great photos of cruck framing. Our framer Dave Bowman explains his approach in "David Bowman Crafts Buildings from Trees," *Northern Woodlands,* May 12, 2022, https://northernwoodlands.org/blog /article/david-bowman-trees.

11. "Shared Equity Innovation," page on web site of Champlain Housing Trust, www .getahome.org/innovation/; Jakob Kendall Schneider et al., "Interrupting Housing Inequality Through Community Land Trusts," *Housing Policy Debate,* June 13, 2022, www.tandfonline.com/doi/full/10.1080/10511482.2022.2055614; Kristen Sharpless and Jim Lavinsky, "Vermont Needs Both Housing and Land Conservation," *VTDigger,* January 3, 2022, https://vtdigger.org/2022/01/03/sharpless-lovinsky -vewrmont-needs-both-housing-and-land-conservation/. Katie Michels and David A. Hinden, "Building Collaboration Among Community Land Trusts Building Affordable Housing and Conservation Land Trusts Protecting Land for Ecological Value," Lincoln Institute of Land Policy working paper WP23KM1, January 2023.

12. Christine McGowan, "A Vermonter's Approach to Sustainable, Affordable Housing," Vermont Sustainable Jobs Fund web site, April 29, 2021, www.vsjf.org/2021 /04/29/a-vermonters-approach-to-sustainable-affordable-housing/; Northern Forest Center, https://northernforest.org/resources/resources/wood-heat-faqs/, makes a more full-throated claim for the social and environmental virtues of rural wood heat.

13. Jeff Spiritos, "Creating Affordable Housing Opportunities with Mass Timber," Dovetail Partners, March 2021, www.dovetailinc.org/portfoliodetail.php?id=605 25fce7bf85; essays in Max Page and Martha R. Miller, eds., *Bending the Future:*

Fifty Ideas for the Next Fifty Years of Historic Preservation in the United States (Amherst: University of Massachusetts Press, 2016). Rutherford H. Platt, *Reclaiming American Cities: The Struggle for People, Places, and Nature Since 1900* (Amherst: University of Massachusetts Press, 2014), provides an excellent history of twentieth-century urban and suburban development, with better twenty-first-century alternatives.

14. Spiritos, "Creating Affordable Housing Opportunities"; Laura Glesby, "Beulah Breaks Ground on Affordable Apts.," *New Haven Independent,* August 10, 2022, www .newhavenindependent.org/article/beulah_breaks_ground_on_69_affordable-_units.

15. "Forest-to-Cities Climate Challenge," New England Forestry Foundation web site, https://foresttocities.org/get-involved/; Meyer et al., "New England's Climate Imperative," on carbon benefits of mass timber.

16. Fred Pearce, "The Hidden Environmental Toll of Mining the World's Sand," *Yale Environment 360* (2019), https://e360.yale.edu/features/the-hidden-environmental -toll-of-mining-the-worlds-sand; Mass Timber Dialogue, "Mass Timber: An Important Climate Solution and Economic Opportunity for Central New England & Eastern New York" (2021), https://merid.org/wp-content/uploads/2021/07/Final -Mass-Timber-Report.pdf, provides an overview and references on the carbon advantages of mass timber construction.

17. "Olver, John W. Design Building" page on University of Massachusetts Campus Planning web site, www.umass.edu/cp/olver-john-w-design-building; "The John W. Olver Design Building at UMass, Amherst," page on UMass Building and Construction Technology web site, https://bct.eco.umass.edu/about-us/the-design -building-at-umass-amherst/.

18. The biophilic benefits of wood buildings are reviewed, with references to supporting studies, in Valerie Montjoy, "The Biophilic Response to Wood: Can It Promote the Wellbeing of Building Occupants?" *ArchDaily,* March 2, 2022, www.archdaily .com/974790/the-biophilic-response-to-wood-can-it-promote-the-wellbeing-of -building-occupants.

19. See Meyer et al., "New England's Climate Imperative," 2022, on the carbon benefits of improved forest management.

20. Foster et al., *Wildlands and Woodlands;* Brian Donahue et al., *A New England Food Vision: Healthy Food for All, Sustainable Farming and Fishing, Thriving Communities* (Durham, N.H.: Food Solutions New England, 2014).

21. Pottern and Barley, "Farms Under Threat," 2020.

22. Jamie Sayen, *Children of the Northern Forest: Wild New England's History from Glaciers to Global Warming* (New Haven: Yale University Press, 2023); John S. Gunn et al., "Evaluating Degradation in a North American Temperate Forest," *Forest Ecology and Management* 432 (2019): 415–26; Jonathan Thompson et al., "Do Working Forest Easements Work for Conservation?" *bioRxiv* (2023), www .biorxiv.org/content/10.1101/2023.08.24.554638v1.article-info.

23. Foster et al., *Wildlands and Woodlands;* Brian Donahue, "Rewilding Walden Woods and Reworking Exurban Woodlands: Higher Uses in Thoreau Country," in *Landscape and the Ideology of Nature in Exurbia,* ed. Kirsten Valentine Cadieux and Laura Taylor (New York: Routledge, 2013).

24. Foster et al., *Wildlands in New England.*

25. Jon Liebowitz and Robert Perschel, "New England Forests Can Sustain Our Climate and Biodiversity—If We Work Together," *CT Insider,* February 3, 2023, www.ctinsider.com/opinion/article/opinion-we-need-work-protect-forests-17762801.php.

26. Ellis, "Half Earth Is Not Nearly Enough." The central tenets of ecological forestry are excerpted in Amanda Mahaffey and Zander Evans, "Ecological Silviculture: Foundations and Applications," Forest Stewards Guild web site, October 14, 2020, https://foreststewardsguild.org/enews/ecological-silviculture-foundations-and-applications.

27. Palik et al., *Ecological Silviculture.*

28. Forest scientists such as Suzanne Simard have argued that trees communicate and cooperate for the good of their offspring, or indeed of the entire ecological community of which they are part. See Suzanne Simard, *Finding the Mother Tree: Discovering the Wisdom of the Forest* (New York: Alfred A. Knopf, 2021). But other ecologists have disputed this interpretation of mycorrhizal networks; see, for example, Kathryn Flynn, "The Idea That Trees Talk to Cooperate Is Misleading," *Scientific American,* July 19, 2021, www.scientificamerican.com/article/the-idea-that-trees-talk-to-cooperate-is-misleading/.

29. A good overview of the ecological history and conservation issues involved is the set of articles in David R. Foster, ed., "Insights from Historical Geography to Ecology and Conservation," *Journal of Biogeography* 29 (2002). For continuing debate among ecologists on, for example, the extent of Native American fire in the Eastern forest, see W. Wyatt Oswald et al., "Conservation Implications of Limited Native American Impacts in Pre-Contact New England," *Nature Sustainability* 3 (January 20, 2020), with subsequent commentary by Marc D. Abrams and Gregory J. Nowacki, "Native American Imprint in Paleoecology," *Nature Sustainability* 3 (July 20, 2020) and "W. W. Oswald et al. Reply," *Nature Sustainability* 3 (July 20, 2020). This exchange contains exhaustive references to the extensive literature on this subject.

30. I present 120 years as an average—the number of years can vary considerably depending on the health and vigor of any particular stand. For production calculations see Littlefield et al., *Illusion of Preservation.* "Foresters for the Birds: Assessing Your Woods for Bird Habitat" page of Massachusetts Department of Conservation and Recreation web site, www.mass.gov/guides/foresters-for-the-birds-assessing-your-woods-for-bird-habitat.

31. On the decline in paper consumption see Howard and Liang, "U.S. Timber Production, 1965–2017," 3.

32. See Peterman's Boards and Bowls, www.spencerpeterman.com, for bowls; Gill CC Woodworks, www.gillccwoodworks.com, for bars; Timber HP, https://timberhp.com, for wood fiber insulation; Cambia Wood, https://cambiawood.com, for thermally modified lumber.

33. The impact of conservation on tax rates is very small in most cases, although slightly greater in the poorest towns. See Alexey Kalinin et al., "Does Land Conservation Raise Property Taxes? Evidence from New England Cities and Towns," Harvard Forest (2022), https://harvardforest.fas.harvard.edu/sites/default/files/jthomps/Land%20Conservation%20and%20Taxes%20Paper%201_13.pdf.

34. Donahue, *Reclaiming the Commons;* "Creating Community Forests, Boosting Local Economy, and Protecting Wildlife" page on Northern Forest Center web site, https://northernforest.org/our-work/strengthening-communities/creating -community-forests/; Katherine R. E. Sims et al., "Assessing the Local Economic Impacts of Land Protection," *Conservation Biology* 33 (2019), https://conbio.on linelibrary.wiley.com/doi/abs/10.1111/cobi.13318.

Chapter 10. Slow Food, Slow Fire, Slow Wood

1. Stephen Pyne, "Welcome to the Pyrocene," *Grist,* August 18, 2021, https://grist .org/wildfires/welcome-to-the-pyrocene/, nicely summarizes Stephen J. Pyne, *The Pyrocene: How We Created an Age of Fire, and What Happens Next* (Oakland: University of California Press, 2021). See also David M. J. S. Bowman et al., "Fire in the Earth System," *Science* 324 (2009): 481–84.

2. Mumford, *Technics and Civilization.* The terms "paleotechnic" and "neotechnic" are from Patrick Geddes, *Cities in Evolution: An Introduction to the Town Planning Movement and to the Study of Civics* (London: Williams and Norgate, 1915).

3. A good historical overview can be found in Glenn Adamson, *Craft: An American History* (New York: Bloomsbury, 2021), along with Glenn Adamson, *Fewer, Better Things: The Hidden Wisdom of Objects* (London: Bloomsbury, 2018). A wonderful school that continues the sloyd tradition in the modern era is the North Bennet Street School in Boston, https://nbss.edu/about/.

4. For a good recent discussion of the thinking of these authors, see Brian Morris, *Pioneers of Ecological Humanism: Mumford, Dubos, and Bookchin* (New York: Black Rose Books, 2017).

5. "Anachronistic species" include those that may have relied on now extinct megafauna for seed dispersal. Common North American examples include osage orange, pawpaw, and honey locust. Black locust, with its large seed pods and curiously limited pre-European range, strikes me as another good candidate. See Connie Barlow, *The Ghosts of Evolution: Nonsensical Fruit, Missing Partners, and Other Ecological Anachronisms* (New York: Basic Books, 2001).

6. See discussion in Canham, *Forests Adrift,* 150–68.

Index

Abenaki, 27, 169

Acton, Massachusetts, 90–91

Adirondack Park, 103

affordable housing: need for, 221; using local wood in, 222

agrarian tradition, attitude toward nature of, 169–75

Agricultural Preservation Restriction, 18, 24–25, 53

agriculture, Northeastern, history of, 30–31, 37–38, 57, 59, 77, 100, 133–34, 143–45

Alcott, Bronson, 3

Allegheny Plateau, Pennsylvania, 95, 127, 141–43

America's Wooden Age, 74, 184–85, 236

Ann Arbor, Michigan, 47

anti-Modernism, 257–59

Arnold Arboretum, 69

Arts and Crafts movement, 47, 257–59

Ashfield stone, 189, 220

Askew Hall, 91, 93

Audubon Society of Massachusetts, 58, 235

Audubon Society of Western Pennsylvania. *See* Todd Sanctuary

ax: broad, 3, 75; felling, 3, 181–82, 184

balloon frame construction, 97, 99–100

balusters, 161–63

bannisters, 161–63

barber chair, 107

barn: at our farm, 11, 19, 96–97; kits for, 100

Barnard, David, 125

Bascom, Moses, 169

Bay House, 47

beaver, 55–56, 172

beech, American, 161–62, 170–71

Benson, Tedd, 47–49

Big Dig, Boston, 48

birch, black, 64, 86, 147, 161, 235, 260; cabinets, 152–53; flooring and trim, 151–53; growth characteristics, 129–31, 153; lumber, 132, 150–53; suppressing (failure of), 148–50; in Pennsylvania, 131, 143; in Weston, 131–32

birch, yellow, 131, 132

Blob, the, 95

bore cut, 106–10

Bowman, David, 83, 92, 105, 114–18, 120–26, 152, 218

Brandeis University, 10, 14, 69, 154

Bransfield, Jonathan, 69

Brick Nog and Plaster, 76, 212

Briggs, Toby, 86–87, 89, 92, 116, 125, 151–52, 160, 162

brother, my. *See* Donahue, Kevin

brother, my other. *See* Donahue, Neil

brush cutter, Husqvarna, 35, 149

Buffalo Creek, 65

Butler County, Pennsylvania, 65

butternut squash, 244

cabin porn, 7, 213

Calvin, John, 173–74

Campbell, Susan, 50–51, 61

Carnegie Museum of Natural History, 65

central hardwood forest, 52–53, 70

chainsaws, working with, 35, 106–13, 164–66, 190–91, 195

cedar, Atlantic white, 76

Chalmers, Tom: as architect, 81–83, 86–87, 152, 162; as farm partner, 23–25, 30–35, 44, 51, 60, 164, 256

Chandler, Joseph Everett, 91–92

cherry, black: at the farm, 96, 260; felling for braces, 105–14; in the house, 9, 127, 152; in Pennsylvania, 95–96, 104–5, 127, 141–43; sawing for braces, 114–16; in the stairs, 160; in Weston, 95

chemical wood industry, 101–2

chestnut, American, 4, 16, 260; blight in, 69

Yale Agrarian Studies Series

JAMES C. SCOTT, SERIES EDITOR

The Agrarian Studies Series at Yale University Press seeks to publish outstanding and original interdisciplinary work on agriculture and rural society—for any period, in any location. Works of daring that question existing paradigms and fill abstract categories with the lived experience of rural people are especially encouraged.

James C. Scott, *Seeing Like a State: How Certain Schemes to Improve the Human Condition Have Failed*

Steve Striffler, *Chicken: The Dangerous Transformation of America's Favorite Food*

James C. Scott, *The Art of Not Being Governed: An Anarchist History of Upland Southeast Asia*

Timothy Pachirat, *Every Twelve Seconds: Industrialized Slaughter and the Politics of Sight*

James C. Scott, *Against the Grain: A Deep History of the Earliest States*

Jamie Kreiner, *Legions of Pigs in the Early Medieval West*

Ruth Mostern, *The Yellow River: A Natural and Unnatural History*

Brian Lander, *The King's Harvest: A Political Ecology of China from the First Farmers to the First Empire*

Jo Guldi, *The Long Land War: The Global Struggle for Occupancy Rights*

Andrew S. Mathews, *Trees Are Shape Shifters: How Cultivation, Climate Change, and Disaster Create Landscapes*

Francesca Bray, Barbara Hahn, John Bosco Lourdusamy, and Tiago Saraiva, *Moving Crops and the Scales of History*

Deborah Valenze, *The Invention of Scarcity: Malthus and the Margins of History*

Brooks Lamb, *Love for the Land: Lessons from Farmers Who Persist in Place*

Jamie Sayen, *Children of the Northern Forest: Wild New England's History from Glaciers to Global Warming*

Michael R. Dove, *Hearsay Is Not Excluded: A History of Natural History*

Gregory M. Thaler, *Saving a Rainforest and Losing the World: Conservation and Displacement in the Global Tropics*

Lee Sessions, *Nature, Culture, and Race in Colonial Cuba*

Merrill Baker-Medard, *Feminist Conservation: Politics and Power in Madagascar's Marine Commons*

James C. Scott, *In Praise of Floods: The Untamed River and the Life It Brings*

For a complete list of titles in the Yale Agrarian Studies Series, visit yalebooks.com /agrarian.